HAZON GABRIEL

NEW READINGS OF THE GABRIEL REVELATION

Society of Biblical Literature

Early Judaism and Its Literature

Judith H. Newman,
Series Editor

Number 29

HAZON GABRIEL
NEW READINGS OF THE GABRIEL REVELATION

HAZON GABRIEL

New Readings of the Gabriel Revelation

Edited by
Matthias Henze

Society of Biblical Literature
Atlanta

HAZON GABRIEL
New Readings of the Gabriel Revelation

Copyright © 2011 by the Society of Biblical Literature

All rights reserved. No part of this work may be reproduced or transmitted in any form or by any means, electronic or mechanical, including photocopying and recording, or by means of any information storage or retrieval system, except as may be expressly permitted by the 1976 Copyright Act or in writing from the publisher. Requests for permission should be addressed in writing to the Rights and Permissions Office, Society of Biblical Literature, 825 Houston Mill Road, Atlanta, GA 30329 USA.

Financial support for the production of this book from the Department of Religious Studies at Rice University is gratefully acknowledged.

Library of Congress Cataloging-in-Publication Data

    Hazon Gabriel : new readings of the Gabriel revelation / edited by Matthias Henze.
       p. cm. — (Early Judaism and its literature ; no. 29)
    Essays include the papers of a conference hosted by the Program in Jewish Studies at Rice University, Houston, Tex., in Feb. 2009.
    Includes selections from the text of the Gabriel revelation and abbreviated annotated English translations.
    Includes bibliographical references and index.
    ISBN 978-1-58983-541-2 (paper binding : alk. paper)
    1. Gabriel revelation—Congresses. 2. Jerusalem in Judaism—Congresses. 3. Eschatology, Jewish—Congresses. I. Henze, Matthias. II. Gabriel revelation. English & Hebrew. Selections.
    PJ5034'.9.H39 2011
    296.1'5—dc22
                                           2011008511

Printed on acid-free, recycled paper conforming to
ANSI /NISO Z39.48–1992 (R1997) and ISO 9706:1994
standards for paper permanence.

In memory of

Hanan Eshel, ז״ל

July 25, 1958 – April 8, 2010

ח׳ באב תשי״ח – כ״ד בניסן תש״ע

Gifted scholar, revered teacher, dear friend

איש חמודות שלום לך
Dan 10:19

Contents

Abbreviations ix
Preface xi

1. The *Jeselsohn Stone*: Discovery and Publication
   David Jeselsohn 1

2. A Hebrew Prophetic Text on Stone from the Early Herodian Period:
   A Preliminary Report
   Ada Yardeni and Binyamin Elizur 11

3. Notes on the So-Called *Gabriel Vision* Inscription
   Elisha Qimron and Alexey (Eliyahu) Yuditsky 31

4. The Apocalyptic and Messianic Dimensions
   of the Gabriel Revelation in Their Historical Context
   Israel Knohl 39

5. *Hazon Gabriel:* A Grammatical Sketch
   Gary A. Rendsburg 61

6. Response to Israel Knohl, *Messiahs and Resurrection
   in "The Gabriel Revelation"*
   Adela Yarbro Collins 93

7. Gabriel and David: Some Reflections
   on an Enigmatic Text
   John J. Collins 99

8. Some Observations on the *Hazon Gabriel*
   Matthias Henze 113

9. Hosts, Holy Ones, and the Words of Gabriel:
   The Angelology of *Hazon Gabriel* in the Context
   of Second Temple and Late Antique Literature
   Kelley Coblentz Bautch 131

10. The Use of Daniel in the *Gabriel Revelation*
   Daewoong Kim 153

11. "Jerusalem" in the *Gabriel Revelation*
   and the Revelation of John
   David Capes... 173

Bibliography 187
Photographs of *Hazon Gabriel*....................................... 189
Contributors 195
Index of Passages 197
Index of Names and Subjects 215
Index of Authors 217

Abbreviations

ABD	*The Anchor Bible Dictionary.* Edited by David Noel Freedman. 6 vols. New York: Doubleday, 1992.
AGJU	Arbeiten zur Geschichte des Spätjudentums und Urchristentums
AnBib	Analecta biblica
AOAT	Alter Orient und Altes Testament
BAR	*Biblical Archaeology Review*
BZAW	Beihefte zur Zeitschrift für die alttestamentliche Wissenschaft
BZNW	Beihefte zur Zeitschrift für die neutestamentliche Wissenschaft
CahRB	Cahiers de la Revue biblique
CEJL	Commentaries in Early Jewish Literature
ConBOT	Coniectanea biblica: Old Testament Series
CRINT	Compendia Rerum Iudaicarum ad Novum Testamentum
DDD	*Dictionary of Deities and Demons in the Bible.* Edited by Karel van der Toorn, Bob Becking, and P. W. van der Horst. 2nd ed. 1999.
DJD	Discoveries in the Judaean Desert
DSD	*Dead Sea Discoveries*
DSSEL	*Dead Sea Scrolls Electronic Library*
GKC	*Gesenius' Hebrew Grammar.* Edited by K. Kautzsch. Translated by A. E. Cowley. 2nd ed. Oxford: Clarendon, 1910.
HAR	*Hebrew Annual Review*
HSM	Harvard Semitic Monographs
HSS	Harvard Semitic Studies
HTR	*Harvard Theological Review*
IEJ	*Israel Exploration Journal*
JAAC	*Journal of Aesthetics and Art Criticism*
JANES	*Journal of the Ancient Near Eastern Society of Columbia University*
JBL	*Journal of Biblical Literature*
JJS	*Journal of Jewish Studies*
Josephus	
Ant.	*Antiquities*
J.W.	*Jewish War*
JQR	*Jewish Quarterly Review*

JR	*Journal of Religion*
JSJSup	*Journal for the Study of Judaism Supplement Series*
JSPSup	*Journal for the Study of the Pseudepigrapha Supplement Series*
JSS	*Journal of Semitic Studies*
NTS	*New Testament Studies*
OLA	Orientalia lovaniensia analecta
Or	*Orientalia*
OTP	*The Old Testament Pseudepigrapha*. Edited by James H. Charlesworth. 2 vols. Garden City, N.Y.: Doubleday, 1983, 1985.
OTS	*Oudtestamentische Studiën*
PEQ	*Palestine Exploration Quarterly*
PTL	*PTL: A Journal for Descriptive Poetics and Theory of Literature*
RevQ	*Revue de Qumran*
RHPR	*Revue d'histoire et de philosophie religieuses*
SBLSCS	Society of Biblical Literature Septuagint and Cognate Studies
SHR	Studies in the History of Religion
SJLA	Studies in Judaism in Late Antiquity
STAC	Studien und Texte zu Antike und Christentum
STDJ	Studies in the Texts of the Desert of Judah
SVTP	Studia in Veteris Testamenti pseudepigraphica
Tacitus	
Hist.	*Historiae*
TDNT	*Theological Dictionary of the New Testament.* Edited by G. Kittel and G. Friedrich. Translated by G. W. Bromiley. Grand Rapids: Eerdmans, 1964–76.
TDOT	*Theological Dictionary of the Old Testament.* Edited by G. J. Botterweck and H. Ringgren. Translated by J. T. Willis. G. W. Bromiley, and D. E. Green. Grand Rapids: Eerdmans, 1974–.
TSAJ	Texte und Studien zum antiken Judentum
VTSup	Supplements to Vetus Testamentum
WBC	Word Biblical Commentary
WUNT	Wissenschaftliche Untersuchungen zum Neuen Testament

Preface

In the spring of 2009, the Houston Museum of Natural Science hosted an exhibit on late Second Temple Judaism and Christian origins titled "The Birth of Christianity: A Jewish Story." One of the objects on display was a gray limestone, presumably an ancient stele, bearing a Hebrew inscription. The stele, which measures about one by three feet, is owned by Dr. David Jeselsohn, a private antiquities collector from Zurich, Switzerland, who had acquired the stone a decade earlier from an antiquities dealer in Jordan. A little over two years prior to the Houston exhibit, two Israeli epigraphers, Ada Yardeni and Binyamin Elizur, had published the text for the first time and named it *Hazon Gabriel*, or *The Gabriel Revelation*. By the time the Houston exhibit opened its doors on December 12, 2008, the text was already well known beyond the scholarly community and quickly became a favorite with the visitors.

The text's popularity was in part due to a front-page article in the *New York Times*, published on July 6, 2008, that featured the stone and its owner. It also reported about Professor Israel Knohl of the Hebrew University in Jerusalem, who was among the first to write on the inscription. Professor Knohl asserted that the *Hazon Gabriel* is a Jewish text from the late first century B.C.E. that speaks about a Messiah who dies a violent death and rises again from the dead on the third day. Since the *Hazon Gabriel* dates from pre-Christian times, Knohl went on to argue that this text changes our understanding of the origins of Christianity (note, however, that in his essay for this volume, "The Apocalyptic and Messianic Dimensions of the *Gabriel Revelation* in Their Historical Context," Knohl disclaims his earlier thesis regarding the resurrection and now no longer maintains that the *Hazon Gabriel* mentions the resurrection of a Messiah on the third day). In February 2009, while the stone was on display at the Houston Museum of Natural Science, Professor Knohl came to Houston, gave a public lecture at the museum, and participated in a small conference on the *Hazon Gabriel* hosted by the Program in Jewish Studies at Rice University. The articles in this volume comprise the papers of the Rice conference plus several important additional essays.

Any modern exegete working on the *Hazon Gabriel* is confronted with two obstacles. The first is that the Jordanian antiquities dealer, who has since passed away, was unable to provide exact information about the provenance of the stele. For some scholars this is reason enough not to consider the inscription at all, an understandable objection. And yet, over the last three and a half years, a number of scholars from different academic disciplines have worked on the stone and its inscription. None of the experts who have examined the text has concluded that the stone is a forgery. In their opinion, the *Hazon Gabriel* is authentic and dates from the late first century B.C.E. or the early first century C.E. The second obstacle is the poor state of the inscription's preservation. The text is only partially legible (about eighty-seven lines, arranged in two columns, are preserved), and in several important places the interpretation of the text depends on how the interpreter reconstructs individual letters or words. Since the publication of the *editio princeps* by Ada Yardeni and Binyamin Elizur in April 2007, Elisha Qimron and Alexey (Eliyahu) Yuditsky have published a new, partial edition of the *Hazon Gabriel*. Their edition includes numerous improved readings that have since been widely accepted. Finally, Israel Knohl has partially modified his own reading in light of these two editions. In most cases, he follows either the edition of Yardeni and Elizur or that of Qimron and Yuditsky, though in some cases he proposes his own independent reading.

The purpose of the present volume is to make accessible in one book all existing editions of the *Hazon Gabriel* together with annotated English translations and to offer some initial interpretations of the text as a whole, its language and most prominent motifs. The first essay is by David Jeselsohn, the owner of the stone, who relates the story of its purchase and of the earliest attempts to decipher it. The next two essays are both co-authored, the first by Ada Yardeni and Binyamin Elizur and the next by Elisha Qimron and Alexey (Eliyahu) Yuditsky. Their essays are abbreviated English versions of the original Hebrew editions of the inscription, together with ample notes on their readings. Israel Knohl's contribution focuses on some central passages that support his messianic interpretation of the *Hazon Gabriel*. In an appendix to his essay, Knohl provides his own edition of the inscription. The next essay, by Gary Rendsburg, gives a comprehensive lexicon of the language of the *Hazon Gabriel*. The essays that follow, by Adela Yarbro Collins, John Collins, Matthias Henze, Kelley Coblentz Bautch, Daewoong Kim, and David Capes, all offer their own interpretations of the composition or examine a distinct aspect thereof. The volume closes with a bibliography of articles and books that have appeared on the *Hazon Gabriel* to date (August 2010).

Several individuals have helped with the production of this volume and deserve recognition. I wish to thank Joel Bartsch and Barbara Hawthorn from the Houston Museum of Natural Science, as well as Glen Rosenbaum, for putting together the exhibit and for bringing the stele to Houston for its first public viewing. David Jeselsohn generously made the stone available to scholars and laypeople alike; he attended the Rice conference; and he kindly agreed to write an essay for this book. Israel Knohl has done much to bring the *Hazon Gabriel* to our attention, and he has been an important motor behind this book, too, for which I am very grateful to him. I would like to thank West Semitic Research for allowing me to reproduce the photos in the back of this volume of a few selected text passages. I am indebted to Judith Newman, editor of the Early Judaism and

Its Literature series, for accepting this volume into the series and for her very prompt and professional editorial help with the manuscript. Leigh Andersen and Bob Buller at the SBL have been prompt and extraordinarily helpful with the practical aspects involved in the production of this volume.

I did most of my work on this book while I was a fellow in residence at the Netherlands Institute for Advanced Study (NIAS) in Wassenaar, The Netherlands. With its tranquil setting and intellectually stimulating atmosphere, NIAS is the envy of every scholar. I am particularly indebted to the formidable library staff at NIAS, Dindy van Maanen and Erwin Nolet.

It is with immense sadness and fond memories that we dedicate this volume to the memory of Hanan Eshel, extraordinary scholar and dear friend. During my visits to Jerusalem to prepare the Houston exhibit, Esti and Hanan always welcomed me to their home and discussed with me the contours of the exhibit and the objects that would be on display, objects Hanan knew so well. His mastery of early Judaism, of its history, literature, and archaeology, was rather exceptional, both in scope and in detail, and his willingness to share his expertise with others was truly generous. With his untimely death we have lost a great mind, a formidable teacher, and a powerful and vocal advocate for the study of early Judaism. Perhaps most importantly, we have lost a wonderful human being.

ברוך דיין האמת

Matthias Henze
Rice University
February 2011

ONE

The *Jeselsohn Stone*:
Discovery and Publication

David Jeselsohn

Never have I imagined that an item of my collection would be published on the front page of the *New York Times*, would have more than a million search results in the Internet, would be the subject of many articles and books, would be exhibited in museums, or would be the star of television films.

I

But let me proceed in chronological order. In order to explain what happened, I must give a brief description of the background, which is my interest in the history of the Jewish people of the Land of Israel and in their archaeological artifacts.

For the last forty years I have been studying, researching, and collecting in these areas. During this time I assembled collections of objects relating to the archaeology of the land of Israel and to Jewish art and culture. The archaeological collection includes primarily ancient oil lamps, coins of the Jews and of the land of Israel, and, most relevant to this article, a collection of written materials—mainly ostraca, seals, and bullae. In the areas of Jewish culture and art my collection consists of Hebrew manuscripts and books, mainly incunabula and early prints as well as Jewish ceremonial art. My interest in these areas was the stimulus for my academic studies of archaeology. In addition, when I still had more discretionary time, I was involved in publishing articles on relevant topics.[1] These interests also led my wife and me to establish the Jeselsohn Epigraphic Centre for Jewish History at Bar Ilan University in Israel under the directorship of the late Professor Hanan Eshel, as well as The David and Jemima Jeselsohn

---

1. For example, I produced the first publication of a YHDH coin, a tiny silver coin from the early third century B.C.E. from Judea with the inscription YHDH (= *Yehuda* = Judea), or the first publication of a *Ḥever Yehudim* (= Community of the Jews) coin from the Hasmonean period. David Jeselsohn, "A New Coin Type with Hebrew Inscription," *IEJ* 24 (1974): 77–78; "Ḥever Yehudim—A New Jewish Coin," *PEQ* 112 (1980): 11–17.

Library, a series of books on antiquity.² Many items from my collection are permanently on loan to museums and exhibitions throughout the world. Recently I have begun to arrange and catalogue the collections toward their eventual scientific publication.³

II

Research and collecting brought me into contact with academics, researchers, collectors, and dealers in many countries. One of the dealers was Ghassan Rihani from Irbid in northern Jordan, who spent a large part of his time in London, where his daughter lived. From London he used to offer me various objects—statues and vessels of bronze, pottery and glass, jewelry, coins, seals, and so forth. He passed away in 2001, and his son Tayeb has continued the business.

This brings us to the stone inscription. One of the deliveries from Rihani about ten years ago included a large wooden crate in which was a stone tablet of 96 x 37 x 14 cm in size, broken into three pieces. On its smoothed surface was a Hebrew inscription written in black ink in two columns. Already upon my first glance at the inscription I was struck by how easily the letters and the words could be read insofar as they were not blurred or semi-erased. At the same time, I was intrigued and frustrated by the fact that, although the words were quite clear, the sentences made little sense. Words like "Lord of the Hosts, God of Israel," "Israel," "Jerusalem," and "my servant David" indicated that this was a religious text, but its meaning was difficult to grasp. The word "chariots," which is quite unusual, caused me to think that this might be a text of the Hekhalot literature, a mystic cabalistic text from the end of antiquity or the beginning of the Middle Ages. I wondered if this was part of the Hekhalot and Chariot literature of the group known as the Chariot Riders, a mystical apocalyptic literature having its origin in the Tannaitic and Amoraic times, that is, during the first to fifth centuries C.E.

Rihani could not supply any reliable information as to the origin of the stone or the place in which it was found. Because the ink on the stone was generally in a good state of preservation, it was clear to me that the stone must have been preserved in a dry climate, devoid of water, humidity, or vegetation. Taking into account the Hebrew paleography and the Jewish connection, I could think of only one area that could reasonably be considered, namely, the area of the Dead

---

2. The library is being published by Yad Ben-Zvi and the Magnes Press of the Hebrew University, both in Jerusalem. The library comprises at present four series, all in Hebrew: (a) Between the Bible and the Mishnah; (b) a series of studies in the ancient period; (c) *Treasures of the Past* (archaeological sites), also in English; and (d) the Cairo Genizah.

3. Ada Yardeni of Jerusalem is working on the collection of more than six hundred Aramaic ostraca of the fourth century B.C.E. from Idumea, that is, southern Judea, and André Lemaire from Paris works on about three hundred Hebrew ostraca of the seventh and sixth centuries B.C.E. from the same area.

Sea, where the annual precipitation is less than 100 mm. It was also clear to me that the stone could not have come from Israel, that is, from the western side of the Dead Sea, and so it was my conclusion that it must have come from the eastern side.

Although I could not date the inscription, I had no doubt about its antiquity and authenticity. Zeev Radovan from Jerusalem, who specializes in archaeological photography, came to Zurich to take photos of the inscription in 2002, and the photos were sent to Ada Yardeni in Jerusalem, an expert in ancient Semitic paleography. She told me that the inscription seemed interesting, but she also could not make much sense of it. And so the inscription was left, so to say, "unattended" in my collection.

In November 2005 I invited Bezalel Porten, professor emeritus of ancient Jewish history, who specializes in Aramaic epigraphy (also of Jerusalem), together with Yardeni and Radovan to come to Zurich and work on my collection of Aramaic ostraca.[4] I used this opportunity to show Yardeni the inscription, which until then she had only known from photos. Her reaction was immediate and unequivocal: it is an authentic inscription from the time of the Dead Sea Scrolls, or, more accurately, from the end of the first century B.C.E. Later she called the inscription "a Dead Sea Scroll in stone."[5]

Yardeni remained in Zurich for a few more days after finishing her work on the Aramaic ostraca, during which time she studied the inscription thoroughly and transcribed it. Upon her return to Jerusalem, she continued to work on it together with Binyamin Elizur, and a year and a half later they published it in the Hebrew quarterly *Cathedra* under the title "A Prophetic Text on Stone from the First Century BCE: First Publication."[6] This was the first time that this respected quarterly published by the Yad Ben-Zvi Institute in Jerusalem had published an archaeological item in color on its cover and the first time that it had included a large overleaf, with an almost life-size transcription of the inscription. The publication of this article was even more noteworthy against the backdrop of the present trend in academic circles to avoid any publication of archaeological artifacts with no secure provenance. The significance of the inscription and the later echoes throughout the world seem to have fully justified this courageous decision.

In the article itself, the authors describe the inscription and come to the conclusion that it is a quasi-biblical, prophetic text with allusions to or citations from the biblical books of Zechariah, Haggai, and Daniel, and in which God speaks to someone who identifies himself as "I Gabriel," probably the angel Gabriel. Because of this, they named the inscription the *Gabriel Revelation*. According

---

4. See n. 3 above.

5. Ada Yardeni, "A New Dead Sea Scroll in Stone? Bible-like Prophecy Was Mounted in a Wall 2,000 Years Ago," *BAR* 34, no. 1 (2008): 60–61.

6. Ada Yardeni and Binyamin Elizur, "A Prophetic Text on Stone from the First Century BCE: First Publication" (in Hebrew), *Cathedra* 123 (2007): 155–66.

to the authors of the article, the author of the inscription was a supporter of the Davidic dynasty. They placed both its composition and its writing at the end of the first century B.C.E.

The article immediately caught the attention of Israel Knohl, professor of biblical studies at the Hebrew University in Jerusalem. In his book *The Messiah before Jesus*, Knohl had already promulgated the theory that there was in Judaism a tradition of a Messiah who died and was resurrected even before Jesus.[7] In line 80 of the inscription, Knohl read after the words "in three days" the word חאיה, meaning "come to life," or "be resurrected." He interpreted the word as the angel Gabriel's call to the killed Messiah, who was the Messiah son of Joseph, to come back to life, that is, to be resurrected three days after his death. Yardeni and Elizur could read with certainty only the first letter of the word, namely, the letter ח. Knohl immediately published an article in the weekly literary supplement of the daily *Ha'aretz*, which appears both in Hebrew and in English, in which he explained his theory and added his identification of the killed Messiah as Simon.[8] Simon was the leader of a Jewish revolt against the Romans in Transjordan in the year 4 B.C.E., who was killed by the Romans, as described by Flavius Josephus in his history of the Jewish War against the Romans in the years 66–70 C.E. (*J.W.* 2.4.2 §§57–59). Knohl concluded his article, writing: "I believe that the discovery and publication of the 'Gabriel Revelation' is of extraordinary importance. It is a discovery that calls for a complete reassessment of all previous scholarship on the subject of messianism, Jewish and Christian alike."

In July 2007, Knohl came to Zurich to examine personally the stone and the various possible variant readings. He then published an article in the *Journal of Religion* in which he elaborated on his thesis.[9]

Although I was convinced that the inscription was old and authentic, I thought that it might be useful to have it examined scientifically. Even if the stone itself could give no useful chronological clues, the accretions, sediments, and patina on its surface could. These layers could also help to determine the area of origin, based on the assumption that the stone remained near the place where it was originally inscribed. Therefore, I contacted Professor Yuval Goren of the Department of Archaeology and the Cultures of the Near East at the Tel Aviv University, who came to Zurich, examined the stone, and published his findings in a detailed scientific article in the *Israel Exploration Journal*.[10] His conclusions

---

7. Israel Knohl, *The Messiah before Jesus: The Suffering Servant of the Dead Sea Scrolls* (S. Mark Taper Foundation Imprint in Jewish Studies; Berkeley: University of California Press, 2000).

8. Israel Knohl, "In Three Days, You Shall Live," *Ha'aretz*, April 19, 2007 (Hebrew and English).

9. Israel Knohl, "'By Three Days, Live': Messiahs, Resurrection and Ascent to Heaven in Hazon Gabriel," *JR* 88 (2008): 147–58.

10. Yuval Goren, "Micromorphologic Examination of the *Gabriel Revelation* Stone," *IEJ* 58 (2008): 220–29.

were that the stone was from the eastern shore of the Dead Sea, probably to the east of the small Lisan peninsula, that the accretion of calcitic sediment on the stone—partly covering the letters—was due to a long natural process in an arid climatic zone, and that "there was no indication of modern treatment of the surface of the stone."[11] This last statement was his objective, cautious, and scientific way of saying that the inscription was authentic.

In view of the above-mentioned aversion to publish artifacts with no secure provenance, the editorial board of the Israel Exploration Society deliberated at length about the appropriateness of publishing Goren's article. Their final positive decision was, as with *Cathedra*, testimony to their courage and to the importance of the inscription.

The articles were published and elicited interest—but nothing more. And I asked myself: Why is that? Why did this discovery have no wider echoes? If Knohl was correct, my thinking was that this was a unique discovery with major implications for both Judaism and—even more so—for Christianity. And even if he was not correct, we now had for the first time a prophetic, quasi-biblical text on stone from the time of the Dead Sea Scrolls, a period in which the biblical canon had not yet been formalized! Could it be because the publications were mostly in Hebrew? Up to that time there were only three articles in English, the two by Knohl and a short article by Yardeni in the *Biblical Archaeology Review*.[12] I gave some thought to publishing a book and to producing a television documentary, similar to what Frieda Tchacos, whom I knew from Zurich, had done for the Gospel of Judas.[13] But nothing came of these plans, and it looked as if the inscription would sink again into oblivion.

III

But—*habent sua fata libelli* or, in our case, *scriptura*—things developed totally differently. In the first half of 2008, I received a phone call from the correspondent of the *New York Times* in Jerusalem, Ethan Bronner. He had heard about the inscription and wanted to interview me, to send a photographer to Zurich, and to publish an article in his newspaper. I agreed, the interview was done, the pictures taken—but again nothing happened for months.

Then came the summer of 2008. During three days in July I attended an international conference that was organized at the Israel Museum in Jerusalem,

---

11. Ibid., 228.
12. Yardeni, "New Dead Sea Scroll in Stone?"
13. Rodolphe Kasser, Marvin Meyer, and Gregor Wurst, *The Gospel of Judas: From Codex Tchacos* (Washington, D.C.: National Geographic, 2006); Herbert Krosney: *The Lost Gospel: The Quest for the Gospel of Judas Iscariot* (Washington, D.C.: National Geographic, 2006); and the television film *The Gospel of Judas*, which was aired on the National Geographic channel on April 9, 2006.

celebrating sixty years of the discovery of the Dead Sea Scrolls.[14] At this conference Knohl spoke about his theory under the title "The Gabriel Revelation and the Birth of Christianity." Even today I do not know if it was by chance or not, but on the first day of the conference, on July 6, 2008, the *New York Times* published on its front page a long article by Ethan Bronner under the heading "Ancient Tablet Ignites Debate on Messiah and Resurrection" with a large photo of the stone and myself. In this article, Bronner described in a factual and balanced way the stone, the inscription, and its interpretations by various scholars, including myself, Yardeni, Goren, Daniel Boyarin, professor of talmudic culture at the University of California, Berkeley, Moshe Bar-Asher, president of the Israeli Academy of Hebrew Language and professor emeritus of Hebrew and Aramaic at the Hebrew University, and Moshe Idel, professor of Hebrew thought at the Hebrew University.

The article had an enormous impact on the conference in Jerusalem and everywhere else. The inscription turned into a hot and central news item on all radio and television stations throughout the world. Newspapers on the following day, July 7, 2008, dedicated their front pages and long articles to the inscription. So, for example, the *International Herald Tribune* published an article entitled "Is 3-day resurrection an idea pre-dating Jesus?" together with a photo of the stone and myself. All newspapers in Israel carried the news. In the following weeks, this wave spread like a media tsunami all over the world from Hong Kong in the east to California in the west, and daily, weekly, monthly, and quarterly newspapers, including *Time* reported widely about this discovery. The interest on the Internet grew explosively, and the links mentioning the *Jeselsohn Stone* or the *Gabriel Revelation* numbered more than one million.

This enormous media interest had three important results. First, I began to receive applications from production firms, vying for the production rights for a documentary television film. Second, museums began to apply for the right to exhibit the stone. And third, and most important, the scholarly world began to direct its attention to the stone through further research, photos, articles, books, and conferences.

As for films: out of the many applications I accepted two, the German cultural channel ZDF (Zweites Deutsches Fernsehen) and the National Geographic Channel. The first film was produced by Friedrich Klütsch with the help of Jürgen Zangenberg, professor of New Testament exegesis at the University of Leiden in the Netherlands, for the firm Tellux Film in Vienna, under the name "Der Auftrag des Erzengels" (The Assignment of the Archangel). This film was quite lavishly produced, with shootings in Switzerland, Israel, and Jordan and with actors and adventurous scenes taken at studios in Morocco. It was broadcast by ZDF for the first time on Easter Sunday, April 12, 2009.

---

14. "The Dead Sea Scrolls and Contemporary Culture—Celebrating 60 Years of Discovery." International Conference, Israel Museum, Jerusalem, July 6–8, 2008.

The second film was produced by Steven Hoggard of Hoggard Films in Boulder, Colorado, under the title "The First Jesus?" and aired for the first time on the National Geographic Channel on September 20, 2009. Both films mainly emphasized the theory of Knohl.

As for museums, I agreed to send the stone to two exhibitions. The first was in the Houston Museum of Natural Science in Houston, Texas, in an exhibition entitled "The Birth of Christianity: A Jewish Story," which ran from December 12, 2008, through April 12, 2009. Fifty-three thousand visitors came to view the exhibition, which included also a series of lectures. It was during that exhibition that I met Matthias Henze, professor of biblical studies at Rice University in Houston, who was one of the curators of the exhibition and who had organized a seminar on the inscription on February 10, 2009. As a matter of fact, this book is the outcome of his initiative and this seminar.

The second exhibition was organized by the Milwaukee Public Museum in Milwaukee, Wisconsin, entitled "Dead Sea Scrolls and the Bible." It ran from December 11, 2009, through June 6, 2010, was attended by 168,000 visitors, and also included a series of lectures. A catalogue on the exhibition was also published.

On the subject of research, although the original photographs by Radovan from 2002 and 2005 were of very good quality, I decided to take advantage of the advanced techniques used by Bruce Zuckerman, professor of religion at the University of Southern California, Los Angeles, and director of the West Semitic Research and InscriptiFact Projects. He used high resolution scanning Multi-Spectral Imaging (MSI) in order to illuminate and digitally document overlapping sections of the stone in various discrete areas of the spectrum, from ultraviolet through visible light to infrared. He was also employing Reflectance Transformation Imaging (RTI), enabling a better examination of the physical texture of the stone. Taking advantage of the presence of the stone in Houston, Zuckerman came twice with his team from Los Angeles and created a series of very detailed photos. The modern technique enabled him even to discover places where the original script was erased in antiquity and then written over, probably because the writer was not satisfied with his original writing. Regretfully, the new photographs could not shed any new light on the difficult reading of the word חאיה in line 80, which was of special importance for Knohl's theory.

Scientific articles began to be published one after another. Goren's article was already mentioned above.[15] Knohl was the most prolific. He first published an article in *Biblical Archaeology Review* under the title "The Messiah Son of Joseph," in which he further explained his views.[16] He then published a revised version of his article in the *Journal of Religion,* mentioned above, and an article in

---

15. Goren, "Micromorphologic Examination."
16. Israel Knohl, "The Messiah Son of Joseph: 'Gabriel's Revelation' and the Birth of a New Messianic Model," *BAR* 34, no. 5 (2008): 58–62, 78.

the Hebrew quarterly *Tarbiz* under the title "Studies in the *Gabriel Revelation*."[17] In this article he elaborated on ideological and literary components of the inscription, finding them to be of utmost importance for the understanding of apocalyptic, messianic, and martyrological developments in both Judaism and Christianity. These components supported his above-mentioned theory of an Ephraimitic Messiah; he suggested that the inscription was not composed by the Qumran sect. In addition, he proposed some alternate readings to those of Yardeni and Elizur.

Knohl then published a book entitled *Messiahs and Resurrection in 'The Gabriel Revelation'* in which he wrote in the introduction: "*The Gabriel Revelation* is an apocalyptic text dated to the turn of the Common Era. The dramatic finding of the apocalyptic text *The Gabriel Revelation* should change the way we view the historical Jesus and the birth of Christianity. It provides the key to understanding the roots of Jesus' messianic conception."[18]

John J. Collins, professor of Old Testament criticism and interpretation at Yale Divinity School, published a critical response to Knohl's messianic interpretation of the inscription in the *Yale Alumni Magazine*.[19] He had already previously been critical of Knohl's messianic thesis.[20]

Moshe Bar-Asher published a learned and thorough article about the language of the inscription.[21] His main findings were that the Hebrew language of the inscription should be placed in the period between the language of the Bible (among its characteristics are defective spellings and the use of the letter *sin* instead of the letter *samek*) and the language of the Mishnah (characterized, *inter alia*, by the construction of the masculine plural and dual endings and masculine plural pronominal forms with a final *nun*, by a gradual omission of guttural consonants, and by the use of a word of Greek origin—the word סימן, from the Greek σημεῖον, "sign," the first attestation of this word in Hebrew). Bar-Asher also elaborated quite widely on the word קיטוט, a new addition to the Hebrew vocabulary, meaning "very small," or "a very short while." His findings support the dating of the inscription to the late Second Temple period, that is, to the first century B.C.E. or the first century C.E.

---

17. Israel Knohl, "Studies in the *Gabriel Revelation*" (in Hebrew), *Tarbiz* 76 (2007): 303–28.

18. Israel Knohl, *Messiahs and Resurrection in 'The Gabriel Revelation'* (Kogod Library of Judaic Studies; London: Continuum, 2009), ix.

19. John J. Collins, "The Vision of Gabriel," *Yale Alumni Magazine* (September/October 2008): 26–27.

20. John J. Collins, "A Messiah before Jesus?" and "An Essene Messiah? Comments on Israel Knohl," in *Christian Beginnings and the Dead Sea Scrolls* (ed. John J. Collins and Craig A. Evans; Acadia Studies in Bible and Theology; Grand Rapids: Baker Academic, 2006), 15–35 and 37–44.

21. Moshe Bar-Asher, "On the Language of 'The Vision of Gabriel'," *RevQ* 23 (2008): 491–524, and a Hebrew version of the article in *Meghillot: Studies in the Dead Sea Scrolls* 7 (2009): 193–226.

Alexey Yuditsky and Elisha Qimron, professor of Hebrew language at the Ben Gurion University in Beer Sheva, one of the leading scholars in the field of the Dead Sea Scrolls and a member of their editorial team, also wrote about the inscription.²² They found a citation from the book of Jeremiah and postulated some different readings. In the disputed line 80, for example, where Knohl reads חאיה, "live," they read the word האות, "the sign." Generally they state that the language of the inscription is neither biblical nor Mishnaic but rather similar to the language of the Dead Sea Scrolls. They sum up their article as follows: "The language of the inscription is not identical with the language of any other Hebrew text. It is most similar to the language of the Dead Sea Scrolls and does not have even one trait typical solely of Mishnaic language. It shows that we are familiar with only a tiny part of the Hebrew language as it was when still spoken."²³

Gary A. Rendsburg, professor of Jewish history at Rutgers University, New Brunswick, N.J., also wrote an article drawing attention to some grammatical and literary aspects of the inscription.²⁴

It is intriguing to follow the magnitude of research and intellectual efforts invested in unlocking the secrets of the stone, and it is astonishing to look at the wealth of information—and of speculations—gleaned from the inscription. There is no doubt in my mind that we shall see even more of this in the future.

---

22. Alexey E. Yuditsky and Elisha Qimron, "Notes on the Inscription 'The Vision of Gabriel'" (in Hebrew), *Cathedra* 133 (2009): 133–44.

23. Yuditsky and Qimron, "Notes on the Inscription," 143 (trans. David Jeselsohn).

24. Gary A. Rendsburg, "Linguistic and Stylistic Notes to the Hazon Gabriel Inscription," *DSD* 16 (2009): 107–16.

TWO

A Hebrew Prophetic Text on Stone from the Early Herodian Period: A Preliminary Report

Ada Yardeni and Binyamin Elizur

About eight years ago, we were informed of the existence of a stone bearing a Hebrew text that was previously unknown.[1] This is a very large piece of limestone (ca. 96 x 37 cm), of light gray color, polished on one side, the other being undressed and formless. The stone is broken into three pieces, considerably differing in size but joining together with hardly any pieces missing. To date the

---

1. Photos of the stone were sent to Ada Yardeni in 2003. Yardeni tried to copy the written text from the photos and was surprised to discover a unique composition, but she could not identify its nature. The photos and the text were given to Binyamin Elizur, who corrected some readings but had no time to deal with the text. It took another three years before Yardeni could see the stone itself and make a hand copy of the original. This helped in confirming most of the readings, but since the writing is worn out in many places, only part of the text could be deciphered and its *Sitz im Leben* remained a mystery. Binyamin Elizur then located most of the extrabiblical sources, mainly with the assistance of the program *Maagarim* of the Historical Dictionary of the Hebrew Language, the texts included in it having been established on the basis of manuscripts, as well as with the help of the concordance of Hekhalot literature edited by Peter Schäfer (*Konkordanz zur Hekhalot-Literatur* [2 vols.; TSAJ 12–13; Tübingen: Mohr Siebeck, 1986, 1988), and with the help of the concordance of personal names appearing in the scrolls from the Judean Desert (*The Texts from the Judaean Desert: Indices and an Introduction to the Discoveries in the Judaean Desert Series*, ed. Emanuel Tov; DJD 39; Oxford: Clarendon, 2002], 237–84). This article was written by Ada Yardeni in consultation with Binyamin Elizur. The Hebrew version was translated into English by Ada Yardeni. We would like to thank Mr. Eugen Y. Han for his helpful comments, as well as Prof. W. van Bekkum for the translation into English of the verses from the *piyyut*, and Dr. Michael Rand for editing the article. Since the publication of our Hebrew version in *Cathedra* ("A Prophetic Text on Stone from the First Century BCE: First Publication" [in Hebrew], *Cathedra* 123 [2007]: 155–66), an article has been published in *Cathedra* in 2009 by Alexey Yuditsky and Elisha Qimron ("Notes on the Inscription 'The Vision of Gabriel'" [in Hebrew], *Cathedra* 133 [2009]: 133–44) in which important corrections have been made to our reading. Only two of these corrections have been inserted here (lines 24 and 31 [see below]).

pieces have not been joined permanently. The main break starts ca. 40 cm from the bottom on the right, slants down to the left, and ends ca. 25 cm from the bottom on the left. A secondary break is found at the right top of the lower piece, creating a sharp-angled triangle (measuring 7 x 25 x 23 cm), its tip pointing to the left.[2]

The provenance of the stone seems to be Jordan, and it is now part of the collection of Dr. David Jeselsohn in Zurich. We hereby thank him for allowing us to examine the stone, to photograph it, to make a hand copy of it, and to publish it in the present preliminary report.

Two columns appear on the polished side of the stone, 3.5 cm apart. Each column is 16 cm wide and ca. 75 cm or more long. The text is written in ink, in a manner resembling the writing of a Torah scroll, in a "Jewish" book hand of the late first century B.C.E. (see below in the paleographic description). Forty-seven thin, straight, horizontal guidelines, running through both columns parallel to the short side of the stone, and four straight, vertical lines bordering the columns on both sides, are incised with a thin, sharp implement in a manner very similar to the guidelines in the scrolls from the Judean Desert. A margin of ca. 1 cm has survived on both the right and left sides of the stone. A margin of about 5 cm has survived at its top, and a larger margin of about 13 cm has survived at its bottom.

The existing text comprises eighty-seven lines of writing, the right column comprising forty-four lines and the left column only forty-three lines, the two last being shorter and delimited by three large, slanting strokes, one below the other, marking the end of the entire text. About three horizontal guidelines at the bottom seem to have been left empty (unless additional lines of text once existed in column A, which are now undetectable).

The text is poorly preserved, with lacunas throughout. The top and the bottom of the text, together with the beginnings of the lines in column A and the ends of the lines in column B, are very worn-out, with only single letters being legible. The readings in many places are conjectural and difficult to restore owing to a lack of parallels.

The undressed surface of the back of the stone indicates that it was installed in a wall in an upright position. The layout of the text, resembling the columns of a scroll (possibly having been copied from a scroll), indicates that it may originally have been much longer—that is, comprising more columns and thus having been written on a series of stones and perhaps installed in the walls of a large chamber. However, no similar finds seem to exist, and since the beginning of column A could not be deciphered, this assumption can be neither confirmed nor refuted.

The text is a literary composition not known from other Jewish sources. Its formulation indicates that it belongs to the prophetic genre. It contains at least

---

2. See the photos in this volume (pp. 189–94). For a drawing of the entire inscription, see *Cathedra* 123 (2007); also online at http://sbl-site.org/assets/pdfs/pubs/Gabriel/Yardeni.pdf.

one biblical citation, from the book of Haggai, and expressions from the books of Zechariah and Daniel (see below). Some expressions, however, seem to be early attestations of expressions known from later sources (e.g., Hekhalot literature, *piyyut*, Talmud, and Midrash; see below). The text also contains expressions that do not seem to have parallels elsewhere. The language shows some Aramaic influence. The text seems to have been composed in the late first century B.C.E. and copied onto the stone (perhaps from a scroll) soon after, as indicated by its script.

Text (doubtful readings appear in gray type)

Column A

1. [ ] [... ......ד
2. [ ] [...[?] .ה...[ ].
3. [ ] [ע] [ב
4. [ ] [כי] [.ארס... ל....ה.
5. [ ] [... ..] [ ]
6. [ ] [ח]?..[.ז .הו .ה..] [י...מל] ? [
7. [ ] [ב..[?].ב. בני ישראל [ ] [?]..ל..ש
8. [בנ...ד[?].ל[?].ל..[?].[?].ל[ ] [ב] [ל] [דא.[?]
9. [ ] [ה.ו[?]דבר יהו]ה.[ ] [.....] [... .ק.] [ה.[?]
10. [ ] [..... ....לב ...תים שאלת...[?]
11. [?]יהוה אתה שאלני כן אמר אלהים צבאות
12. [ ]..[ני מבית ישראל ואגדה בגדלות ירושלם
13. [כן] אמר יהוה אלהי ישראל הנה כול הגאים
14. ......על ירושלם ו.שמתו... מ....ג...
15. [א]חת שתין שלוש ארבעין נביאין והשבין
16. [ו]ההסידין עבדי דוד בקש מן לפני אמ/פרים
17. [ ].שים האות אני מבקש מן לפנך כי אמר
18. [י]הוה צבאות אלהי ישראל גני..וכרי.
19. קדשה לישראל לשלשת ימין תדע כי אמר
20. יהוה אלהים צבאות אלהי ישראל נשבר הרע
21. מלפני הצדק שאלני ואגיד לכה מה הצמח
22. הרע הזה לו/יבנסד/ר/ך אתה עומד המלאך הוא
23. כסמכך אל תורה ברוך כבוד יהוה אלהים מן
24. מקומו עוד מעט קיטוט היא ואני מרעיש את
25. .. השמים ואת הארץ הנה כבוד יהוה אלהים
26. צבאות אלהי ישראל אלה המרכבות שבע
27. [ע]ל שער ירושלם ושערי יהודה ונ... למען
28. ....ל... מלאכה מיכאל ולכול האחרין בקשו
29. .ילב.. כן אמר יהוה אלהים צבאות אלהי
30. ישראל אחד שנין שלושה ארבעה חמשה ששה

31. [שב]עה אל מלאכה..... מה זו אמר העץ
32. [ ].....   [ ].ל.ד. פכ....... ואלוף השני
33. [ ]שמר על.. ירשלם ..... שלושה בגדלות
34. [ ].[?]וה[?]   [...].לו.[?].[?]ה..א.[ ]. ד.ך
35. [...] ויו בד עו...שראה איש.ן.[ ]
36. שסמן ממירושלם]   [. ..... שהוא
37. .. אני על .אי.[?] אב/מר.אותגלות
38. אתגלות .צל.[?]. אלהים ע...א.ן וארא ה
39. ג.[א]....[ירושלם יאמר יהוה
40. צבאות ..א.ל.. ....ל...חנארו.ורח.[?]
41. [ ]   [דם שירם .....
42. [ ]   [.א.ן הנגי. בכול
43. [ ]   [...ב ש.ו. .
44. [ ]   [ש.[?]

Column B

45. [ ]   [
46. [י[הוה]   [
47. [..[ ].י.[ ]   [
48. [..ל. .ע]   [
49. [..[?].ד.[ ]..   [
50. [.[ ]...[ ].[ ]   [
51. [עמך ר/דעוך   [
52. .ן ה[מ]לאכים]   [מן ..על[ ].ד/.ה.
53. על עמו/י ומחה ....ה[ ]..[ ].[ ]שג
54. [ ]שלשת ימין זה שאמ.. [.]הוא
55. אלה[ ].[..[ ]שֹל.[ ]...[ ]..[ ]   [
56. ר]או נא[?]ה.צ.....[ ]
57. סתום דם טבחי ירושלם כי אמר יהוה צבא[ות]
58. אלהי ישראל כי אמר יהוה צבאות אלהי
59. ישראל מא.. ל.. אל.... ל.[ ].[ ].[ד.[?]
60. [ ].[ ]לני רוח הנרא..תן .שק. ל.[?]
61. ..[ל אשריא....תץ ש...[?]
62. בה א..[ ]   ..[ב ד.[?]..[[
63. א [ ].א. אב.[?].א.[ ]...[ ].[ ]   [
64. ..[ ].[ ]ה ה/חביב .. ל...[ ]   [
65. שלושה קדושי העולם מן מק.[[
66. [ ].ו שלום אמר עליך אנחנו בטוחין ..[?]
67. בשר לו על דם זו המרכבה שלהן .. ל.[ ]

A HEBREW PROPHETIC TEXT ON STONE 15

68. אוהבין רבים ליהוה צבאת אל<ה>י ישראל ..
69. כה אמר יהוה צבאת אלהי ישראל .מ....[?]
70. נביאים שלחתי אל עמי שלושה ואני אומר
71. שראיתי ברכ. ל..לך דבר. ברן [...ב..[?]
72. המקום למען דוד עבד יהוה] [..א.[ ]..[ ]
73. את השמים ואת הארץ ברוך ש...... .[ ]
74. אנשים עושה חסד לאלפים מ.... חסד.] [
75. שלושה רועין יצאו לישראל .ל...[ ].[ ]
76. אם יש כהן אם יש בני קדושים ..ה..] [
77. מי אנכי. אני גבריאל המ.ל.כי.לי ..מל] [
78. תצילם נבי...ם גר..ם לשות.ן [ ] .ב. [ ]
79. מלפניך שלושה הא[ת]ות שלושה ... א[ק] [ ]
80. לשלושת ימין חא.. אני גבריאל ... ל..[?]
81. שר השרין ד..ן ארובות צרים א] [. א..[?]
82. ל.ראו/.ת ה...לשנם מן [ ]....ן וה.ב.ג.מ[?]
83. לי מן שלושה הקטן שלקחתי אני גבריאל
84. יהוה צבאת אל<ה>י] [..[ ]
85. אז תעמדו א .]..ל..[ ].. [..א........[?]
86. ...ל.... \
87. ב....עו\לם
88. \

Translation (Semitic sounds in capitals and\or italics)

Column A

(Lines 1–6 are unintelligible)
7. […]the sons of Israel …[…]…
8. […]… […]…
9. […]the word of YHW[H …]…[…]
10. […]… I/you asked …
11. YHWH, you ask me. Thus said the Lord of Hosts:
12. […]… from my(?) house, Israel, and I will tell the greatness(es?) of Jerusalem.
13. [Thus] said YHWH, the God of Israel: Behold, all the nations are
14. … against(?)\to(?) Jerusalem and …,
15. [o]ne, two, three, forty(?) prophets(?) and the returners(?),
16. [and] the Ḥasidin(?). My servant, David, asked from before Ephraim(?)
17. [to?] put the sign(?) I ask from you. Because He said, (namely,)
18. [Y]HWH of Hosts, the God of Israel: …
19. sanctity(?)/sanctify(?) Israel! In three days you shall know, that(?)/for(?) He said,

20. (namely,) YHWH the Lord of Hosts, the God of Israel: Evil has been broken (down)
21. before justice. Ask me and I will tell you what ²²this bad ²¹plant is,
22. *lwbnsd/r/k* (=?) you are standing, the messenger/angel. He
23. ... (= will ordain you?) to Torah(?). Blessed be the Glory of YHWH the Lord, from
24. his place. "In a little while," *qyṭuṭ*(= a brawl?/tiny?) it is, "and I will shake the
25. ... of? heaven and the earth". Here is the Glory of YHWH the Lord of
26. Hosts, the God of Israel. These are the chariots, seven,
27. [un]to(?) the gate(?) of Jerusalem, and the gates of Judah, and ... for the sake of
28. ... His(?) angel, Michael, and to all the others(?) ask/asked
29. .... Thus He said, YHWH the Lord of Hosts, the God of
30. Israel: One, two, three, four, five, six,
31. [se]ven, these(?) are(?) His(?) angel .... "What is it," said the tree(?)
32. ...[...]... and (the?) ... (= leader?/ruler?), the second,
33. ... Jerusalem.... three, in\of the greatness(es?) of
34. [...]...[...]...
35. [...]..., who saw a man ... working(?) and [...]...
36. that he ... [...]... from(?) Jerusalem(?)
37. ... on(?) ... the exile(?) of ...,
38. the exile(?) of ..., Lord ..., and I will see
39. ...[...] Jerusalem, He will say, YHWH of
40. Hosts, ...
41. [...]... that will lift(?) ...
42. [...]... in all the
43. [...]...
44. [...]...

Column B

(Lines 45-50 are unintelligible)
51. Your people(?)/with you(?) ...[...]
52. ... the [me]ssengers(?)/[a]ngels(?)[...]...
53. on\against His/My people. And ...[...]...
54. [...]three days(?). This is (that) which(?) ...[...]He(?)
55. the Lord(?)/these(?)[...]...[...]
56. see(?) ...[...]
57. closed(?). The blood of the slaughters(?)/sacrifices(?) of Jerusalem. For He said, YHWH of Hos[ts],
58. the Lord of Israel: For He said, YHWH of Hosts, the God of
59. Israel: ...
60. [...]... me(?) the spirit?/wind of(?) ...

61. ...[...]...
62. in it(?) ...[...]...[...]
63. ...[...]...[...]
64. ...[...]... loved(?)/... ...[...]
65. The three saints of the world\eternity from/of ...[...]
66. [...]... peace he? said, to\in you we trust(?) ...
67. Inform him of the blood of this chariot of them(?) ...[...]
68. Many lovers He has, YHWH of Hosts, the God of Israel ...
69. Thus He said, (namely,) YHWH of Hosts, the God of Israel ...:
70. Prophets have I sent to my people, three. And I say
71. that I have seen ...[...]...
72. the place for the sake of(?) David the servant of YHWH[...]...[...]
73. the heaven and the earth. Blessed be ...[...]
74. men(?). "Showing mercy unto thousands," ... mercy [...].
75. Three shepherds went out to?/of? Israel ...[...].
76. If there is a priest, if there are sons of saints ...[...]
77. Who am I(?), I (am?) Gabriel the ...(=angel?)... [...]
78. You(?) will save them, ...[...]...
79. from before You, the three si[gn]s(?), three ...[....]
80. In three days ..., I, Gabriel ...[?],
81. the Prince of Princes, ..., narrow holes(?) ...[...]...
82. to/for ... [...]... and the ...
83. to me(?), out of three - the small one, whom(?) I took, I, Gabriel.
84. YHWH of Hosts, the God of(?)[Israel ...]...[....]
85. Then you will stand ...[...]...
86. ...\
87. in(?) ... eternity(?)/... \

Description of the Text

The text is very fragmentary, but it seems to be a collection of short prophecies dictated to a scribe, in a manner similar to prophecies appearing in the Hebrew Bible. However, although the inscription contains many biblical expressions, the language sounds more like Mishnaic Hebrew than Biblical Hebrew (e.g., there is no use of *waw*-consecutive to express already finished and still unfinished actions), and it shows some Aramaic influence. The text is written in the first person, possibly by someone calling himself Gabriel (lines 77, 80, 83; cf. Dan 8:16; 9:21) and is addressed to someone in the second person singular. One of the short prophecies is almost an exact quotation from Hag 2:6 (lines 24–25). The author cites the "word of YHWH" (line 9), and many prophecies open with the words "thus/therefore said the Lord/YHWH of Hosts, the Lord of Israel" (lines 11, 13, 17–18, 19–20, 29–30, 57–59, 69). The name Jerusalem is mentioned several times (lines 12, 14, 27, 36, 39, 57) in different contexts.

The text contains an expression that may perhaps refer to a historical event. This expression is *dm ṭbḥy Yrwšlm* (= *dam ṭibĕḥê Yĕrûšālēm*? [Line 57]). The word *ṭbḥy* seems to be the construct form of *ṭĕbaḥ* ("slaughter" or "sacrifice"). If this text was indeed composed in the first century B.C.E., as indicated by its script and language, there is more than one event to which this expression may refer. It seems more plausible, however, to understand the word *ṭbḥy* as referring to the flesh of the sacrifices in the Jerusalem temple, that is, to the feasts held in Jerusalem. Unfortunately, the text does not contain enough information to indicate the precise time of its composition.

The word *glwt* ("exile"), which seems to appear in lines 37, 38, 39, perhaps indicates that the author was forced to leave Jerusalem and reside in exile.

The text seems to contain a number of allusions to various groups of unnamed people, among them "the prophets, the returners(?) and the Ḥasidin(?)" (lines 15–16; cf. Ps 149:5–6),[3] "the others" (line 28), "the three saints of the world/eternity(?)" (line 65), "many lovers," etc. (line 68; cf. "the lovers of the Lord"),[4] "three prophets" (line 70; this expression appears in several sources referring to different prophets of unknown identity),[5] "three shepherds" (line

---

3. יעלזו **חסידים** בכבוד ירננו על־משכבותם, רוממות אל בגרונם וחרב פיפיות בידם.
"Let the **saints** be joyful in glory. Let them sing aloud upon their beds. Let the high praises of God be in their mouth, and a double-edged sword in their hand."

4. Emil Puech, "525. 4QBeatitudes," *Qumran Cave 4.XVIII: Textes hébreux (4Q521–4Q528, 4Q576–4Q579)* (ed. E. Puech; DJD 25; Oxford: Clarendon, 1997), 131.

5. Cf. ידאג ירמיה ;לחכמה יצפה ישעיה ;לחסידות יצפה בחלום 'מלכ הרוא .הם **נביאים שלשה**
מן הפורענות.
"**Three** are the **prophets**: the one who sees kings in a dream—he may look forward to piety; [the one who sees] Isaiah—he may look forward to wisdom; [the one who sees] Jeremiah—let him fear retribution" (*b. Ber.* 57b).

אמר רבא בר בר חנא אמ' ר' יוחנן. "שלשה נביאים עלו עמהם מן הגולה. אחד שהעיד להם על המזבח ואחד שהעיד להם על מקום המזבח, ואחד שהעיד להם שמקריבים אע"פ שאין בית."
"Rabbah bar bar Hannah said in R. Johanan's name, '**Three prophets** went up with them from the exile: one testified to them about [the dimensions of] the altar; another testified to them about the site of the altar; and the third testified to them that they could sacrifice even though there was no Temple'" (*b. Zebah.* 62a).

דבר־אחר. "דברי קהלת בן דוד". **שלשה נביאים** על ידי שהית נבואתן דברי קנתורין נתלית נבואתן בעצמם. ואילו הן. "דברי קהלת". דברי עמוס". "דברי ירמיה".
"Another interpretation of 'the words of Koheleth son of David' (Qoh. 1:1): There are **three prophets** to whom, because their prophecy consisted of words of reproach, it is attributed personally, *viz.*, 'The words of Koheleth,' 'The words of Amos,' [and] 'The words of Jeremiah'" (*Qoh. Rab.* 1,1,2).

שלשה נביאים הם. אחד תבע כבוד האב ולא תבע כבוד הבן. ואחד תבע כבוד הבן ולא תבע כבוד האב. ואחד תבע כבוד האב וכבוד הבן.
"**Three** are the **prophets**: one demanded the honor of the Father but did not demand the honor of the son, and one demanded the honor of the son but not the honor of the Father, and one demanded the honor of the Father and the honor of the son" (*ʾAbot R. Nat.* ver. B, 47 [Ed. Schechter, p. 65a]).

זה אחד משלשה **נביאים** שאמ' כלשון הזה. אליהו ומיכה ומשה.

75; cf. Zech 11:8; it appears also in later sources,⁶ but it is difficult to know to whom the text referred).

The text also mentions "My servant, David" (line 16), and "David the servant of YHWH" (l. 72), indicating that the author supported the Davidic dynasty. The "bad plant" (lines 21–22; cf. Jer 23:5; 33:15; Zech 3:8; 6:9–15) possibly refers to the Messiah of a different dynasty. In line 16, one can perhaps restore the name *'prym* (Ephraim[?]). If the name indeed appears, it may have referred to the Messiah son of Joseph, as opposed to the Messiah of the tribe of Judah.⁷

The reference to "His(?) messenger/angel Michael" (line 28) may be based on the book of Daniel (Dan 10:13, 21; 12:1; in extrabiblical sources, Michael is often mentioned together with Gabriel).⁸ In Dan 12:1 Michael is referred to as השר הגדול ("the great Prince" [= "the patron angel"?]).⁹ In Dan 8:25 שר שרים ("the Prince of Princes") appears. This expression appears in line 81, the context being obscure. It is difficult to explain the letter *he* at the end of the word מלאכה before the name Michael in line 28. (Could it perhaps be the Aramaic article or the Aramaic possessive suffix that entered this Hebrew text?)

In addition to the citation from the book of Haggai mentioned above, the text contains biblical expressions and words alongside expressions and words unknown from the Bible.

Expressions appearing in the Bible or resembling biblical expressions are the following: ואגדה בגדלות (line 12; *wě'aggidâ biggědūlôt*; cf. ואגידה לך גדלות, Jer. 33:3); עבדי דוד (line 16; *ʿabdî Dāwid*; cf. 1 Kgs 11:32; 14:8; Ezek 34:24; 37:24; and sometimes with the word order דו(י)ד עבדי, e.g., 2 Sam 3:18; 1 Kgs 11:32, etc.); לשלשת ימין (lines 19, 80; *lišlōšet yāmîn*; cf. Exod 19:15; Ezra 10:8, 9; Amos 4:4); ברוך כבוד יהוה (line 23; *bārûk kěbôd YHWH min měqômô*; Ezek 3:12; please note that the correct reading in line 24 מקומו has been offered lately by Alexey Yuditsky and Elisha Qimron instead of our reading מושבו); המרכבות שבע (line 26; *hammerkābôt šebaʿ*; as against ארבע מרכבות, Zech 6:1;¹⁰ but see also שבעה

"This is one of **three prophets** who spoke thus: Elijah, and Micah and Moses" (*Midr. Tanḥ*, ed. Buber, Qorah 3, p. 96).

ירמיה היה אחד **משלשה נביאים** שנתנבאו באותו הדור. ירמיהו וצפניהו וחולדה הנביאה. ירמיהו היה מתנבא בשוקים וצפניה בתוך הבית בתי כניסיות וחולדה אצל הנשים.

"Jeremiah was one of **three prophets** who prophesied in his generation: Jeremiah, and Zephaniah, and Huldah the prophetess. Jeremiah prophesied in the city squares, Zephaniah in the Temple and in synagogues, and Huldah among the women" (*Pesiq. Rab.* 26 ed. Ish Shalom, p. 129b). "Jeremiah, Zephaniah, and Huldah"—Parma MS. See Jer 1:2; Zeph 1:1; 2 Kgs 22:3, 4; and 2 Chr 34:8, 22.).

6. "שלשה רועים" אילו משה ואהרן ומרים.
"'**Three shepherds**': these are Moses and Aaron and Miriam" (*Tanḥ.*, Huqqat 8)."

7. Cf. *Pesiq. Rab.* 36–37 (ed. Ish Shalom, pp. 161b–163a).

8. Cf., e.g., *Gen. Rab.* 1 (ed. Theodor-Albeck, p. 5).

9. Cf. *Tg. Job* 25:2; *Tg. Ps.* 137:7; *b. Ḥag.* 12b ומיכאל השר הגדול, "and **Michael, the great prince**").

10. Cf. אמר ריש לקיש האבות הן הן המרכבה

מרכבות in a later source);[11] יהוה צבאות אלהי ישראל (line 69; *YHWH ṣĕbā'ôt 'ĕlōhê Yiśrā'ēl* [with variations in lines 11, 13, 17–18, 19–20, 29–30, 57–59] = 2 Sam 7:27; Isa 21:10; 37:16); למען דוד עבד יהוה (line 72?; *lĕma'an Dāwid 'ebed YHWH*; cf. 1 Kgs 11:13: למען דוד עבדי ולמען ירושלם); עושה חסד לאלפים (line 74; *'ôśeh ḥesed la'ălāpîm* = Exod 20:6; Deut 5:10; Jer 32:18); שלושה רועי (line 75; *šĕlôśâ rô'în*; cf. Zech 11:8: ואכחד את שלשת הרעים בירח אחד ותקצר נפשי בהם וגם נפשם בחלה בי ["And I cut off the three shepherds in one month, and my soul loathed them and their soul also abhorred me"]; אם יש[12] (line 76; *'im yēš* = Gen 44:26); שר השרין (line 81; *śar haśśārîn*; cf. שר השרים Dan 8:25 = Michael; this expression appears in several extrabiblical sources).[13]

"Resh Lakish said: the forefathers, it is they who are the Chariot" (*Gen. Rab.* 47:6 [ed. Theodor-Albeck, p. 475], et al.).

11. Cf. א' ר' לוי משום ר' יוסה מעוניה שא' ר' מאיר: "שבעה רקיעים ברא הק' ושבעה מרכבות ...

"R. Levi said in the name of R. Yosi the Ma'onian that R. Me'ir said: The Holy One Blessed Be He created seven firmaments and **seven chariots** . . ." (*Re'uyot Yehezke'el* 11 [ed. Wertheimer, *Batei Midrashot*, II, Jerusalem, 1953, p. 130]).

12. Cf. n. 5 above.

13. Cf. in Hekhalot literature:

א' מטטרון מלאך שר הפנים ומלאך שר התורה ומלאך שר החכמה ומלאך שר התבונה ומלאך שר המלכים! ומלאך שר הרוזנים ומלאך שר הכבוד מלאך שר המלכים מלאך **שר השרים** רמים וגבוהים רבים ונכבדים שבשמים ובארץ.

"Thus said Metatron, the angelic prince of the countenance, the angelic prince of the Torah, the angelic prince of wisdom, the angelic prince of insight, the angelic prince of !kings!, the angelic prince of rulers, the angelic prince of the [Divine] majesty, the angelic prince of kings, the angelic **prince of princes**, high and exalted, distinguished and respected in heaven and on earth" (*Synopse zur Hekhalot-Literatur* [ed. Peter Schäfer; TSAJ 2; Tübingen: Mohr Siebeck, 1981], §78 [= Hugo Odeberg, *3 Enoch, Or The Hebrew Book of Enoch* (Cambridge: Cambridge University Press, 1928; repr., Library of Biblical Studies; New York:Ktav, 1973), 73]).

וזה הנער מלאך שלו שר הפנים מלאך שר התורה שר החכמה שר התבונה שר המלוכה שר הכבוד שר ההיכל שר המלכים שר הרוזנים **שר השרים** רמים וגבוהים רבים ונכבדים שבשמים ובארץ.

"Now this youth is His angel, the prince of the countenance, the angelic prince of the Torah, the prince of wisdom, the prince of insight, the prince of kingship, the prince of [Divine] majesty, the prince of the Temple, the prince of kings, the prince of rulers, **the prince of princes**, high and exalted, distinguished and respected in heaven and on earth" (Schäfer, *Synopse*, §389).

See also:

בששי ברא בהמות וחיה ורמש. ושבע חיות ושקצים ורמשים שנ'[אמר] תוצא הארץ נפש חיה למינה בהמ'[ה] ורמ'[ש] וגו'. אחר כולם ברא אדם למשול בכולן. דבר דיבר והכין צבאיו וכל אחד ואחד ציוה על עבודתו. גידל מלאך בראש כולם **וגבריאל בראש השרים**.

"On the sixth [day] he created Behemoth and beasts and crawlers and the seven beasts and the abominations and the crawlers, as it is said: Let the earth bring forth living creatures in accordance with their types, cattle and crawlers *and so forth* (Gen 1:24). And after all these he created man to rule over them all. He spoke the word and set up His hosts, and commanded each one to his particular task. He [also] elevated an angel to be at the head of them all, **Gabriel, as the head of princes**" (Schäfer, *Synopse*, §847).

Other biblical words: צמח (line 21; *ṣemaḥ*; cf. Jer 23:5; 33:15; Zech 3:8; 6:12 [cf. הוא צמח הוא מנחם],[14] possibly referring to the Messiah); העץ (line 31; *hāʿēṣ*? [= the tree]; the corrected reading— העץ instead of our reading הצץ—has been offered lately by Yuditsky and Qimron); עמי (line 70; *ʿammî*); אות (line 17; *ʾôt*; letter[?]/sign[?]; cf., e.g., אשר שמת אתות ומפתים, "Who has set signs and wonders" [Jer 32:20]); צדק (line 21; *ṣedeq*;. cf. אפרים משיח צדקנו[15] and Isa 41:10]); הקטן (line 83. *haqqāṭān*; cf. 1 Sam 16:11; 17:14).

Expressions not appearing as such in the Hebrew Bible: אתה שאלני (line 11; *ʾattâ šaʾalēnî*; perhaps a case of Aramaic influence); גדלות ירושלם (line 12; *gĕdûlôt Yĕrûšālēm* [see Jer 33:3]; the word גדלות appears in the Bible but not together with the name of the city); נביאין והשבין [ו]החסידין (lines 15–16; *nĕbîʾîn wĕhaššābîn* [*wĕ*]*haḥăsîdîn* [the latter probably referring to a certain social or political group]); בקש מן לפני (line 16; *biqqēš min lĕpānay* [?]/*lipnê*[?]); אני מבקש מן לפנך (line 17; *ʾănî mĕbaqqēš min lĕpānêkā*; cf. Aramaic מן קדמך,[16] but cf. also מלפני in line 21 and מלפניך in line 79]); נשבר הרע מלפני הצדק (lines 20–21; *nišbar hāraʿ millipnê haṣṣedeq*; see צדק above); מה הצמח הרע הזה לי/ובנסר/ך (lines 21–22; *mâ haṣṣemaḥ hāraʿ hazzeh lî/lô benesek* [?]; the reading is conjectural); כסמכך אל תורה (line 23; *kĕsōmĕkākā ʾel tôrâ*; the meaning here is unclear; the root סמך in the meaning "to ordain" appears in Talmudic Hebrew);[17] כן אמר (line 29; *kēn ʾāmar* [as in Aramaic],[18] as against biblical כה אמר); מה זו (line 31; *mâ zô*; cf. biblical מה זה [e.g., Exod 4:2] and מה זאת [e.g., Gen 3:13]); אחד שנין שלושה ארבעה חמשה ששה [שב]עה אל מלאכה (lines 30–32; *ʾeḥād, šĕnayin, šĕlôšâ, ʾrbāʿā, ḥămiššâ, šiššâ,*

In *piyyut*:

שלמה סוליאן, סדר עבודה, [א...] במרומים [...] מלא עולמים. ס'[גולה] תען שירים / בעטותו בגדים מאושרים / סוקרת בו בפנים מזהירים / בדמות פני **מיכאל שר סרים**.

"The treasured [nation] resounds with song / as He dons sublime garments, / beholds Him with radiant faces, / the image of Michael, the **prince of princes**" (Naoya Katsumata, "An Additional Seder ʿAvoda for Yom Kippur by Shelomo Suleiman Al-Sinjari," *Frankfurter Judaistische Beiträge* 29 [2002]: 41, lines 231–32).

דוסא החזן, יוצר בלק: ויבא שר השרים בהקדימך / עוז מיכאל תמימך / "מי האנשים האלה עמך".
"And the **prince of princes** came at Your bidding, / the mighty Michael, Your blameless [angel], / 'Who are these men with you?' (Num. 22:9])" (Ezra Fleischer, *The Yozer, Its Emergence and Development* [in Hebrew; Jerusalem: Magnes, 1984], 732).

14. Y. *Ber.* II 5a (Jerusalem: Academy of the Hebrew Language, 2001), 18, line 42.

15. *Pesiq. Rab.* 37 (ed. Ish Shalom, p. 163a).

16. Cf., e.g., XḤev/SE 7:6; see Ada Yardeni, *Textbook of Aramaic, Hebrew and Nabatean Documentary Texts from the Judaean Desert and Related Material* (2 vols.; Jerusalem: Hebrew University, 2000), vol. B, III Concordance, p. 127.

17. Cf., e.g., *b. Sanh.* 13b.

18. Cf., e.g., Bezalel Porten and Ada Yardeni, *Textbook of Aramaic Documents from ancient Egypt* (4 vols.; Jerusalem: Hebrew University/Winona Lake, Ind.: Eisenbrauns, 1986–99), 96, A6.2:22, et passim.

[šib]ʿâ, ʾel(eh?) malʾāk(?) . . . ; seven angels are mentioned in Hekhalot literature);[19] איש תהפכות ואלוף השני (line 32; wĕʾallûf haššēnî (?); cf. the midrash to Prov 16:28 ישלח מדון ונרגן מפריד אלוף, "A quarrelsome man sows strife, and a whisperer alienates friends";[20] this is an adoption of a biblical title referring to Edomite tribal leaders [cf. Genesis 36]; the word אלוף appears in Hekhalot literature in the context of angels);[21] סתום דם טבחי ירושלם (line 57 = sātûm?/sātôm? dam ṭibĕḥê[?] Yĕrûšālēm; the precise meaning of סתום in this context is obscure, either ending the preceding verse or perhaps referring to the interruption of the sacrifice practice at the Jerusalem temple); שלושה קדושי העולם (line 65; šĕlôšâ qĕdôšê hāʿôlām), עליך אנחנו בטוחין (?; line 66; ʿālêkā ʾănaḥnû bĕṭûḥîn?; the reading is conjectural);[22] בשר לו על דם זו המרכבה שלהן (line 67; baśśēr lô ʿal dam zô hammerkābâ šellāhēn); אוהבין רבים ליהוה (line 68; ʾôhăbîn rabbîm laYHWH; cf. ואהבת את יהוה אלהיך, Deut 6:5); נבי־אים שלחתי אל עמי שלושה (line 70; nĕbîʾîm šālaḥtî ʾel ʿammî šĕlôšâ; the word order seems to be influenced by Aramaic); שראיתי (line 71; šerāʾîtî; postbiblical language showing Aramaic influence; cf. biblical אשר, ʾăšer); שלושה רועין יצאו לישראל (line

---

19. Cf. שליט שבעה מלאכין על נורא. תרמוס אוריאל ואפיאל גבריאל נוריאל פנאל וסרפיאל. "There are **seven angels** [appointed] over the fire: TRMWS, Uri'el, 'PY'el, Gabri'el, Nuri'el, PN'el, and SRPY'el" (Schäfer, *Synopse*, §493).

20. Cf. "יפריד אלוף" שהפריד אלופו של עולם. "Alienates friends: he alienated the Friend of the world" (*Gen. Rab.* 20:2 [ed. Theodor-Albeck, p. 182]).

21. Cf. אמר רבי ישמעאל. אמר לי מטטרון מלאך שר הפנים. למעלה מהן משני השרים הגדולים הללו יש שר אחד **אלוף** ונכבד [...] שאין כיוצא בו בכל השרים כלם. רכביאל יו"י שמו שהוא עומד אצל המרכבה. "R. Ishmael said: Metatron, the angelic prince of the Countenance, said to me, 'Above them, i.e., these two great princes, there is one prince, **venerable (?)** and respected. . . the like of whom is not found amongst all the princes. His name is RKBYʾel, YWY, for he stands near the Chariot'" (Schäfer, *Synopse*, §30);

אמר ר' ישמעאל. אמר לי מטטרון מלאך (ה) שר הפנים. למעלה מהן יש(ר) שר אחד גדול ותקיף חייליאל יו"י שמו. שר אדיר ונורא שר **אלוף** וגבור שר גדול ונורא. "R. Ishmael said: Metatron, the angelic prince of the Countenance, said to me, 'Above them there is a prince, great and powerful, ḤYYLYʾel YWY is his name—a strong and awesome prince, a **venerable (?)** and heroic prince, a great and awesome prince'" (Schäfer, *Synopse*, §31);

אמר ר' ישמעאל. אמר לי מטטרון מלאך שר הפנים. למעלה מהן יש שר אחד גדול ונורא גבור ונכבד **אלוף** ונערץ. "R. Ishmael said: Metatron, the angelic prince of the Countenance, said to me, 'Above them there is a prince, great and awesome, heroic and respected, **venerable (?)** and mighty'" (Schäfer, *Synopse*, §39);

אמר ר' ישמעאל. אמר לי מטטרון מלאך שר הפנים. למעלה מהם יש שר אחד מופלא ואדיר רב יקר גבור ועריץ ו**אלוף** ונגיד. "R. Ishmael said: Metatron, the angelic prince of the Countenance, said to me, 'Above them there is a prince, wonderful and powerful, great, precious, heroic and mighty, and **venerable (?)** and princely'" (Schäfer, *Synopse*, §§41–42).

22. Cf. כי על רחמיך הרבים אנו בטוחים. "For we trust in Your great mercy." *A Prayer before the Thirteen Attributes, Selihot according to Polish Rite* (ed. Daniel Goldschmidt; Jerusalem: Mossad Harav Kook, 1965), 7.

75; šĕlôšâ rôʿîn yāṣĕʾû lĕyisrāʾēl; the expression יצא ל, "to go out to" or "to arise from," is unusual for Hebrew, which typically employs יצא מן); אם יש כהן אם יש בני (line 76; ʾim yēš kōhēn ʾim yēš bĕnê qĕdōšîm; אם יש is attested in the Bible [e.g., Gen 44:26] but not in this particular syntagm); מי אנכי אני (line 77; the reading is conjectural; the expression מי אנכי is attested in the Bible [e.g., Exod 3:11]; cf. also מי אנכי in 2 Sam 7:18; cf. מי אני in the parallel verse in 1 Chr 17:16); שלשה הא[ת]ות (line 79; šĕlôšâ hāʾôtôt [perhaps האותיות]; this expression appears in several extra-biblical sources);[23] מן שלושה הקטן (line 83; min šĕlôšâ haqqāṭān; מן shows Aramaic influence); שלקחתי אני (line 83[?]; šelāqaḥtî; note ש as against biblical אשר).

---

23. In Hekhalot literature: א׳ר ישמעאל. שאלתי לר׳ נחונייא בן הקנה. היאך חכמתו של שר התורה. אמ׳ לי [...]. ו(ש)[כ]שאתה מתפלל בסוף הזכר שלשה (שמות) אותיות.׳; נ״א: אותות > שמזכירין חיות בשע[ה] שצופות ורואות בארכם יהוה אלהי ישראל. גלי איי אדיר אדדר יהיאל זיך בניבא.
"R. Ishmael said: I asked R. NeHunya b. Haqana, 'How does the wisdom of the prince of the Torah [come about]?' He said to me: [...]. And when you pray, at the end, mention (the) **three letters** that mention the Hayyot when they behold and see >RKS, the Lord, the God of Israel: GLY ʾYY ʾDYR ʾDDR YHYʾL ZYK BNYBʾ'" (*Maʿase Merkava*, 56; Gershom Scholem, *Jewish Gnosticism: Merkabah, Mysticism and Talmudic Tradition* [New York: Jewish Theological Seminary of America, 1965], 109 = Schäfer, *Synopse*, §564).

וכשאת׳ מתפלל תפילה אחרת {ו}הזכר איתי׳ שמזכירין גלגלי המרכבה שאומרים שירה לפני כסא הכבוד. הך פז יפא פף יאו גהוא שביבא. זהו קנין שכל אדם שמזכירין קונה חכמה לעולם. וכי יכול אדם לעמוד בו. אלא **שלש אותיות** <נ״א: אותות> כתב משה ליהושע ברום ושתה. אם אינך יכול לעמוד חקוק אותם בחוק ואל תצטער בדברי גיבורים.
"And when you pray another prayer, {and} mention the letters that mention the wheels of the Chariot, which sing before the Throne of Majesty: HS PZ YPʾ PP YʾW GHWʾ SBYBʾ. Any man mentioning this thing (lit. acquisition) acquires wisdom forever. And does a man have power to withstand it (i.e., this incantation)? Now Moses wrote **three letters** in the cup (?) for Joshua and he drank. If you cannot withstand [it], make an engraving of them (lit. engrave them an engraving) and do not be troubled by the words of the heroes." *Maʿase Merkava*, 57; Scholem, *Jewish Gnosticism*, 109.

In *piyyut*:

יי טוב טעם לעמו דיבר / טיכוס **שלושה אותות** העיבורים עיבר / ירח ועונג ושמעו חיבר / יען אם יאבו לשמוע עמים תחתיהם ידבר.
"God spoke good sense to His people, / prescribing the order of the **three signs** of calendar reckoning. / He joined moon, pleasure [= Sabbath] and [the lection] *Shimʿu,* / such that if they are pleased to obey, He would subdue nations under them" (*Maʿariv* for '*Shimʿu*' and New Moon [ed. Menachem Zulay, *Erez Israel and Its Poetry* (Jerusalem: Magnes, 1995), 336]).

טעם פחז **שלשה אותות** זללתה / יחד פזרת ונזרתה.
"You have belittled the meaning of the **three letters** of [the word] *pakhaz* ('disturbance'), / both [*khet*] scattering [*peh*] and being dispersed [*zayin*]" (Simʿon bar Megas [ed. Joseph Yahalom, *Liturgical Poems of Simʿon bar Megas* (Jerusalem: Israel Academy of Sciences and Humanities, 1984), 146]).

אותות שלשה היום נישתלשו / באום שלישיה בשלוש קודשו.
"**Three signs** today are gathered threefold. Among the triune nation they are thrice sanctified" (E. B. Qilir [ed. S. Elizur, "'שלשה אותות' – A Qilirian Qedushta for Shabbat-Hanuka and Rosh-Hodesh," *Jerusalem Studies in Hebrew Literature* 8 (1985): 178]).

החדש הזה לשמור / כסכם אסופי הר המור / וא{ו}תם אל יגמור / **שלשת אותות[י]ו** בו (י)[ל]שמור.
"This month is to be observed / by the consensus of those gathered at Mt. Moriah [=the San-

The following words are not attested in the Bible in the orthography encountered in our text: הגאים (line 13; *haggōʾîm*; cf. biblical הגוים [e.g., Hag 2:7]; cf. also הגואין in a Bar Kokhba letter);[24] לכה (line 21; *lĕkâ*; cf. biblical לך; the long forms of the personal pronouns are common in the scrolls from the Judean Desert); קיטוט (line 24; *qîṭûṭ*[?]; the form belongs to the root קטט, "to fight, etc.," or is a variant of במעט קט, Ezek 16:47).

It is difficult to determine the *Sitz im Leben* of this text and its precise nature. Richard C. Steiner, to whom I showed a draft of this article, suggested that it might perhaps be "an apocalyptic text, based on the apocalyptic texts in Zechariah and Daniel. . . . Could he [i.e., the Gabriel of our text] be the angel Gabriel who explains to Daniel the meaning of his visions in Daniel 8-9?" [e-mail, May 7, 2006]. In a late text called *Ma'ase Dani'el alaw ha-Shalom* a few expressions appear that echo certain expressions in our text.[25] However, no text known to date shows an unambiguous relationship with the text on the stone. One may conjecture that the text includes hints of a rivalry between two messianic groups.[26]

---

hedrin]. / And may God give them full leave / to observe the **three signs** on it" (E. B. Qilir, Qedushta for Shabbat HaHodesh, '*Atiyat Et Dodim*' [Israel Davidson, *Thesaurus of Mediaeval Hebrew Poetry* (New York: Ktav, 1924), A 8904]).

24. P. Yadin 51:6; see Yardeni (n. 16 above), vol. A, p. 167.

25. Cf. והגידו לכו וגבריאל למיכאל אלהים יאמר אז ... האלהים לפני וגבריאל מיכאל יתיצבו אז לישראל.
"Then **Michael and Gabriel** will stand up before God" . . . "then God will say to **Michael and Gabriel**: 'Go and speak to Israel'" (Adolph Yelinek, *Beit Hamidrash 5* [in Hebrew; Vienna: Brider Winter, 1873], 127; and cf. Jehuda Even Shmuel Kaufman, *Midreshei Ge'ulah* [in Hebrew; Tel Aviv: Mossad Bialik, 1943], 224).

הקודש וממקום מציון יצא גדול ורעש משמים יופיע וה'.
"And God will appear from heaven, and a loud **noise** will come out from Zion and from the Place of Holiness" (Yelinek, *Beit Hamidrash 5*, 128; Even Shmuel, *Midreshei Ge'ulah*, 225; cf. line 24).

האלה האותות השלשה את איפה עשה.
"Do, then, these **three signs**" (Yelinek, *Beit Hamidrash 5*, 127; Even Shmuel, *Midreshei Ge'ulah*, 224; cf. line 79).

השמים ארבות את ויפתח חסדו אלהים להם ישלח אז.
"Then God will send His grace upon them and open the ***Arubbot*** of heaven" (Yelinek, *Beit Hamidrash 5*, 127; Even Shmuel, *Midreshei Ge'ulah*, 224; cf. line 81). However, one has to keep in mind that this is a late Persian composition, from the mid-tenth century (940; see Even Shmuel, *Midreshei Ge'ulah*, 202), that is, about one thousand years later than our inscription, and it was translated into Hebrew in the mid-nineteenth century (by Abraham Kohen Kaplan, probably for Yelinek; see Yelinek, *Beit Hamidrash 5*, 117 note; Even Shmuel, *Midreshei Ge'ulah*, 207), that is, about two thousand years later than our inscription.

26. If this interpretation is correct, one may cite another phrase from *Ma'ase Dani'el alaw ha-Shalom*:

תחת ירושלים החרבה יוריד ירושלים הבנויה משמים ונצר מגזע ישי הוא המשיח בן דוד יראה [...] ומשיח בן יוסף יומת ונס משיח בן דוד יתנוסס'
"Instead of the destroyed Jerusalem He will bring down from heaven the built Jerusalem, and

There seems to be no doubt that the author belonged to the group supporting the Davidic Messiah. Since our text is formulated in the name of Gabriel, one may perhaps refer to it (temporarily) as "Gabriel's Vision."

PALEOGRAPHY

The script of this text is a "Jewish" formal hand, typical of the Herodian period, written by a professional scribe. However, the handwriting looks rather careless. This may be due to the inconvenient conditions created by writing in ink on a hard and large surface. The stone being undressed in the back, it may have stood erect when the scribe copied the text, possibly from a scroll. But even if it was lying on the floor or on a raised surface, it would presumably have been difficult to write on it in an elegant script because of its large size. The script may be securely dated to about the late first century B.C.E. or the early first century C.E. It shows many affinities with the scripts of the Dead Sea Scrolls. In the comparative script chart (p. 26), we indicate only two other alphabets, chosen at random, of two manuscripts of the *Damascus Document* from Qumran (4Q269 [PAM 43.268], 4Q270 [PAM 43.295-99]), dating to about the early first century C.E.

Following is a description of the main characteristics of the script appearing on the stone. The letters are suspended from the incised guidelines similarly to the treatment in the Qumran scrolls. The spacing between the lines and the columns, as well as the relative size of the letters, show a striking similarity of proportion to that in the scrolls. (They are slightly more than double in comparison to the same parameters as evidenced in 4Q270. However, the columns on the stone seem to be proportionally narrower.) The spacing between the guidelines is about 17–18 mm. The average height of *het* is about 5–6 mm, the letters varying a little in size. The average number of letters in a line is 30–33.

The most important letters for the dating of this script to the period of the Dead Sea Scrolls are *lamed*, with a small and narrow body, and the long and narrow final *mem*, with the "sting" on its "roof" and the open lower left corner (see, e.g., the word *Yrwšlm* in line 39).

The earliest features of this script are typical of the late first century B.C.E. These are mainly the long and open final *mem*, with its left stroke beginning high above the "roof" and ending occasionally above the base stroke; the relatively long medial *kaf*; the triangular loop at the top of *yod* and *waw*; the backward-leaning *alef, gimel,* and *ṣade*; the slanting base of *tet*; and the wavy final *nun*.

---

an offspring of the family of Yishai, the Messiah son of David, will see [...] and the Messiah son of Joseph will be killed and the flag of the Messiah son of David will flutter" (Yelinek, *Beit Hamidrash 5*, 128; Even Shmuel, *Midreshei Ge'ulah*, 225); but see what Even Shmuel wrote concerning this verse (*Midreshei Ge'ulah*, 207–8).

4Q269	4Q270	Hazon Gabriel
PM 43.268	PM 43.295–99	

The alphabet of the *Hazon Gabriel*, compared with 4Q269 and 4Q270

The latest features of this script are typical of the early first century C.E. Among these we may cite a number of extra ornamental additions on certain letters, mainly the ornaments on the right stroke of *alef* and *ṣade* as well as the ornamental additions on top of the left down stroke of the seven letters known as *shaʿatnez getz* (*shin, ayin, tet, nun, zayin, gimel,* and *ṣade*); the occasional occurrences of the "tail" of *bet*; the almost horizontal base strokes of *bet, kaf, mem, nun,* and *ṣade*; the closed and short *samek*; and the short *tav* with the left down stroke bending its bottom in an angle to the left.

Following are the descriptions of individual letters.[27]

Alef leans backward, a feature inherited from its ancestor, the Aramaic *alef*. The medial stroke slants down slightly to the right while the right and left "arms" stretch in opposite directions, the left one starting near the top of the medial stroke and terminating above the imaginary base line. Both "arms" occasionally have additional ornaments in the form of a small stroke that joins the main stroke in a to-and-fro movement (cf. a similar phenomenon in 4Q269; the *alef* of 4Q270 has only the right ornamental addition).

Bet has an almost horizontal "roof" starting with a high serif. Its horizontal base stroke, drawn from left to right, occasionally ends beyond its meeting point with the right down stroke, creating a small "tail" at the lower, right corner. This feature appears sporadically in the second century B.C.E. and becomes characteristic of *bet* in ca. the first century C.E.

Gimel leans backward, its down stroke being almost erect, and its left "leg" stretches forward in a convex curve. This feature sporadically appears in the second century B.C.E. and is typical of the *gimel* of the first century. An additional short stroke occasionally appears to the right of its top, typical of the "Jewish" Herodian book hand.

Dalet has a quite distinctive serif slanting down toward the left end of its "roof." Its right down stroke starts above its meeting point with the right end of the "roof." The letter appears mostly in an erect position.

He has a wavy "roof" formed with one stroke rather than two, the latter being typical of the Herodian *he* (cf. both 4Q269 and 4Q270). The wavy "roof" of *he* is typical of the semiformal hand from the Hasmonean to the post-Herodian periods.

Waw mostly differs from the shorter *yod*, both occasionally having a triangular "loop" to the left of their top, typical of the "Jewish" Herodian script (cf. both 4Q269 and 4Q270; this feature is common in a certain type of ossuary inscription as well as in the Copper Scroll). The letter mostly stands upright.

Zayin has a thickened top, perhaps made with a to-and-fro movement (cf. both 4Q269 and 4Q270).

Het is made with a wavy right down stroke, starting above the right end of

---

27. Cf. the tracing of the inscription, and see also the alphabetical charts showing the development of the "Jewish" scripts, in Yardeni, *Textbook*, vol. B, 166–211.

the crossbar. This right down stroke is typical of *het* already in the Aramaic script of the mid-fourth century B.C.E., and continues into the "Jewish" script of the Herodian period. The left down stroke occasionally begins at the left end of the crossbar or somewhat above it.

Tet is already a small letter. It has a straight, slanting base stroke and a short left down stroke unlike the round base and the high left down stroke of the Aramaic *tet*. At the top of its left down stroke an additional ornament occasionally appears, drawn with a to-and-fro movement. This ornamental addition—as well as that on top of the left down stroke of *gimel, zayin, nun, ayin,* and *ṣade*—is the origin of the ornamental additions on top of the left down stroke of these seven letters in later Torah scrolls and sacred documents. The right stroke begins inside the letter and curves clockwise until it touches the right end of the base stroke.

Yod resembles *waw*, but is mostly shorter.

Medial *kaf* is somewhat longer than *bet*. Around the middle of the Herodian period, they became equal in height. Unlike *bet*, its base line does not exceed its meeting point with the down stroke.

Final *kaf* resembles *dalet* but is considerably longer.

Lamed is typical of the "Jewish" book hand evidenced in the Dead Sea Scrolls. It has a small and short "body" and a high "mast" with a thickened top, occasionally made like the triangular "loop" of *waw* and *yod*.

Medial *mem* is already of medial height as a result of the process of leveling the height of the letters in the early Herodian period. It has an almost horizontal base stroke and a straight and upright "back." Its serif seems to be already an independent stroke, its "roof" and left down stroke having merged together into one stroke beginning at the top of the "back" and slanting down to the left, but terminating high above the left end of the base stroke. This form of *mem* is typical of the late Herodian period.

Final *mem* occasionally appears in medial position (cf. the epitaph of King Uzziah with the final *mem* in the word *lmptḥ*). The long final *mem* appears sporadically in the Herodian period and is typical of the "Jewish" script of the Hasmonean period. A clear example of an early form of final *mem*, still open at its lower left corner, appears, for example, in line 41. In our inscription there are a few cases of a cursive, round final *mem* (see, e.g., *hgʾym* in line 13, and *ʾlhym* in line 29; cf. also, e.g., 4Q448 [early first century B.C.E.; Yardeni, *Textbook*, vol. A, 253]).

Medial *nun* has an ornamental addition at the top of its vertical stroke and an almost horizontal base stroke, forming an angular corner (cf. 4Q269 and 4Q270).

Final *nun* has an ornamental addition similar to that of the medial *nun*.

Samek is already small and closed at its lower left corner (cf. 4Q269 and 4Q270). Open forms of *samek* still appear sporadically in documents dating to around the beginning of the Christian era.

Ayin appears in various sizes, that is, a smaller form (e.g., *ʿbdy* in line 16) and a larger form (e.g., *ʿl* in line 67), as a result of the careless writing. The letter leans backwards (cf. 4Q270). Its right stroke bends at its top to the left, whereas its left stroke occasionally has an ornamental addition at its top made with a to-and-fro movement, the letter being part of the seven *sha'atnez getz* letters (see above, in the discussion of *tet*).

Medial *pe* is relatively short. Its typical "nose" is relatively short (cf., e.g., *lpny* in line 16 and *lpnk* in line 17). Since it has no serif it is easily distinguishable from *bet* and *kaf*.

Final *pe* seems to appear in line 32. Unlike medial *pe*, it has a clear "nose" (unless the reading ᵓ*lwp* is wrong and it is a *waw* with a triangular "loop").

Medial *ṣade* occasionally has the tops of its strokes bending toward each other in a manner similar to *ayin*. The letter leans backwards, its left stroke bending at its bottom in an angle to the left, creating an almost horizontal base, while its right stroke stretches back to the right. The ornament occasionally appearing at the end of the right "arm" is made similarly to that at the right "arm" of *alef*, whereas the top of its left stroke sometimes has an ornamental addition, also made with a to-and-fro movement similarly to the other *sha'atnez getz* letters.

Final *ṣade* resembles medial *ṣade* but for its long left stroke, which in some cases curves to the left.

Qof has proportions similar to the *qof* of 4Q269 and 4Q270. It has an almost triangular "body," its size resembling that of *lamed*. The right stroke slants down toward the relatively short and somewhat wavy "leg," sometimes touching it.

Resh clearly differs from *dalet* in that it has no protrusion at its upper right corner (similarly to 4Q269 and 4Q270).

Shin has a vertical left stroke, often exceeding its meeting point with the right "arm." As a result of the careless writing, its right "arm" occasionally bends at its top. Since the letter leans backwards, the lower part of its right "arm" looks like an almost horizontal base stroke, but for the most part the letter retains its triangular form. The middle stroke also sometimes has an ornamental addition in a form that is also found on top of the right arm of *alef* and *ṣade*, and the left stroke sometimes also has an ornamental addition made with a to-and-fro movement, similar to the other *sha'atnez getz* letters.

Tav bends its left down stroke at its bottom to the left, creating a right angle with its "foot" (similarly to 4Q270). Its left down stroke starts high above its "roof," and sometimes cuts through the "roof" as the result of the careless writing.

THREE

Notes on the So-Called *Gabriel Vision* Inscription

Elisha Qimron and Alexey (Eliyahu) Yuditsky

The present paper is an abbreviated version of the article in Hebrew published in *Cathedra* 133 (2009): 133–44. The Hebrew version suggested a new reading and interpretation in a number of passages of the so-called *Gabriel Vision* inscription as well as a linguistic discussion of some of its distinctive features. This English shortened version, however, also includes a few improvements. It has been prepared especially for the volume dedicated to the early Judaism and its literature. We would like to thank the editor, Prof. Matthias Henze, for inviting us to present our paper.

11 יהוה אתה שאלני כו אמֹר אלהים צבאות
12 טֹו .... בית ישראל ואגדה בגדלות ירושלם..
13 [כו] אמר יהוה אלה[י] ישראל הנה כול הגאים
14 צֹובֹאִֹים עֹל ירושלם ו....
15 [א]חת שתין שלוש ארבע הֹנביאין והֹשבין
16 [ו]החסידין עבדי דוד בקש מן לפני אמֹרים
17 [הש]יֹבֹנֹי האות אני מבקש מן לפנֹך כו אמר
18 [י]הוה צבאות אלהי ישראל בֹנֹי ב[י]דֹי בֹרִֹית
19 חֹדשה לישראל לשלשת ימין תדע כו אמר
20 יהוה אלהים צבאות אלהי ישראל נשבר הרע
21 מֹלפני הצדק שאלני ואגיד לכה מה הצמח
22 הֹרֹע הזה לו ב.סֹדֹ אתה עומד המלאך הוא
23 בסמכך אל תירה ברוך כבוד יהוה אלהים מן
24 מקומו עוד מעט קיטוט היא ואני מרעיש את
25 הֹשמֹים וֹאת הארץ הנה כבוד יהוה אלֹהֹים..
26 צבאות אלהי ישראל אלה המרכבות שמֹע
27 [קו]ֹל שֹוֹדֹ ירושלם ואת ערי יהודה ינחם למען
28 צֹבֹ[א]ֹת [ה]ֹמלאךֹ מיכאל ולכול האהבין בֹקשו
29 [מלפניך] כו אמר יהוה אלֹהֹים צבאות אלהי
30 [ישר]אל אחד שנין שלושה ארבעה חמשה ששה
31 ...[ויש]ראל מֹלאךֹ .... מהו ואמרה עץ
32 .... יֹ]רֹושלֹםֹ כימֹוֹת עולם וֹאֹראה שני

64 שלוש[ה .... העולם של]ושה ... העולם]
65 שלושה קדושי העולם מ...
66 י]רושלים אמר עליך אנחנו בטוחין [לו על]
67 בשר לו על דם זו המרכבה של...
68 אוהבין רבים ליהוה צבאות אלי ישראל...
69 כה אמר יהוה צבאות אלהי ישראל [שלושה]
70 נביאים שלחתי אל עמי שלושה רועין [וא]ח̇ר
71 שראיתי ב......... [ואשיבם] אֹל
72 המקום למ̊ען דוד עבד יהוה [הנה] א[תה עשית]
73 את השמים ואת הארץ בכוחך [הגדול ובזרועך]
74 הנטוה עושה חסד לאלפים מ[...
75 שלושה רועין יצאו לישראל [......חסידין]
76 אם יש בהן אם יש בֹם קדושין...
77 מי אתה אני גבריאל...
78 תצילם נבי[א ור]ועה יצילו אותך [אני מב]ק̊ש
79 מלפניך שלושה רֹעים שלושה [נבי]א̇י̇ן
80 לשלושת ימין חאוֹת אני גבריאל

The Annotated Vocalized Text of the Inscription and Its Translation[1]

11 יהוה אַתָּה שְׁאֵלָנִי. כֹּו אָמַר אֱלֹהִים צְבָאוֹת:
(of) YHWH you ask me, thus said the Lord of Hosts

12 ..טו .... בֵּית יִשְׂרָאֵל, וְאַגִּדָה בִּגְדֹלוֹת יְרוּשָׁלָם.
... the House of Israel and I will recount the greatness of Jerusalem

13 [כֹּו] אָמַר יהוה אֱלֹהֵי יִשְׂרָאֵל: הִנֵּה כֹּל הַגֵּאִים
[Thus] said YHWH the God of Israel: Soon all the nations

14 צוֹבְאִים עַל יְרוּשָׁלַם וּ......
fight against Jerusalem and ...

---

1. Notes to the text refer to the articles of Ada Yardeni and Binyamin Elizur, Israel Knohl, and Ronald Hendel; see Ada Yardeni and Binyamin Elizur, "טקסט נבואי על אבן מן המאה הראשונה לפסה"נ, הודעה ראשונה" [A Prophetic Text on Stone from the First Century BCE: Preliminary Publication], *Cathedra* 123 (2007): 155–66; Israel Knohl, "עיונים ב'חזון גבריאל'" [Studies in the *Vision of Gabriel*], *Tarbiz* 76 (2007): 303–28, Ronald Hendel, "Note to 'Vision of Gabriel,'" *BAR* 35, no. 1 (2009): 8. The inscription language has been treated by Moshe Bar-Asher and Gary Rendsburg; see Moshe Bar-Asher, "על הלשון ב"חזון גבריאל"" [On the Language of "The Vision of Gabriel"], *Meghillot: Studies in the Dead Sea Scrolls* 7 (2009): 193–226; Gary A. Rendsburg, "Linguistic and Stylistic Notes to the Hazon Gabriel Inscription," *DSD* 16 (2009): 107–16.

THE SO-CALLED *GABRIEL VISION* INSCRIPTION 33

15 [אַ]חַת, שְׁתַּיִן, שָׁלוֹשׁ, אַרְבַּע. הַנְּבִיאִין וְהַשָּׁבִין
[O]ne, two, three, four. The prophets and the elders

16 [וְ]הַחֲסִידִין. עַבְדִּי דָוִד בִּקֵּשׁ מִן לְפָנַי: אֲמָרִים
[and] the pious ones. David, my servant, asked me:

17 [הֲשֵׁ]יבֵנִי, הָאוֹת אֲנִי מְבַקֵּשׁ מִן לְפָנֶךָ. כֹּה אָמַר
Answer me, I ask you for the sign. Thus said

18 [יְ]הוה צְבָאוֹת אֱלֹהֵי יִשְׂרָאֵל: בְּנִי! בְּ[יָ]דִי בְּרִית
[Y]HWH of Hosts, the God of Israel: My son, I have a new

19 חֲדָשָׁה לְיִשְׂרָאֵל, לִשְׁלֹשֶׁת יָמִין תֵּדַע. כֹּה אָמַר
testament for Israel, by three days you shall know. Thus said

20 יהוה אֱלֹהִים צְבָאוֹת אֱלֹהֵי יִשְׂרָאֵל: נִשְׁבַּר הָרַע
YHWH, God of Hosts, the God of Israel: Evil will be defeated

21 מִלְּפְנֵי הַצֶּדֶק, שְׁאָלֵנִי וְאַגִּיד לְךָ מָה הַצֶּמַח
by justice; ask me and I shall tell you what this bad

22 הָרַע הַזֶּה. לוֹ בְּ.סד אַתָּה עוֹמֵד, הַמַּלְאָךְ הוּא
plant is. Not by ... you exist, (but) the angel supports you,

23 בְּסָמְכֶךָ, אַל תִּירָה! בָּרוּךְ כְּבוֹד יהוה אֱלֹהִים מִן
do not fear! Bless by the glory of YHWH (the) God from His

24 מְקוֹמוֹ. עוֹד מְעַט קִיטוֹט הִיא, וַאֲנִי מַרְעִישׁ אֶת
place. In a little while I shall shake

25 הַשָּׁמַיִם וְאֶת הָאָרֶץ. הִנֵּה כְּבוֹד יהוה אֱלֹהִים
Heaven and earth. Readily the glory of YHWH the God of

26 צְבָאוֹת אֱלֹהֵי יִשְׂרָאֵל, אֱלֹהַּ הַמֶּרְכָּבוֹת שֹׁמֵעַ
Hosts, the God of Israel, the God of the chariots will listen to

27 [קוֹ]ל שׁוֹד יְרוּשָׁלַם וְאֶת עָרֵי יְהוּדָה יְנַחֵם. לְמַעַן
the [cr]y of Jerusalem and will console the cities of Judah for the sake of

28 צְבָ[א]ת [הַ]מַּלְאָךְ מִיכָאֵל, וּלְכֹל הָאֹהֲבִין בקשׁו
the Hosts of Michael [the] angel and for all the lovers *bqšw*

29 [מִלְּפָנֶיךָ]. כֹּה אָמַר יהוה אֱלֹהִים צְבָאוֹת אֱלֹהֵי
[You]. Thus said YHWH, the God of Hosts, the God of

30 [יִשְׂרָ]אֵל: אֶחָד, שְׁנַיִן, שְׁלוֹשָׁה, אַרְבָּעָה, חֲמִשָּׁה, שִׁשָּׁה
[Isr]ael: one, two, three, four, five, six

31 ... [וַיִּשׁ]אַל מַלְאָךְ .... מַהוּ? וָאֹמְרָה: עֵץ
... angel ... [ask]ed ... What is this? And I said: a tree

32 ....יְ.רוּשָׁלַם כִּימוֹת עוֹלָם. וָאֶרְאֶה שְׁנֵי
... [Je]rusalem [shall be] as in early times. I saw two

Line 11: כו — Yardeni and Elizur read בן. This reading is preferable both materially and linguistically; expressions such as כה אמר ה' are usual in the Bible, whereas an expression such as בן אמר ה' does not occur in early Hebrew sources.

Line 12: There are six illegible letters at the beginning of the line. Syntactically, before the form ואגדה an imperative is expected, such as הטו.

Ibid: The line after בית is probably incidental to the inscription. Thus, one should read בית ישראל instead ביתי ישראל.

Line 14: At the beginning of the line, the word צובאים fits the traces and the size of the lacuna. For the expression כול הגאים צובאים על ירושלם, compare Isa 29:7: אֲשֶׁר יִגֹּף ה' אֶת כָּל הָעַמִּים אֲשֶׁר, and Zech 14:12: הֲמוֹן כָּל הַגּוֹיִם הַצֹּבְאִים עַל אֲרִיאֵל, צָבְאוּ עַל יְרוּשָׁלָ͏ִם.

Line 15: ארבע הׄנביאין — Yardeni and Elizur read ארבעין נביאין. However, the traces identified as –ין belong to the next word. The reading ארבע הׄנביאין, that is, אַרְבַּע הַנְּבִיאִין, is grammatically preferable.

Lines 16–17: אמרׄים [הש]יׄבֹנוׄ לְהָשִׁיב — The restoration is based on Prov 22:21: אֲמָרִים אֱמֶת לְשֹׁלְחֶיךָ. Compare also Job 22:14. Yardeni and Elizur read [..] אפרים שים, yet the second letter in אמרים can hardly be pe.

Line 17: כו rather then כי; see the note to line 11.

Lines 18–19: בֹּנׄיׄ בן[י]דׄי בְּרִית חֹדשה לישראל — This suggested reading is doubtful. Yardeni and Elizur read גנים.וכרים קדשה לישראל. In personal communication Yardeni noted that the reading חדשה is materially problematical, yet in the new digital photographs the first letter best be read as ḥeth.

Line 19: כו rather then כי; compare the note to line 11.

Lines 20–21: נשבר הרע מׄלפני הצדק — The phrase means "Evil is going to be shattered by justice." The expression נשבר מלפני originates in Aramaic; compare Tg. Onq. Deut 20:3: ולא תיתברון מן קדמיהון. See also Z. Ben-Hayyim, "ישנים גם חדשים מן צפוני מדבר יהודה" [New Ancient Scrolls Discovered in the Judean Desert] Leshonenu 42 (1978): 280–81. Compare also the expression שב"ר לפני in the Dead Sea Scrolls: 4Q372 2:12 כי שברו יהוה; 4Q373 1:6 כי נשבר לפניו אלהינו לפני. The verb נשבר indicates a near future.

Line 21: We presume that the word ואגיד reflects the long form וָאַגִּידְךָ as ואגדה in line 12.

Lines 21–22: מה הצמח הֹרֹע הזה — The phrase possibly refers to a vision that the author has had. Thus, הצמח הרע is probably צמח רע מראה, "ugly plant," which is a sign of the great distress that befalls Israel before its salvation. Compare Gen 41:20, 27; 1QapGen 13:16.

Line 22: The word לו ב..סֹדׄ is problematic. The letters לוב.ס are quite clear. Between ב and ס there are traces of one or more letters. The last letter looks like ד or ר, but it could be damaged ה or ך as well. For the syntactic construction, one should compare Deut 9:5: לֹא בְצִדְקָתְךָ וּבְיֹשֶׁר לְבָבְךָ אַתָּה בָא לָרֶשֶׁת אֶת אַרְצָם. That is to say, you are not standing by yourself, but the angel is supporting you. Compare also Dan 8:18: וַיִּגַּע בִּי וַיַּעֲמִידֵנִי [גבריאל] עַל עָמְדִי; Dan 10:13: וְהִנֵּה מִיכָאֵל אַחַד הַשָּׂרִים; Dan 10:18–19: וַיֹּסֶף וַיִּגַּע בִּי כְּמַרְאֵה אָדָם וַיְחַזְּקֵנִי וַיֹּאמֶר אַל תִּירָא; הָרִאשֹׁנִים בָּא לְעָזְרֵנִי

THE SO-CALLED *GABRIEL VISION* INSCRIPTION   35

אִישׁ חֲמֻדוֹת. Compare אל תירא here to אל תירה in line 23. In light of these passages it seems that the two initial letters לו should be interpreted as לא. The cluster ב.סד probably reflects a phrase beginning with the particle -ב, say, (אתה עומד) לו במסד. Compare Isa 28:16: אֶבֶן בֹּחַן פִּנַּת יִקְרַת מוּסָד מוּסָּד הַמַּאֲמִין לֹא יָחִישׁ.

Line 24: מקומו — Yardeni and Elizur read מושבו. All the letters besides ק are quite clear. There is no difference between the expression ברוך כבוד ה' אלהים מן מקומו and Ezek 3:12: בָּרוּךְ כְּבוֹד ה' מִמְּקוֹמוֹ. The preference of מן over -מ is probably an Aramaism.

Line 27: [קו]ל שׂוֹד — "cry"; compare Jer 6:7: חָמָס וָשֹׁד יִשָּׁמַע בָּהּ עַל פָּנַי. Cf. also Jer 9:18, 20:8, Ps 12:6.

Ibid: ושערי יהודה ינחם — Elizur and Yardeni read ...וא̇ת ערי יהודה ינ. For ינחם compare Zech 1:17: כִּי נִחַם יהוה עַמּוֹ; Isa 52:9: וְנִחַם ה' עוֹד אֶת צִיּוֹן וּבָחַר עוֹד בִּירוּשָׁלָ͏ִם גָּאַל יְרוּשָׁלָ͏ִם. For the parallelism ירושלים//ערי יהודה, compare Jer 33:10; Zech 1:12.

Line 28: צְבָ[א]וֹת [ה]מלאך מיכאל — This new suggested reading is admittedly doubtful. Yardeni and Elizur read מלאכה מיכאל...

Ibid: אוהבין ולכול האהבין — Yardeni and Elizur read ולכול האחרין. Compare in the line 68.

Lines 28–29: [מלפניך] בקשו — restored according to lines 16, 17.

Line 29: כו rather then כן; see the note to line 11.

Line 31: [שב]עה Yardeni and Elizur read - [...]ויש[אל מלאךְ̇.... מהו ואמרה עץ אל מלאכה ... מה זו אמר הצץ. Before מהו presumably stood the object of the vision. The reading at the beginning of the line is doubtful. If the reading מהו ואמרה עץ, that is, מַהוּ? וָאָמְרָה: עֵץ, is correct, we have another future conversive form of the first person singular with the ending ‎–ה, which is usual in the Dead Sea Scrolls, in Late Biblical Hebrew, and in the Samaritan Pentateuch. For עץ, compare הצמח in line 21.

Line 32: י[ְ]רוּשָׁלַ͏ִם- י[ְ]רוּשָׁלִַם כִּימוֹת עוֹלָם וָאֵרָאָה שְׁנֵי is written with superlinear *yod*, which accords with the Masoretic vocalization; compare the note to line 66. The expression כימות עולם refers to the tree (עץ), which symbolizes rest and longevity. Compare Isa 65:22: כִּי כִימֵי הָעֵץ יְמֵי עַמִּי; see also Amos 9:11. The last word is likely to be a *nomen regens* שְׁנֵי. Yardeni and Elizur read a few isolated letters in the middle of the line; at the end of the line they read אלוף שני.

64   שְׁל̇וֹשׁ[ָ]ה .... הָעוֹלָם, שְׁל̇[וֹ]שָׁה ... הָעוֹלָם,
[Thre]e ...., thr[ee] ...

65   שְׁלוֹשָׁה קְדוֹשֵׁי הָעוֹלָם מ...
three holy ones from past generations ...

66   [יְ]רוּשָׁלַיִם. אמר: עָלֶיךָ אֲנַחְנוּ בְּטוּחִין, [לֹו עַל]
[Je]rusalem saying: (only) on You we rely, [not on]

67   בָּשָׂר, לוֹ עַל דָּם. זוֹ הַמֶּרְכָּבָה שֶׁל...
flesh (and) not on man. This is the chariot ...

68 אוֹהֲבִין רַבִּים לִיהוה צְבָאֹת אֱלֹהֵי יִשְׂרָאֵל ...
YHWH of Hosts, the God of Israel has many lovers ...

69 כֹּה אָמַר יהוה צְבָאֹת אֱלֹהֵי יִשְׂרָאֵל: [שְׁלוֹשָׁה]
Thus said YHWH of Hosts, the God of Israel:

70 נְבִיאִים שָׁלַחְתִּי אֶל עַמִּי, שְׁלוֹשָׁה רוֹעִין. [וְאַ]חַר
I sent [three] prophets to my people, three shepherds. And after

71 שֶׁרָאִיתִי בְ... [וַאֲשִׁיבֵם] אֶל
that I saw ... [I returned them] to

72 הַמָּקוֹם לְמַעַן דָּוִד עֶבֶד יהוה. [הִנֵּה] אַ[תָּה עָשִׂיתָ]
the place for the sake of David, the servant of YHWH. Y[ou made]

73 אֶת הַשָּׁמַיִם וְאֶת הָאָרֶץ בְּכוֹחֲךָ [הַגָּדוֹל וּבִזְרוֹעֲךָ]
heaven and earth with your great [might and outstretched]

74 הַנְּטוּיָה. עוֹשֶׂה חֶסֶד לַאֲלָפִים מִ[...]
arm. You show kindness to the thousandth generation ...

75 שְׁלוֹשָׁה רוֹעִין יָצְאוּ לְיִשְׂרָאֵל [.....] חסידין
Three shepherds will come forth for Israel ...

76 אִם יֵשׁ בָּהֶן, אִם יֵשׁ בָּם קְדוֹשִׁין...
If there are [pious ones] among them, if there are holy ones among them ...

77 מִי אַתָּה? אֲנִי גַּבְרִיאֵל...
Who are you? I am Gabriel ...

78 תַּצִּילֵם. נָבִי[א וְר]וֹעֶה יַצִּילוּ אוֹתָךְ. [אֲנִי מְבַ]קֵּשׁ
you shall save them. A proph[et and a she]pherd will save you. [I as]k

79 מִלְּפָנֶיךָ שְׁלוֹשָׁה רוֹעִים, שְׁלוֹשָׁה [נְבִי]אִין.
from You three shepherds, three [pro]phets.

80 לִשְׁלוֹשֶׁת יָמִין הָאוֹת. אֲנִי גַּבְרִיאֵל...
In three days the sign will be (given). I am Gabriel ...

Lines 64–65: ...[שְׁלוֹשׁ]ה .... הָעוֹלָם שֶׁלּ[וֹשָׁה ... הָעוֹלָם] שלושה קדושי העולם — In these lines the phrase שלושה ... העולם is repeated (apparently three times), but its kernel survived only in the last case (קדושי). Other scholars identify in line 64 only the word חביב, which is probably a misreading.

Line 66: [יְ]רוּשלים — See the note to line 32. Yardeni and Elizur read וּשׁלום []. Lines 66–67: עָלֶיךָ אֲנַחְנוּ בְּטוּחִין [לוֹ עַל] בָּשָׂר לוֹ עַל דָּם — "(only) on you we rely, [not on] flesh (and) not on man." Compare Jer 17:5–7: כֹּה אָמַר ה' אָרוּר הַגֶּבֶר אֲשֶׁר יִבְטַח בָּאָדָם וְשָׂם בָּשָׂר זְרֹעוֹ וּמִן יהוה, יָסוּר לִבּוֹ ... בָּרוּךְ הַגֶּבֶר אֲשֶׁר יִבְטַח בַּה'; וְהָיָה ה' מִבְטָחוֹ; Zohar, Vayakhel, 225: לא על אינש רחיצנא ולא על בר אלהין סמיכנא, אלא באלהא דשמיא. For the syntactic construction and the content compare lines

22–23. Yardeni and Elizur do not restore the text and suggest a different interpretation.

Lines 69–71: [שלושה] נביאים שלחתי אל עמי שלושה רועין [וא]חׄר שראיתי — Knohl reads נביאים שלחתי אל עמי שלושה רועי שראיתי; Yardeni and Elizur read שלושה רועין. The phrase ... נביאים שלחתי אל עמי שלושה ואני אומר שראיתי is in apposition to the preceding נביאין [שלושה] and occurs again in line 79. For the collocation of the nouns נביא and רועה compare Jer 2:8.

Lines 71–72: [ואשיבם] אֶל המקום — restored according to Jer 32:37.

Lines 72–74: [הנה] א[תה עשית] את השמים ואת הארץ בכוחך [הגדול ובזרעך] הנטוה עושה חסד לאלפים מ[] — These lines contain a citation of Jer 32:17–18: הִנֵּה אַתָּה עָשִׂיתָ אֶת הַשָּׁמַיִם וְאֶת־הָאָרֶץ בְּכֹחֲךָ הַגָּדֹל וּבִזְרֹעֲךָ הַנְּטוּיָה ... עֹשֶׂה חֶסֶד לַאֲלָפִים וּמְשַׁלֵּם עֲוֹן אָבוֹת אֶל־חֵיק בְּנֵיהֶם אַחֲרֵיהֶם... Compare also Jer 32:36–42.

Line 74:]לאלפים מ — One is tempted to restore [מ]שלם עון אבות according to Jer 32:18. But such a restoration does not fit the positive context here or the existing traces.

Lines 75–76: שלושה קדושי [חסידין] אם יש בהן אם יש בֹם קדושין — Compare אם יש כהן אם יש בני קדושים in line 65. Yardeni and Elizur read העולם.

Line 77: מי אתה — This reading fits the next phrase אני גבריאל. Presumably we have here a dialogue between the seer and the angel, yet the required introductory verb ויאמר is missing. Yardeni and Elizur read מי אנוכי.

Lines 78–79: תצילם נבי[א ור]ועה יצׄילו אותך [אני מב]קֹש מלפניך שלושה רוֹעים [נבי]אׄין שלושה. For the restoration מלפניך [אני מבקש], compare lines 16, 17, 82. Yardeni and Elizur read תצילם נבי...ם גר...ם לשות []. ב [] מלפניך שלשה הא[ת]ות שלשה ... אק

Line 80: לשלושת ימין האוֹת — Knohl reads לשלושת ימין חאיה, while Hendel suggests reading לשלושת ימין האות; compare האות אני מבקש in line 17 and לשלושת ימין תדע in line 19. It should be added that the construction לשלושת ימין האות has a parallel in the Bible: Exod 8:19: לְמָחָר יִהְיֶה הָאֹת הַזֶּה.

Ibid: אני גַבְרִיֹאֵל — The reading of גבריאל is not clear on the photographs.

Further New Readings

Line 33: ירושלם — Yardeni and Elizur read ירשלם.

Line 35: In the middle of the line we read וארא[ה] איש א[ח]ד עומד. Compare Dan 10:5: וָאֶרָא וְהִנֵּה אִישׁ אֶחָד. Yardeni and Elizur read שראה איש ... עובד. The phrase in Daniel includes the particle הנה between the verb רא"י and the noun, as is usual in the Bible, whereas the inscription omits this particle here and in line 32.

Line 36: At the beginning of the line we read יר[וֹשׁלם].

Ibid: The words את ירושלם finish the line. Between the break and these words three letters can be recognized, perhaps עֹזֹב[.

Lines 37–38: [אָמַר זֹאות גלות ...[וז]אוֹת גלות [...] וֹ[אֵלֹה העניאין ואראה – Concerning two exiles, compare Jer 24:1–10. Yardeni and Elizur read אבר.אותגלות... אתגלות.

Line 41: The penultimate word seems to be וארה. Yardeni and Elizur read שירם.

Line 53: At the beginning of the line we read על עמו ובחר. Compare Isa 14:1: וְנִחַם ה' עֹוד אֶת צִיּוֹן וּבָחַר עֹוד; Zech 1:17: כִּי יְרַחֵם ה' אֶת יַעֲקֹב וּבָחַר עֹוד בְּיִשְׂרָאֵל בִּירוּשָׁלָם. Yardeni and Elizur read על עמו ומחר.

Line 57: כו rather then כי; see the note to line 11.

Line 59: In the middle of the line after the damaged section, some letters have remained. They can be deciphered as [אמר אֱלֹהִים or אמר לִיהֹוָה].

Line 60: At the beginning of the line, one can read and restore שלם[ירו.

Line 82: At the beginning of the line, we read לֹ האות or לִי האות. Yardeni and Elizur read למראות.

Ibid: After the break we read קָשִׁים מלפנֹיךָ הנה [מב], that is, מְבַקְשִׁים מִלְּפָנֶיךָ הִנֵּה. For the restoration, compare lines 16, 17, 78.

Line 83: At the beginning of the line, we read לימין שלושה. Compare לשלושת ימין in line 80. For the syntactic construction, compare Gen 7:4: כִּי לְיָמִים עֹוד שִׁבְעָה; and especially in Late Biblical Hebrew 2 Chr 21:19: לְיָמִים שְׁנַיִם; 2 Chr 29:17: לְיָמִים שְׁמוֹנָה. Yardeni and Elizur read לי מן שלושה.

FOUR

The Apocalyptic and Messianic Dimensions of the *Gabriel Revelation* in Their Historical Context

Israel Knohl

1. The Apocalyptic Scene

The *Gabriel Revelation* (*HazGab*) is a multidimensional text. It has an apocalyptic dimension together with two different messianic dimensions. Each of these dimensions is mainly based on one specific biblical text. The apocalyptic scene of the *Gabriel Revelation* is contained mainly in lines 13–16, 24–29, 41–42. It is principally based on Zechariah 14. The first part of the apocalyptic scenario is the description of the gentiles who encamp around Jerusalem and the groups of people exiled from the city [broken or doubtful letters are underlined].

13 [Thus] said the Lord, God of Israel, now all the nations
14 <u>encamp on</u> Jerusalem and from it <u>are exi</u>[led]
15 one two three forty Prophets and the elders
16 and the Hasidim

This scene is clearly based on Zech 14:2: "For I will gather all the nations against Jerusalem to battle, and the city shall be taken and the houses plundered and the women ravished; half of the city shall go into exile, but the rest of the people shall not be cut off from the city".

Lines 24–31 describe the appearance of God, who shakes the earth, and the descent of the angels in chariots at the gates of Jerusalem.

24 .... In a little while, I will shake
25 .. the heavens and the earth. Here is the glory of the Lord God
26 of Hosts, the God of Israel. These are the seven chariots
27 at the gate of Jerusalem and the gates of Judea they will <u>re</u>[st] for
28 my <u>three</u> angels, Michael and all the others.

This picture is mainly based on Zech 14:3–5:[1]

> Then the Lord will go forth and fight against those nations as when he fights on a day of battle. On that day his feet shall stand on the Mount of Olives which lies before Jerusalem on the east; and the Mount of Olives shall be split in two from east to west by a very wide valley; so that one half of the Mount shall withdraw northward, and the other half southward. And the valley of my mountains shall be stopped up, for the valley of the mountains shall touch the side of it; and you shall flee as you fled from the earthquake in the days of Uzziah king of Judah. Then the Lord your God will come and all the holy ones with him.

The "holy ones" who will accompany God are the angels, which, according to the *Gabriel Revelation*, will descend in their chariots.

Finally, we have the fragmentary lines 41–42. The readable words in these lines: "would become maggoty," "abhorrence,"[2] "the diseased spot," testify that the main subject here is the plague God will inflict upon the nations. This plague is described in Zech 14:12: "And this shall be the plague with which the Lord will smite all the peoples that wage war against Jerusalem: their flesh shall rot while they are still on their feet, their eyes shall rot in their sockets, and their tongues shall rot in their mouths."

Thus, the apocalyptic scene of the *Gabriel Revelation* is based mainly on the book of Zechariah, and it does not contain any significant innovation beyond the biblical elements it uses. The main innovation of the *Gabriel Revelation* lies in its messianic dimensions which are dealt bellow.

2. The Holy/new Covenant and "Ephraim" the son of God

Alexey Yuditsky and Elisha Qimron recently published an article with new suggested readings of the text of the *Gabriel Revelation*.[3] The main new evidence adduced by Yuditsky and Qimron is the extensive use that the *Gabriel Revelation* makes of chs. 31–33 of Jeremiah.[4] These chapters contain the most important prophecies of consolation and redemption in the book. Most of these prophecies were delivered during the horrors of the Babylonian siege of Jerusalem. The content of these chapters therefore suits the aims of the author of the *Gabriel Revelation*, who promises redemption against the backdrop of the siege and the slaughter that took place in his own day in Jerusalem.[5] As will become clear

---

1. In lines 24–25, however, we clearly have a quotation from Hag 2:6.
2. This word probably refers to the punishment of the wicked ones in Isaiah 66:24.
3. Alexey Yuditsky and Elisha Qimron, "Notes on the Inscription 'The Vision of Gabriel'" (in Hebrew), *Cathedra* 133 (2009): 133–44.
4. Ibid., 135. Besides the parallels discussed bellow, one should also note the use of Jer. 33:3 in *HazGab* 12.
5. See lines 13–14, quoted above, about the siege. Yuditsky and Qimron ("Notes," 136)

further on, the recognition of the links between the *Gabriel Revelation* and these chapters in Jeremiah helps us to understand the *Gabriel Revelation* as a whole and to resolve several of the major questions concerning it.

As he is wont to do with other biblical passages, when the author of the *Gabriel Revelation* uses verses from Jeremiah, he does not quote them literally but adapts them to his needs. Yuditsky and Qimron point out the explicit use of Jer 32:17–18 in *HazGab* 72–75.[6] However, the author does not cite these verses in their entirety: he omits the words "nothing is too wondrous for you" at the end of v. 17, and he quotes only the first three words from v. 18: עושה[7] חסד לאלפים, "who showest steadfast love to thousands."[8]

With the aid of new photographs of the text of the *Gabriel Revelation*, Yuditsky and Qimron also succeed in deciphering several words in line 18 that were very hard to read. They suggest the following reading for the end of line 17 to the beginning of line 19:

כו[9] אמר [י]הוה צבאות אלהי ישראל, בני! ב[י]די ברית חדשה לישראל.
Thus said the Lord of Hosts, the God of Israel, "My son! I have a new covenant for Israel."

Generally speaking this reading is persuasive,[10] but I am not sure about their reading of the first word of line 19. The first editors of the *Gabriel Revelation*, Yardeni and Elizur, read this word as קדשה, "holy," while Yuditsky and Qimron suggest reading it as חדשה, "new." Even after studying the new photographs of

---

have suggested that we should read here הנה כול הגאים צובאים על ירושלים, "now all the nations are encamping on/besieging Jerusalem."

6. Yuditsky and Qimron, "Notes," 135.

7. In the *Gabriel Revelation* the plene spelling is used for the word עושה, while in the Bible the spelling is defective: עשה.

8. These words naturally remind us of the biblical language of the Ten Commandments: "showing steadfast love to thousands of those who love me and keep my commandments" (Exod 20:6; see also Exod 34:7 and Deut 5:10).

9. Regarding their reading of the word כו, as a byform of כה, see the discussion in Yuditsky and Qimron, "Notes," 137. Ada Yardeni and Binyamin Elizur ("A Prophetic Text on Stone from the First-Century BCE: First Publication" [in Hebrew], *Cathedra* 123 [2007]: 155–56) read hear כי.

10. The word that Yuditsky and Qimron read as בני, "my son," is read by Yardeni and Elizur as גני, "my gardens." However, the first letter of this word is not consistent with the usual form of the letter ג in this inscription. As Yardeni and Elizur noted ("Prophetic Text," 164), the letter ג in this text has two legs; the right leg is almost upright, while the left leg is rounded inward. The letter in question, however, lacks two distinct legs in its bottom section; instead, it has in its bottom an almost horizontal line. Admittedly, the upper horizontal line of the letter is very short relative to the way the letter ב is normally written, but note that it resembles the ב in צבאות on line 84, whose upper horizontal line is also very short. In view of these considerations I believe that Yuditsky and Qimron's reading of בני is preferable to Yardeni and Elizur's reading of גני.

the stone it is difficult, in my opinion, to determine whether the first letter of this word is a ח or a ק, and both readings are possible. If we accept Yuditsky and Qimron's reading of ברית חדשה, "new covenant," then the *Gabriel Revelation* is certainly drawing on Jer 31:31, "Behold, a time is coming—declares the Lord—when I will make a new covenant with the House of Israel and the House of Judah." But even if we prefer the reading "holy," I believe that the verse from Jeremiah still reverberates in the *Gabriel Revelation*. We have already noted that the author of the *Gabriel Revelation* frequently changes and adapts the language of the biblical verses on which he bases himself. Thus, we can understand the expression ברית קדשה to mean "holy covenant" and treat it as a conflation of the "new covenant" in Jeremiah with the "holy covenant" ברית קדש in Dan 11:28, 30.

In the lines before the statement about the "holy/new covenant," *HazGab* 16–17, we read about God's speech to David. Yardeni and Elizur read this speech as follows:

עבדי דוד בקש מן לפני אפרים [ ] שים האות אני מבקש מן לפנך.
My servant David, ask of Ephraim [ ] place the sign; (this) I ask of you.

I would like first to note that both the mention of "Ephraim" and the expression שים האות, "place the sign," are evidently taken from the above-mentioned chapters of Jeremiah. "Ephraim" is mentioned four times in ch. 31 of Jeremiah, and ch. 32 contains the expression אשר שמת אתות, "you have put signs." This expression appears in Jer 32:20, very close to vv. 17–18 of this chapter, which, as noted above, are explicitly cited in the *Gabriel Revelation*. Thus, the fact that both "Ephraim" and שמת אתות ("you have put signs") appear in Jeremiah 31–32 reinforces the plausibility of the reading that Yardeni and Elizur propose for lines 16–17.[11]

The expression אשר שמת אתות, "you have put signs," in Jer 32:20 refers to the punishment of the Egyptians by God. It seems that the author of the *Gabriel Revelation* uses the expression שים האות, "put the sign," with a similar meaning, that is, as the expression of a punishment and a disaster that are brought upon an evil entity. If this is indeed the case, we should probably connect this expression

---

11. Yuditsky and Qimron ("Notes," 137) suggest that instead of אפרים [ ] שׁ[ים האות, "Ephraim [ ] place the sign," we should read אמרים [הש]יבני, "give a reply," in keeping with Prov 22:21. But this reading is impossible. I just examined a special new photograph of the right section of *HazGab* 15–18, in which the remnants of the letters at the beginning of line 17 are sharply defined. The remnants are definitely consistent with Yardeni and Elizur's reading of שים, but not with Yuditsky and Qimron's reading יבני. One can clearly see that the last marks before the next word in the line, האות, may be the remnants of a ם, while under no circumstances could they be ני (there is a vertical line at whose base a horizontal line goes out to the right). And as we have seen, the link between the reading proposed by Yardeni and Elizur and the passages in Jeremiah 31–32 greatly increases the plausibility of their reading. The shape of the פ in the word אפרים should be compared with the way this letter is written in the word מלפני in line 21.

with the statement about the breaking of evil in *HazGab* 20–21: "By three days you shall know, for thus said the Lord of Hosts, the God of Israel, the evil is to be broken before righteousness." The connection between "the sign" and "by three days" is evident in *HazGab* 80, "By three days the sign."[12]

I have suggested completing the word at the beginning of line 17, to read ו[שים], "[that he] place."[13] In light of this completion we can read the line as follows:

עבדי דוד בקש מלפני אפרים [וי]שים האות . אני מבקש מן לפנך,

My servant David, ask of Ephraim [that he] place the sign; (this) I ask of you.

God asks his servant David to ask "Ephraim" to place the sign. This request of Ephraim appears in the *Gabriel Revelation* immediately before God says, "My son, I have a holy/new covenant for Israel." Ephraim is twice described as the son of God in ch. 31 of Jeremiah (31:8 [Eng. 9], 17–19 [Eng. 18–20]). Thus, God's declaration, "My son, I have a holy/new covenant for Israel," is probably addressed to "Ephraim." Hence, the "son of God" to whom the holy/new covenant is given is "Ephraim."

It seems also that the "son of God"/"Ephraim" is the main figure to whom the statements ascribed to God in the *Gabriel Revelation* are addressed. The lines which seem to contain the words addressed by God to Ephraim are 11–15, 18–27. Besides this, we have the words addressed by God to David (lines 16–17) and probably also to the angels (in lines 28–29). The last section of the text (lines 77–87) contains the speech of the angel Gabriel.

As noted above, Jeremiah describes Ephraim as the firstborn son of God (Jer 31:8 [Eng. 9], 17–19 [Eng. 18–20]). He is also described there as a suffering and tormented son who says to his father, "Thou hast chastened me, and I was chastened" (v. 18). It is clear that "Ephraim" refers in the book of Jeremiah to the collective entity of the northern kingdom of Israel. For this reason he is paired in Jeremiah with other collective entities such as "Israel" or "Judah." Thus, the suffering of "Ephraim" in Jeremiah is the suffering of the inhabitants of the northern kingdom who were exiled by the Assyrians.

Unlike Jeremiah, the author of the *Gabriel Revelation* combines "Ephraim" not with a collective entity but rather with the personal and messianic figure "my

---

12. I now accept the reading האות ("the sign") of the third word of line 80. This reading was first suggested by Ronald Hendel, "The Messiah Son of Joseph. Simply 'Sign,'" *BAR* 35 (2009): 8; and Yuditsky and Qimron ("Notes," 140–41). In my previous publications, I have argued for the reading חאיה ("live"). I still maintain that the reading חאיה ("live") is possible graphically. Yet the inner connections between lines 17–21 and line 80 support the reading האות ("the sign").

13. See Israel Knohl, *Messiahs and Resurrection in 'The Gabriel Revelation'* (Kogod Library of Judaic Studies; London/New York: Continuum, 2009), 10.

servant David": "My servant David, ask of Ephraim" (line 16). Hence, we may infer that in the *Gabriel Revelation* the figure of Ephraim is not a collective figure but rather a personal figure. Since "my servant David" is a personal and messianic title (see Ezek 34:23-24; 37:24-25), it seems that Ephraim of the *Gabriel Revelation* is also a personal and messianic title. This personal messianic figure is probably to be identified with the "son of God" whom God tells about the "holy/new covenant."

3. The Catastrophic Messianism

Another biblical text (besides Zechariah 14 and Jeremiah 31–33) that served as a significant source for the *Gabriel Revelation* is Dan 8:16-27. These verses contain the first revelation of the angel Gabriel to Daniel. There are several points of contact between the *Gabriel Revelation* and these biblical verses. The words of encouragement in lines 22-23, "the angel is supporting you. Do not fear," echo Dan 8:17-18 in the depiction of the revelation scene. "So he came near where I stood; and when he came, I was frightened and fell upon my face. . . . As he was speaking to me, I fell into a deep sleep with my face to the ground; but he touched me and set me on my feet." The figure of the "evil branch" in HazGab 21-22 is probably connected to the figure of the "king of bold countenance" in Dan 8:23. The announcement about the breaking of evil in lines 20-21 mirrors the announcement about the breaking of the "king of bold countenance" in Dan 8:25. The instruction to "seal up" (סתום) in line 57 probably echoes the similar instruction in Dan 8:26. Finally, the reference to שר השרין, "prince of the princes," in line 81 clearly relies on the שר שרים, "prince of princes," in Dan 8:25, "and he shall even rise up against the prince of princes."

According to the account in *HazGab* 81, the "prince of princes" became as דומן ארובות צרים, "dung in the rocky crevices." The biblical word דֹּמֶן or דּוּמָן always refers to an unburied corpse (see 2 Kgs 9:37; Jer 8:2; 9:21; 16:4; 25:33; Ps 83:11). Thus, we may infer that the "prince of princes" of the *Gabriel Revelation* is neither a divine entity nor an angel but rather a human being. This human being, probably an earthly leader of Israel, was killed and was not buried properly. For this reason his body decomposed and became דומן, that is, dung.

It seems that the author of the *Gabriel Revelation* used his interpretation of the Scriptures of Daniel to develop a notion of *catastrophic messianism*.[14] He probably read the verses in the book of Daniel to mean the following: The "king of bold countenance" will fight against the people of Israel who are "the people of the saints" of Dan 8:24; and, as this verse states, he will destroy and kill many of them. As this catastrophe unfolds, an earthly leader of Israel, "the prince of princes," will be defeated and killed by the evil king, as Dan 8:25 states. The final

---

14. See Gershom G. Scholem, *The Messianic Idea in Judaism and Other Essays on Jewish Spirituality* (New York: Schocken Books, 1971; repr., 1995), 8–18.

salvation will arrive only after all these calamities, when the evil king will be miraculously smitten "but, by no human hand, he shall be broken" (Dan 8:25). Thus, according to this reading of the Scriptures, the killing of many Israelites and the defeat and death of the leader, the "prince of princes" is an essential part of the redemptive process and the final event preceding the miraculous annihilation of the evil king!

4. A Possible Historical Context for the Forming of the Concept of Catastrophic Messianism

Yardeni and Elizur have dated the text of the *Gabriel Revelation* on the basis of its paleography and language to the time around the turn of the Common Era.[15] This estimate provides us with only the latest possible date for the composition of the *Gabriel Revelation*, since the surviving inscription may have been copied from an earlier text. However, Yardeni and Elizur also determine, based on the text's language, that it was composed "around the end of the first century BCE."[16] This dating of the language was accepted also by Moshe Bar-Asher.[17] Hence, we may assume that the text was composed and written around the turn of the Common Era.

There are indications that the *Gabriel Revelation* was written against the backdrop of a military conflict. The mention of "the slaughtered of Jerusalem" (line 57) and of "the nations who encamp around Jerusalem" (lines 13–14) might refer to a bloody event instigated by gentiles in Jerusalem. In fact, in the late first century B.C.E. a gentile army was indeed responsible for massive bloodshed in both Jerusalem and throughout the country—the rebellion that broke out in April of the year 4 B.C.E., following the death of King Herod the Great. The insurgents sought to free themselves from the yoke of the Roman-supported Herodian line. The insurrection began in Jerusalem and spread throughout the province. It was finally crushed by the Roman army under the command of Varus, governor of Syria. Thousands were killed or sold into slavery and parts of the temple were burned (see Josephus, *J.W.* 2.1–5 §§1–79; *Ant.* 17.10 §§250–98; *T. Mos.* 6:8–9).

Josephus tells us that this revolt was led by three men, all of whom possessed aspirations to the throne;[18] that is, the three had messianic preten-

---

15. Yardeni and Elizur, "Prophetic Text," 156.
16. Ibid., 156.
17. Moshe Bar-Asher, "On the Language of 'The Vision of Gabriel'," *RevQ* 23 (2008): 492–524.
18. On the leaders of the revolt, see William R. Farmer, "Judas, Simon and Athrogenes," *NTS* 4 (1958): 147–55; Menahem Stern, "Herod and the Herodian Dynasty," in *The Jewish People in the First Century: Historical Geography, Political History, Social, Cultural and Religious Life and Institutions* (ed. S. Safrai and M. Stern; 2 vols.; CRINT; Philadelphia: Fortress, 1974, 1976), 1: 280; Richard A. Horsley, *Bandits, Prophets and Messiahs: Popular Movements in the*

sions.[19] The *Gabriel Revelation* mentions the "three shepherds" who were sent to Israel (see lines 70, 75). Since the Hebrew רועה, "shepherd," might refer to a king or a messianic leader (see Jer 3:15; 23:1; Ezek 34:2-23),[20] it is possible that the "three shepherds" are the three messianic leaders of this rebellion. While at the time of the rebellion each of these leaders had a different group of supporters, after the rebellion they could be seen as one unit of "three shepherds," similar to the three shepherds mentioned in the book of Zechariah (11:8).

The text reconstruction of the poorly preserved line 40, "That his mist will fill most of the moon," might refer to a lunar eclipse. A lunar eclipse indeed took place a short time before the outbreak of the revolt of 4 B.C.E. Not long before Herod's death, two sages, Judas and Matthias, encouraged their disciples to pull down the golden eagle that was fixed by King Herod above the temple gate. Judas, Matthias, and their disciples were captured after removing the eagle. They were brought before Herod, who sentenced some forty of them to death (Josephus, *J.W.* 1.33.2-4 §§648-55; *Ant.* 17.6.2-4 §§151-67). Josephus further remarks: "And on that same night there was an eclipse of the moon" (*Ant.* 17.6.4 §167). Most scholars agree that the reference is to the lunar eclipse that occurred on the March 13, 4 B.C.E.[21] The revolt began a month later, during Passover. It is therefore possible that the reference to the lunar eclipse in line 40 and the mention of the blood that turns into a chariot in line 67 reflect this event. The sanguine moon on the night of the lunar eclipse of March 13, 4 B.C.E. was probably taken as a sign that the righteous people who gave their life for pulling down the effigy from the temple gate had ascended to heaven and were seen on the moon. Adela Yarbro Collins has suggested that *T. Mos.* 10:8-9 is an allusion to the pulling down of the golden

---

Time of Jesus (Harrisburg, Pa.: Trinity Press International, 1999), 111-17; Nikos Kokkinos, *The Herodian Dynasty: Origins, Role in Society and Eclipse* (JSPSup 30; Sheffield: Sheffield Academic Press, 1998), 227, no. 79.

19. See Stern, "Herod and the Herodian Dynasty," 280; Martin Hengel, *The Zealots: Investigations into the Jewish Freedom Movement in the Period from Herod I until 70 A.D.* (trans. David Smith; Edinburgh: T&T Clark, 1989), 292, 328-29; Horsley, *Bandits, Prophets and Messiahs*, 114-17; Horsley, "Popular Messianic Movements around the Time of Jesus," *CBQ* 46 (1984): 484-87. See also the more skeptical view of Martin Goodman, *The Ruling Class of Judaea: The Origins of the Jewish Revolt against Rome, A.D. 66-70* (Cambridge: Cambridge University Press, 1995), 92.

20. One of the three leaders of the revolt, Athronges, was a shepherd by vocation.

21. See the discussion and literature in Daniel R. Schwartz, *Studies in the Jewish Background of Christianity* (WUNT 60; Tübingen: Mohr Siebeck, 1992), 157-58. I cannot accept his suggestion that the lunar eclipse mentioned by Josephus occurred not on the night of the execution but rather "on the night Matthias ben Theophilus dreamed his fateful dream" (ibid., 161). The syntax and structure of Josephus's story clearly point to the fact that the notion of the lunar eclipse is connected to the burning of the "other Matthias" mentioned in the previous sentence and not to the story about the dream of Matthias ben Theophilus that was told earlier.

eagle.[22] It is thus possible that the *Gabriel Revelation* and the *Testament of Moses*, compiled around the same time, refer to this event.

Finally, we should examine the possible identification of the "prince of the princes" in line 81. It seems that in the *Gabriel Revelation* this title refers to an earthly leader of Israel.[23] The Jewish and Roman sources tell us about Simon of Transjordan, who was probably prominent among the three leaders of the revolt.[24] He proclaimed himself king and was seen as such by his supporters, who undoubtedly viewed him as the fulfillment of their messianic hopes. Josephus describes Simon's death after being defeated on the battlefield: "Simon himself, endeavoring to escape up a steep ravine, was intercepted by Gratus [Herod's military commander], who struck the fugitive from the side a blow on the neck, which severed his head from his body" (*J.W.* 2.4.2 §59). According to the account in *HazGab* 81, the "prince of princes" became as "dung in the rocky crevices" after his death. Thus, the mention of the "rocky crevices" close to that of the death of the "prince of princes" might allude to the killing of Simon—the leader of the revolt who had assumed the mantle of royalty—in the rocky crevices of Transjordan.

It is thus possible that the *Gabriel Revelation* was composed shortly after 4 BCE, against the backdrop of the crushing of the revolt.

Our understanding of the possible historical context of the *Gabriel Revelation* may shed light on the aim and orientation of this composition, as well as on the conditions that led to its inscription on the stone. I assume that this text was composed and written within a group of followers of the messianic leader Simon, who was killed in Transjordan in 4 B.C.E. The stone was probably found in a desert area across in Jordan, not far from the eastern shore of the Dead Sea.[25]

The text of the *Gabriel Revelation* possibly reflects the struggle of the members of this group with the crisis that followed the killing of their messianic leader and the merciless crushing of the rebellion by the Roman army. Such an event would naturally lead the followers of the slain leader to question his messianic pretensions and to take his death as evidence that he was a false messiah. The author of the *Gabriel Revelation*, however, disqualifies such a view as he shapes the ideology of catastrophic messianism based on Gabriel's address to Daniel. According to this ideology, the defeat of the messianic leader is an essential part

---

22. Adela Yarbro Collins, "The Composition and Redaction of the Testament of Moses," *HTR* 69 (1976): 186. See further John J. Collins, "The Testament (Assumption) of Moses," in *Outside the Old Testament* (ed. M. de Jonge; Cambridge: Cambridge University Press, 1985), 148, 157.

23. The meaning of this title in the book of Daniel is a different and separate issue.

24. Simon's prominent role among the leaders of the rebellion is evident in that he is the only one mentioned by the Roman historian Tacitus (*Hist.* 5.9.2), who also states that Simon crowned himself as king. See further E. Mary Smallwood, *The Jews under Roman Rule: From Pompey to Diocletian. A Study in Political Relations* (SJLA 20; Leiden: Brill, 1976), 111, no. 26.

25. See Yuval Goren, "Micromorphologic Examination of the *Gabriel Revelation* Stone," *IEJ* 58 (2008): 220–29.

of the redemptive process. The blood of the slain messiah paves the way for the final salvation.

5. Why "Ephraim"?

Above I have identified Jer 31:9, 18–20 as a source for considering Ephraim as God's firstborn—the tormented, suffering, and beloved son. A similar image of Ephraim as the beloved son of God is found in Hos 11:1-9. Hosea says: "Yet it was I who taught Ephraim to walk.... How can I give you up, Ephraim?... My heart recoils within me; / my compassion grows warm and tender." Yet, at the same time, Hosea also describes Ephraim as one who was killed (13:1, 14).

Elsewhere in the Bible, however, we also find a different portrait of Ephraim, the image of the mighty warrior: "Then Ephraim shall become like a mighty warrior" (Zech 10:7). This image is related to the depiction of Joseph, Ephraim's father, as a mighty bull or wild ox:

> His firstling bull has majesty,
>   and his horns are the horns of the wild ox,
> with them he shall push the peoples,
>   all of them, to the ends of the earth,
> such are the ten thousands of Ephraim.... (Deut 33:17)

By merging these two biblical images of Ephraim, we arrive at the figure of a mighty warrior possessing the messianic titles of God's firstborn and beloved son. However, Ephraim the mighty warrior is also a suffering, afflicted, and even dying son of God.

Joseph Heinemann has argued that the original image of Ephraim as Messiah was that of a mighty warrior, and that only Bar Kokhba's defeat in 135 C.E. generated the motif of the death of this Messiah.[26] It seems, however, that the discovery of the *Gabriel Revelation* indicates otherwise. As we recall, in lines 16–18 we read the following: "My servant David, ask of Ephraim [that he p]lace the sign; (this) I ask of you." God requests of his servant David to approach Ephraim and ask him to place the "sign." This is an astonishing scene: David functions here as a servant who is sent by his master, God, to ask Ephraim to place the "sign." From the context of the following lines of the *Gabriel Revelation* (18-19), it appears that Ephraim enjoys a higher status than David since he is the son of God while David is the servant of God. Thus, the servant David is only a messenger sent to Ephraim, while the latter, rather than David, is entrusted with the performance of the decisive act.

The redemptive process must begin, but the necessary trigger is Ephraim's

---

26. See Joseph Heinemann, "The Messiah of Ephraim and the Premature Exodus of the Tribe of Ephraim," *HTR* 68 (1975): 1–15.

placement of "the sign." As we have stated above, it seems that this sign is the defeating of the forces of evil "by three days." This fits the image of the biblical Ephraim as a mighty warrior. Yet the heavy impact of Jeremiah 31–33 on the *Gabriel Revelation* suggests that we also look at the other aspect of the biblical Ephraim, that is, the suffering and dying son of God. This might lead us to assume that Ephraim of the *Gabriel Revelation* is the heavenly image of the "prince of the princes" whose unburied corpse became dung in the rocky crevices (line 81). As stated above, the "prince of princes" in the *Gabriel Revelation* is an earthly leader of Israel, probably a messianic leader, who was killed by the enemy. This slain leader conforms to a high degree with the image of biblical Ephraim, a warrior and a suffering and dying son of God.

We suggested earlier that the "prince of princes" in the *Gabriel Revelation* is Simon of Transjordan, the messianic leader who was killed in 4 B.C.E. Simon, like the other messianic leaders of that revolt, was not a descendant of the house of David. He probably also lacked a priestly lineage. Thus, he could be seen neither as a Davidic Messiah nor as a priestly Messiah. Prior to the rebellion in 4 B.C.E., he was a slave or servant of Herod, and he is described as a tall and physically strong man (Josephus, *Ant*. 17.10.6 §273).

This is probably the reason for the search for another messianic title and image, a title that can be applied to a messianic leader who is neither the "son of David" nor "the son of Aaron" but is a strong man and a mighty warrior who fought against the enemy for the liberation of Israel. Yet this strong and brave warrior was defeated and killed on the battlefield. As we have seen above, by merging the different biblical images of Ephraim, we arrive at the figure of a mighty warrior possessing the messianic titles of God's firstborn and beloved son who is at the same time also a suffering and dying son of God. This is the reason, in my view, why the author of the *Gabriel Revelation* decided to use "Ephraim" as a messianic title.

In rabbinic Judaism there are various mentions of a suffering and slain Messiah called "Ephraim," the "Messiah son of Joseph," or the "Messiah son of Ephraim."[27] In my view, "Ephraim" of the *Gabriel Revelation* is the source of these messianic titles and figures.

6. The *Gabriel Revelation* as the New/Holy Covenant

I would like now to go back and consider God's statement according to the new reading of lines 18–19: "My son! I have a new/holy covenant for Israel." What is this new/holy covenant that God wants to give his son for Israel? I suggest that

---

27. For "Ephraim," see *Pesiq. Rab.* 36 (trans. William G. Braude: New Haven: Yale University Press, 1968), 678–79; on the "Messiah son of Joseph," see *b. Sukkah* 52a; on the "Messiah son of Ephraim," see Alexander Sperber, ed., *The Bible in Aramaic: Based on Old Manuscripts and Printed Texts* (4 vols. in 5; Leiden: Brill, 1992), 4:495.

the content of the holy/new covenant is the text of the *Gabriel Revelation* itself. This could explain the manner in which the *Gabriel Revelation* is written: just as the Ten Commandments of the Sinai covenant were written on two stone tablets, the new/holy covenant of the *Gabriel Revelation* is written on a stone tablet.[28] The tablets of the Sinai covenant are said to have been "tablets that were inscribed on both sides: they were inscribed on the one side and on the other" (Exod 32:15). The *Gabriel Revelation* was written in two columns: the right column begins at the right edge of the stone tablet and the left column ends at its left edge. Perhaps the author of the *Gabriel Revelation* sought in this way to apply the words of the verse in Exodus "they were inscribed on the one side and on the other."[29]

We have claimed above that the "son of God" who is the receiver of the holy/new covenant is to be identified with "Ephraim" the suffering and dying messianic leader. According to the statement in *HazGab* 18–19, the son of God is receiving the holy/new covenant for Israel; that is, he will have to give and preach this holy/new covenant to the people of Israel. Do we have in the Hebrew Bible a basis for the concept of a slain Messiah who is giving a holy/new covenant to Israel?

As we have seen above, the verses of the first speech of Gabriel to Daniel (Dan 8:23–26) play a major role in the *Gabriel Revelation*. This is certainly connected with the role of the angel Gabriel who is the speaker in the last section of the *Gabriel Revelation* (lines 77–87). I believe, however, that the second speech of Gabriel to Daniel (Dan 9:22–27) is also very significant for the understanding of the *Gabriel Revelation*. In the last two verses of this speech we read the following words:

> And after the sixty-two weeks, an anointed one shall be cut off, and shall have nothing; and the people of the prince who is to come shall destroy the city and the sanctuary. Its end shall come with a flood, and at the end there shall be war; desolations are decreed. And he shall make a strong covenant with many for one week. . . .

Modern scholars understand that the one who "shall make a strong covenant with many" והגביר ברית לרבים is Epiphanes, and the reference here is to his alliance with the hellenizing Jews.[30] However, in the eyes of a Jewish reader in the

---

28. As the beginning of the text inscribed on the stone has not been preserved, it may be that there was a second tablet that contained the beginning of the work.

29. Ibn Ezra may refer to the possibility that the tablets were written in two columns in his short commentary on Exodus. "And others say that the words of God were split up on the tablet." But as Asher Weiser notes, the "split up" (נחלקים) is not found in several manuscripts of the commentary (*Perushei ha-Torah le-Rabeinu Avraham Ibn Ezra* [Jerusalem: Rabbi Kook Institute, 1976/77], 2:348 n. 83).

30. See John J. Collins, *Daniel: A Commentary on the Book of Daniel* (Hermeneia; Minneapolis: Fortress, 1993), 357.

turn of the Common Era, this verse could be read in a different way. We have mentioned above the Danielic phrase ברית קדש, "a holy covenant," as a possible source of the expression "new/holy covenant" in *HazGab* 18–19. The "holy covenant" is mentioned in Dan 11:28, 32. In the same chapter (11:33), we read also that "those among the people who are wise shall make *many* understand" (ומשכילי עם יבינו לרבים). The group called "the many" (הרבים) is mentioned positively also in Dan 12:3. In light of all these positive appearances of "covenant" and "the many," it was almost natural to read the words of Dan 9:27, "he shall make a strong covenant with many" (והגביר ברית לרבים), in a positive way, that is, as a reference to a "holy covenant" that is given to the righteous people of Israel.

But who, then is the one who "makes a strong covenant with many"? The obvious candidate for this task would be the "dying Messiah" who is mentioned in the previous verse (Dan 9:26, "an anointed one shall be cut off"). Thus, the verses of the second speech of Gabriel to Daniel could easily be read as a source for the concept of a slain Messiah who is giving a holy covenant to Israel. It is possible that the reference to the breaking of the "prince of the covenant" in Dan 11:22 was understood in the same fashion. This way, it could serve as another source for the concept of a covenant that is given by a slain Messiah.

7. The *Gabriel Revelation* and the *Testament of Moses*

The author of the *Gabriel Revelation* exhibits well-developed apocalyptic thinking. He speaks in the name of God and also uses the tetragrammaton frequently. He also mentions prophets as an existing reality (line 15). It is thus difficult to believe that the author was a Pharisee. At the same time, his style is different from that of the Qumran community, and there are no indications of Qumranic concepts or terms in this composition. Further, the reference to "Ephraim" as a positive and significant figure in the *Gabriel Revelation* contradicts the use of "Ephraim" in the Dead Sea Scrolls as a negative title for the Pharisees.[31] The author's political views and his belief in resurrection indicate that he is definitely not a Sadducee either. If the *Gabriel Revelation* was indeed written shortly after 4 B.C.E., then it predates the time of the formation of the "fourth philosophy" of the Zealots.[32] Hence, we cannot attribute this composition to any known Jewish sect of the period.

We can, however, point to another composition redacted in the same period, which shares many of the views of the *Gabriel Revelation* and probably belongs to similar apocalyptic circles: the *Testament of Moses* (*T. Mos.*). These two compositions share a similar understanding of their time. Immediately after the

---

31. See David Flusser, "Pharisees, Sadducees and Essenes in Pesher Nahum," in *Essays in Jewish History and Philology in Memory of Gedaliahu Alon* (in Hebrew; ed. M. Dorman et al., Tel Aviv: Dvir, 1970), 133–68.

32. That is, the year 6 C.E.; see *Ant.* 18.1.1 §§4–10.

description of the cruel crushing of the 4 B.C.E. revolt in *T. Mos.* 6:8–9, we find the following remark: "When this has taken place, the times will quickly come to an end" (7:1).[33] As Kenneth Atkinson notes: "The author apparently believed that the partial destruction of the temple and the other tumultuous events that followed Herod the Great's death were signs that signaled the beginning of the final age of History."[34] I believe that these same words can be applied to the author of the *Gabriel Revelation*.

In the final part of *T. Mos.* 7:1, we read: "The four hours shall come."[35] John J. Collins has noted that the "four hours" in *T. Mos.* 7:1 are probably an apocalyptic formulation based on Dan 7:25. He suggests further that "in the present passage it may mean that TM was written less than four years after the attack under Varus."[36] We have suggested above that the *Gabriel Revelation* was written shortly after 4 B.C.E. Thus, it seems that the *Testament of Moses* and the *Gabriel Revelation* were probably written at about the same time.

The main difference between the two texts seems to lie in their attitude to the leaders of the revolt of 4 B.C.E. In the surviving chapters of the *Testament of Moses*, these leaders are not mentioned and Taxo is a nonmilitant model.[37] In contrast, according to our interpretation, the *Gabriel Revelation* expresses great admiration for these leaders, particularly Simon of Transjordan. At the same time, both compositions agree that the final salvation will follow the battle of the heavenly army and will not be brought about by human hands.[38]

---

33. See J. Priest, "Testament of Moses," *OTP* 1:930.

34. Kenneth Atkinson, "Taxo's Martyrdom and the Role of the *Nuntius* in the *Testament of Moses*: Implications for Understanding the Role of Other Imtermediary Figures," *JBL* 125 (2006): 461–62. See also idem, "Herod the Great as *Antiochus Rededvivus*: Reading the *Testament of Moses* as an Anti-Herodian Composition," in *Of Scribes and Sages: Early Jewish Interpretation and Transmission of Scripture* (ed. Craig A. Evans; 2 vols.; Library of Second Temple Studies 50; London: T&T Clark, 2004), 141.

35. See Robert H. Charles, "The Assumption of Moses," in *The Apocrypha and Pseudepigrapha of the Old Testament in English: With Introductions and Critical and Explanatory Notes to the Several Books* (ed. R. H. Charles; 2 vols.; Oxford: Clarendon, 1913), 2:419.

36. John J. Collins, "The Date and Provenance of the Testament of Moses," in *Studies on the Testament of Moses: Seminar Papers* (ed. George W. E. Nickelsburg; SBLSCS 4; Cambridge, Mass.: Society of Biblical Literature, 1973), 17 n. 8. See also Atkinson, "Taxo's Martyrdom," 461-62.

37. See Collins, "Date and Provenance," 30; idem, "Testament (Assumption) of Moses," 148–49. It is possible that this nonmilitant conception is the result of the crushing of the revolt and the killing of its leaders; see David M. Rhoads, "The Assumption of Moses and Jewish History," in Nickelsburg, *Studies on the Testament of Moses*, 56–57. I agree with Johannes Tromp (*The Assumption of Moses: A Critical Edition with Commentary* [SVTP 10; Leiden: Brill, 1993], 124) that none of the numerous suggestions made to solve the enigmatic name Taxo is convincing. This is true, in my view, also of the recent suggestion to explain it as a title of Jesus (Edna Israeli, "'Taxo' and the Origin of the *Assumption of Moses*," *JBL* 128 [2009]: 735–57).

38. I accept the view that the *nuntius* in *T. Mos.* 10:2 is an angel, probably Michael. See Collins, "Testament (Assumption) of Moses," 156; Atkinson, "Taxo's Martyrdom," 472–73.

Yet there is still a very significant agreement between the *Gabriel Revelation* and the *Testament of Moses* with regard to the final event that will bring redemption and salvation. In the ninth chapter of the *Testament of Moses* we read about Taxo, who tells his sons that they should die rather than transgress the commandments of the Lord: "For if we do this, and do die, our blood will be avenged before the Lord" (9:7).[39] This is immediately followed by the description of the arrival of the eschatological war and salvation. Jacob Licht had pointed out the significance of the linkage between Taxo's blood and vengeance.[40] According to his interpretation, "the sense of Taxo's speech and the virtue of his deed appear to be this: God cannot allow innocent blood to be shed unavenged. Let us therefore die innocently, and we shall thus surely promote Divine vengeance and deliverance."[41] Thus, the shed blood of Taxo and his sons paves the way for divine vengeance and redemption. As noted above, the author of the *Gabriel Revelation* shapes the ideology of catastrophic messianism based on his interpretation of Gabriel's address to Daniel. According to this conception, the defeat of the messianic leader is an essential part of the redemptive process. The blood of the slain messianic leader, the "Prince of Princes," paves the way for the final salvation.

Finally, I would like to point to a similarity between the *Gabriel Revelation* and the *Testament of Moses* in their relationship with the formative figure of Moses. The *Testament of Moses* is presented as the testament given by Moses to Joshua, shortly before the end of Moses' life. As I have argued above, the *Gabriel Revelation* was meant to be seen as the tablet of the new/holy covenant, formed after the model of Moses' tablets. Thus, the authors of the *Testament of Moses* and the *Gabriel Revelation*, who lived after a major trauma, wished to tie their vision about the coming divine vengeance and redemption to the authority of Moses.

Appendix

What follows is my proposed reading and English translation of the major passages of the *Gabriel Revelation*. The reading is based on an examination of the inscription itself and photographs of it. I found that in most cases the transcription and reading of Yardeni and Elizur are accurate. The places where I suggest a different reading are indicated by notes. I have also noted the places where I have adopted the reading of Yuditsky and Qimron (Yuditsky and Qimron gave their reading of lines 11–32, 64–80). Letters that are illegible are indicated by a dot; broken or doubtful letters are underlined.

---

39. Priest, "Testament of Moses," 931.
40. Jacob Licht, "Taxo, or the Apocalyptic Doctrine of Vengeance," *JJS* 12 (1961): 96-100.
41. Ibid., 97. Priest claims that the association between blood and vengeance does not prove that Taxo intended "to compel God to exercise His vengeance" ("Testament of Moses," 923), as Licht (p. 98) had argued. However, see John J.Collins, *The Apocalyptic Imagination: An Introduction to Jewish Apocalyptic Literature* (2nd ed.; Grand Rapids: Eerdmans, 1998), 131.

Column 1

11 [?]יהוה אתה שאלני כן אמר אלהים צבאות
12 [ ]..ני מביתי ישראל ואגדה בגדלות ירושלם
13 [ ] אמר יהוה אלהי ישראל הנה כול הגאים
14 ..... [לים] מוג [ה]ומתוב [ ] צובאים[42] על ירושלם ר
15 אחת שתין שלוש ארבעין נביאין והשבין
16 [ו]החסידין עבדי דוד בקש מן לפני אפרים[43]
17 [וי]שים[44] האות אני מבקש מן לפנך כי אמר
18 יהוה צבאות אלהי ישראל בני[45] ב[רי]די ברית
19 ח\קדשה[46] לישראל לשלשת ימין תדע כי אמר
20 יהוה אלהים צבאות אלהי ישראל נשבר הרע
21 מלפני הצדק שאלני ואגיד לכה מה הצמח
22 הרע הזה לובנסד אתה עומד המלאך הוא
23 בסמכך אל תירה ברוך כבוד יהוה אלהים מן
24 מושבו עוד מעט קיטוט היא ואני מרעיש את
25 השמים ואת הארץ הנה כבוד יהוה אלהים ...
26 צבאות אלהי ישראל אלה המרכבות שבע
27 [ע]ל שער ירושלם ושערי יהודה ינחו למען
28 שלושה מלאכה מיכאל ולכול האחרן בקשו
29 אילכם כן אמר יהוה אלהים צבאות אלהי
30 ישראל אחד שנין שלושה ארבעה חמשה ששה
31 [שב]עה אל מלאכה ..... מה זו אמר הצץ
32 ואלוף השני ....[ל.ד.פכ..] [ ]....
33 שמר על ירשלם ...... שלושה בגדלות
34 [ד.ד ?].והו.[ ] שלושה .ד .והו.[ ]
35 [...] וי[עובד... שראה איש . ן...] [ ]
36 שסמן מירושלם]   .שהוא שבו
37 .. אני על.אי..[?] אפר ואות גלות ..
38 [א]ות גלות .צל י.ל אלהים עון אז. וראו
39 [...א....ג]   ירושלם אמר יהוה
40 ..למלא טחבו רוב ירח.. ....א.ל
41 [   ] דם שירם הצפוני
42 [   ] דראון הנגע. בכול

---

42. Following Yuditsky and Qimron ("Notes," 136–37); Yardeni and Elizur have not read this word.
43. See n. 11 above.
44. Ibid.
45. See n. 10 above.
46. See the discussion of the two options, above pp. 41–42.

Column 2

```
                                                         [
54 ל[   הוא  ] שאמ[רתי  זה ימיץ שלשת ]ל
55 אלה[   ] [..של] [...] [..] [..] [
56 ראו נא   הצפ[וני] חנ[ונה]       [
57 סתום דם טבחי ירושלם כי אמר יהוה צבא[ות]
58 אלהי ישראל כן אמר יהוה צבאות אלהי
59 ישראל מא..ל...אל. ] .[. ] .[ד..?]
60 ה.לני.ך יחמול ..רחמו קרב[ין]..[                ]
61 [?]ל אשריא......תץ ש ...[?]
62 בת.ל  א.  ע..נ  ]                    [
63 א.[  ] אב.[?].א.[ ]...[  ].[  ]
64 ]ה/חביב...ל ...[  ]..[..]
65 שלושה קדושי העולם מן מק. ]            [
66 [  ]ו.שלום אמר עליך אנחנו בטוחין [  ]
67 [  ] בשר לו על דם זו המרכבה שלהן ..ל.
68 אוהבין רבים ליהוה צבאת אל<ה>י ישראל
69 כה אמר יהוה צבאת אלהי ישראל .מ.......
70 נביאים שלחתי אל עמי שלושה רועי אומר
71 שראיתי ברכ. ל..לך דבר. ברן [...ב..?]
72 המקום למען דוד עבד יהוה ] .[א.]..
73 את השמים ואת הארץ בכוחך [הגדול ובזרועך]
74 הנטו\יה47 עושה חסד לאלפים מ.....חסד. [ ]
75 שלושה רועיץ יצאו לישראל ..ל...[ ]..[ ]
76 אם יש כהן אם יש בני קדושים ...ה.. [ ]
77 מי אנכי אני גבריאל המל.כי .לי ..מל] [
78 תצילם נבי..ם גרי..ם ושתיץ [..ב.]    [
79 מלפניך שלושה .... שלושה ... אק ] [
80 לשלושת ימין האות48 אני גבריאל ... ..ל.[?]
81 שר השרין דומן ארובות צרים א ].[ א...[?]
82 למראות ה...לשנם מן [....]ן ואהבי ג.מ. [?]
83 לי מן שלושה הקטן שלקחתי אני גבריאל
84 יהוה צבאת אלה[וי יש[ראל]             [
85 אז תעמדו א.[ ].ל ] [..א........[?]
86 יול .א .....\
87 ב..... עלם \
```

---

47. The distinction between י and ו in this inscription is difficult. Yuditsky and Qimron read here הנטו, but it is possible to read הנטיה as a defective form of הנטויה in Jer 32:17.

48. See n. 12 above.

Column 1, lines 11–42

11 [?] Lord you have asked me, so said the God of Hosts
12 [ ] .. from my house Israel and I will talk about the greatness of Jerusalem
13 [Thus] said the Lord, God of Israel, now all the nations
14 <u>encamp on</u> Jerusalem and from it <u>are exi</u>[led]
15 one two three forty Prophets and the elders
16 and the Hasidim. My servant David, ask of Ephra<u>im</u>
17 [that he] place the sign; (this) I ask of you. For thus said
18 the Lord of Hosts, the God of Israel, My son! I have a new/holy covenant for Israel
19 By three days you shall know, for thus said
20 the Lord of Hosts, the God of Israel, the evil is to be broken
21 before righteousness. Ask me, and I shall tell you, what is this
22 wicked branch, plastered white.[49] You are standing, the angel
23 is supporting you. Do not fear.[50] Blessed is the glory of the Lord God from
24 his seat. In a little while, I will shake
25 the heavens and the earth. Here is the glory of the Lord God
26 of Hosts, the God of Israel. These are the seven chariots
27 at the gate of Jerusalem and the gates of Judea they will <u>re</u>[st][51] for
28 my <u>three</u>[52] angels, Michael and all the others, look for
29 your powe<u>r</u>.[53] So said of the Lord God of Hosts, the God
30 of Israel. One two three four five six
31 [se]ven for my angels….. what is this? He said, the frontlet
32 …. [ ] ………. and the second chief
33 <u>watches</u> over.. <u>Jerusalem</u> …… three in the greatness

---

49. Yardeni and Elizur suggested a number of alternative readings for this word, but in my opinion the word לובנסד, "plastered white," can be read clearly. For a possible meaning of this expression see Knohl, *Messiahs and Resurrection*, 13.

50. Yardeni and Elizur read this as בסמכך אל תורה. In my opinion one should definitely read here בסמכך אל תירה, "is supporting you. Do not fear" (see Ps 54:6 [Eng. 4]). My reading was adopted by Yuditsky and Qimron ("Notes," 134, 136).

51. Yardeni and Elizur read here : …ינ; I read ינחו, "rest."

52. Yardeni and Elizur did not read this word at all.

53. At the beginning of line 29, Yardeni and Elizur read the letters י, ל, and כ. Before these letters they mark another letter that they could not make out, which in my opinion is an א. After the letters that Yardeni and Elizur read, there are two lines that slant downward, and I believe that these are the remnants of a ם. The word in its entirety is therefore אילכם, "your might." The word before it is בקשו, "look for" (at the end of line 28); the combination of the two words yields בקשו אילכם, "look for your might." In view of the context, this phrase can be understood as a request that God makes of the angels. The descent of the angels in chariots to the gates of Judea and Jerusalem was portrayed prior to this; it is a descent that should be understood as a preparation for war against the eschatological enemy. It therefore seems that in the context of the preparations for war, God turns to the angels and says בקשו אילכם, namely, "find and prepare your forces."

34 .... three[54] [ ] .....
35 [ ] ..... that he saw a man ... works[55] [
36 that he .... [ ] that a sign from Jerusalem[56]
37 I on ...[ ] ashes[57] and a sign of exile ..
38 [s]ign of exile .... God sin ... and see[58]
39 ...... [ ] Jerusalem said the Lord
40 .... That his mist will fill most of the moon[59]

---

54. Yardeni and Elizur read only ...לו here, but in my opinion the word שלושה, "three," is discernible.

55. Concerning the words איש...עובד, "a man ... works," in this line, compare Zech 13:5: איש עבד אדמה, "a tiller [worker] of the soil." Yardeni and Elizur read here עובד, "works."

56. Yardeni and Elizur marked the whole word מירושלם, "from Jerusalem," as dubious, but in my opinion the first few letters are clearly legible.

57. Yardeni and Elizur read here אבר. I suggest the reading אפר (ashes).

58. Yardeni and Elizur read this line as אתגלות. צל . [?]. אלהים ע...א.ן. וארה, while I read: [א]ות גלות. צל י.ל אלהים עון או. וראו

59. Yardeni and Elizur read the second half of this line as ל....חנארו.ורח.[?]. In my opinion, the ל, which the editors read, is followed by the letters מ, ל, א, and ט. Subsequently the editors read the letter ח, and I agree with them. Next the editors read נ, א, ר, and ו. I agree with them regarding the last two, but in my opinion the first letters are not נ and א but ב and ו. Following them there is a letter that the editors did not read, which in my opinion is a ב. Finally, the editors read ו, ר, and ח, a reading that I would like to correct slightly to י, ר, and ח. According to my revisions, the line reads as follows: למלאטחבורוביירח. I suggest this be read as the phrase "למלא טחבו רוב ירח". Obviously, due to the difficulty in reading the letters this is only guesswork. Can this sentence be understood? The key word here is the word טחב. This word appears in talmudic literature only once, in a parable that explains the first verses of Leviticus 16: "When a sick person goes to the doctor he tells him, 'Do not drink cold [liquids] and do not lie בטחב'" (Sifra, beginning of Aharei Mot [ed. Weiss, p. 79b]). From the context we can deduce that בטחב indicates a moist, damp place. Another occurrence is in several manuscripts of the Targum of Job 37:11: אף ברי יטריח עב = "He also loads the clouds with moisture" = ברם בטחבות מטרח עייבא. See: David M. Stec, The Text of the Targum of Job: An Introduction and Critical Edition (AGJU 20; Leiden: Brill, 1994), 259. In view of this occurrence and in view of the existence of a similar word in Arabic that means "a light cloud," Alexander Kohut concluded that טחב is likely to mean "a mist" or "a light cloud." Alexander Kohut, Arukh Hashalem 4 (Vienna, 1881–82; repr., Jerusalem: Makor, 1969–70), 21. See also Marcus Jastrow's explanation, s.v. טחבות (A Dictionary of the Targumim, the Talmud Babli and Yerushalmi, and the Midrashic Literature (2 vols.; New York: Pardes, 1950; repr., New York: Judaica Press, 1975), 527. The phrase למלא טחבו רוב ירח can therefore be understood as follows: טחבו, "his light cloud," will cover most of the moon. There may be a parallel to this in מאחז פני כסה פרשז עליו עננו, "He covers the face of the moon, and spreads over it his cloud" (Job 26:9). Some have understood the word כֶּסֶה in this verse as denoting the full moon, on the basis of Ps 81:4 and Prov 7:20, and the Ugaritic. See the list in David J. A. Clines, Job 21–37 (WBC 18A; Nashville: Thomas Nelson, 2006), 622–23. Consequently, it may be that the verse in Job and the phrase in the Gabriel Revelation describe the same phenomenon: the deity covers the face of the full moon with his cloud or his mist. Both sources would be speaking of a lunar eclipse, which can take place only at mid-month on יום הכסה, the day of the full moon. I have suggested elsewhere (Knohl, Messiahs and Resurrection, 47–48) that the phrase "Announce him about blood, this

41 [ ] blood that the northerner would become maggoty[60]
42 [ ] abhorrence the diseased spot[61] . in all

Column 2

54 [by] three days this is what [I have] said He
55. these are [
56 please see the north[erner] enca[mps] [
57 Seal up the blood[62] of the slaughtered of Jerusalem. For thus said the Lord of Hos[ts]
58 the God of Israel, So said the Lord of Hosts the God of
59 Israel [
60 ... He will have pity .. His mercy are ne[ar][63]
61 [ ] blessed ? ...
62 daughter ? ...[64]
63 ...
64 [ ] ...[ ] beloved ?
65 Three holy ones of the world from.... []
66 [ ] *shalom* he said, in you we trust ... [?]
67 Announce him about blood, this is their chariot.
68 Many are those who love the Lord of Hosts, the God of Israel
69 Thus said the Lord of Hosts, the God of Israel ....[?]

---

is their chariot" refers to the lunar eclipse that took place shortly before the death of Herod. It may be that the phrase למלא טחבו רוב ירח is also connected to this event. The words רוב ירח refer to a partial eclipse, and the eclipse in question was indeed a partial eclipse (but in fact the occultation was less than 50 percent). In any event, the problematic state of this line of the inscription does not permit us to say anything for certain. Michael Segal [in an oral communication] suggested that טחבו may be a case of metathesis and that we should read למלא טבחו רוב ירח, "the blood of the *slaughtered* will cover most of the moon."

60. Knohl, *Messiahs and Resurrection*, 20.
61. Ibid, 20–21.
62. Yardeni and Elizur marked the words סתום דם as doubtful (except for the ס at the beginning of the line), but in my opinion the reading is certain.
63. Yardeni and Elizur read this line as [ ] הלני רוח הנרא..תן. שק. ל.[?], but I find their transcription and reading problematic. The letter they called a ר at the beginning of the word רוח is not a ר but a ך. Its leg clearly stretches below the line. After a short space, the letters י, ח, and מ are clearly legible. The subsequent letters ו and ל are questionable. After this there appear two letters that are illegible. Following them the letters ר and ח are clearly visible. The letters מ and ו that come next are less clear. Next comes a clearly legible ק, followed by what may be a ר and a ב. I suggest completing the word קרב[ין], "near," here. The phrase therefore reads יחמול רחמו קרב[ין]. = "He will have pity .. His mercy is near." From the context it emerges that the subject is the deity, who will show compassion in the future because his mercy is near. Regarding the spelling רחמו rather than רחמיו, compare כי רבים רחמו (2 Sam 24:14). With the reconstructed collocation רחמו קרבין compare רחמוי קריבין (*y. Ta'an*. 2:1 [65a; Hebrew Language Academy edition, p. 713, line 20]; *Pesiq.Rab Kah*., *Va-tomer ziyyon* [ed. Mandelbaum, p. 283]).
64. Yardeni and Elizur read this line as [ ]..[?].ד.ב.[   ]..בה א.

APOCALYPTIC AND MESSIANIC DIMENSIONS

70 prophets. I sent to my people my th<u>ree</u> <u>shepherds. I will say</u>[65] (?)
71 that I have seen bless[ing]… ….. Go say(?)
72 The place <u>for</u> David the servant of the Lord [   ]...[   ] .. [ ]
73 The heaven and the earth, [with Your great] might [and]
74 <u>outstretched [arm]</u>[66]. Showing steadfast love to thousands …. steadfast love. [ ]
75 Three shepherds went out for Israel … [   ]…
76 If there is a priest, if there are sons of holy ones ….[   ]
77 <u>Who am I</u>? I am Gabriel …….. [   ]
78 You will rescue them………….. <u>for two</u>[67] [] …[   ]
79 from be<u>fore</u> you the three ….[68] three .. [   ]
80 By three days, the <u>sign</u>,[69] I Gabriel … ….. [?]
81 prince of the princes, the d<u>ung</u>[70] of the rocky crevices []… ..[   ]
82 to the <u>visions</u> (?) <u>… their tongue</u> (?) [ ] … <u>those who love me</u>
83 to me, from the three, the small one that I took, I Gabriel
84 Lord of Hosts G<o>d of Is[rael] [
85 then you will stand …86 … \\[71]
87 … <u>wo</u>rld ? \\

---

65. I read these two words as רועי אומר, "my shepherds. I will say"; Yardeni and Elizur read them as ואני אומר, "And I will say." Yuditsky and Qimron read here רועין ואחר "shepherds and after."

66. Following Yuditsky and Qimron, 135, 137.

67. Yardeni and Elizur read לשות.ן.

68. Yardeni and Elizur read here הא[ת]ות (the signs), Yuditsky and Qimron read רועים (shepherds).

69. Yardeni and Elizur read here ….ה, for my past and current readings of this word see n. 12 above.

70. Yardeni and Elizur read here: ד..ן. In my opinion, the remnants of the left part of the letter ם are recognizable, as well as the head of the letter ו. The biblical word דמן or דומן always refers to an unburied corpse; see above p. 44.

71. Yardeni and Elizur read in this line: \ …. ….ל….. . The vertical signs at the end of lines 86-87 mark the end of the inscription.

FIVE

HAZON GABRIEL: A GRAMMATICAL SKETCH

Gary A. Rendsburg

0. INTRODUCTION

The following grammatical sketch of the *Hazon Gabriel* (*HazGab*) inscription is based on the readings provided by Alexey (Eliyahu) Yuditsky and Elisha Qimron, whose analysis covered primarily lines 11–32 and 64–80.[1] While an occasional string of letters in the remaining lines of the epigraph may yield a word here or there, in the main we refrain from invoking such evidence, given the extremely fragmentary nature of these sections (lines 1–10, 33–63, 81–87) and the overall difficulty of reading the ink on the stone.[2] The only exception is a string of four-

---

It is my distinct pleasure to thank Steven Fassberg (Hebrew University) and Matthew Morgenstern (University of Haifa) for their generously reading the pre-final version of this article, for their many constructive comments and criticisms, and for providing several key bibliographic sources (most importantly the 2009 dissertations by Uri Mor and Gregor Geiger, both cited herein—as the reader will see, my ability to consult the former in particular was a special boon to my research). Note the abbreviations DSSEL = Dead Sea Scrolls Electronic Library (2006 edition); Maʾagarim = Maʾagarim: Mifʿal ha-Millon ha-Histori la-Lašon ha-ʿIvrit = The Hebrew Language Historical Dictionary Project (Jerusalem: Academy of the Hebrew Language, 1998–), online at http://hebrew-treasures.huji.ac.il/.

1. Alexey (Eliyahu) Yuditsky and Elisha Qimron, "Heʿarot ʿal ha-Ketovet ha-Mekuneh 'Ḥazon Gavriʾel,'" *Cathedra* 133 (2009): 133–44, along with the abridged English version in the present volume.

2. Notwithstanding our great confidence in the expert reading skills of Ada Yardeni (for which see Ada Yardeni and Binyamin Elizur, "Ṭeqsṭ Nevuʾi ʿal ʾEven min ha-Meʾa ha-Rišona lifne Sefirat ha-Noṣerim: Hodaʿa Rišona," *Cathedra* 123 [2008]: 155–66), as indicated, I utilize herein the study of Yuditsky and Qimron, as the most up-to-date statement on the matter. The readings presented by Yardeni and Elizur served, by and large, as the basis for four earlier treatments: Israel Knohl, "ʿIyyunim be-'Ḥazon Gavriʾel,'" *Tarbiz* 76 (2007): 303–28; Israel Knohl, "'By Three Days, Live': Messiahs, Resurrection, and Ascent to Heaven in Hazon Gabriel," *JR* 88 (2008): 147–58; Moshe Bar-Asher, "ʿal ha-Lašon be-'Ḥazon Gavriʾel,'" *Meghillot: Studies in the Dead Sea Scrolls* 7 (2009): 193–226; and Gary A. Rendsburg, "Linguistic and Stylistic Notes to the Hazon Gabriel Inscription," *DSD* 16 (2009): 107–16. (To be sure, Knohl also introduced his own readings into his article, most famously with חאיה, "live," in line 80, whereas Yardeni

teen words in lines 57–59, for which there is general agreement on the reading; and thus this passage will be included in our investigation. In general, we do not include partially reconstructed words, except where absolutely certain, e.g., יש[ראל], "[Isra]el," in line 30, נבי[אין], "[pro]phets" in line 79, and so on.[3] In addition, we shall not comment on the very enigmatic לו ב.ס.ד (line 22), except in one place as an aside (see §2.2.7).[4]

It is only natural to compare the language of *Hazon Gabriel* with the linguistic profiles of other varieties of ancient Hebrew, namely, (a) Biblical Hebrew (BH), in particular, in its Tiberian Masoretic garb—at times to be divided between Standard Biblical Hebrew (SBH) and Late Biblical Hebrew (LBH); (b) Qumran Hebrew (QH), representing the language of the Dead Sea Scrolls (DSS); (c) the Hebrew of the Judean Desert documents (HJDD), that is, Naḥal Ḥever, Wadi Murabbaʿat, and other sites; and (d) Mishnaic Hebrew (MH), including the language of not only the Mishnah but of other Tannaitic works as well. We will make such comparisons along the way (with occasional nods to Samaritan Hebrew [SH] and to the Hebrew of Ben Sira as well); and then at the article's end we will provide a summary assessment of the language of *Hazon Gabriel*.

1. Phonology and Orthography

1.1. Plene and Defectiva Spelling[5]

As one can see from the following lists, the scribe of *HazGab* favors *plene* over *defectiva* orthography, very much in keeping with the spelling tendencies in the DSS.

The fuller spelling system occurs in the following vocables:[6]

כול	(13)
צובאים	(14)
שלוש	(15)
הנביאין	(15)

---

and Elizur read only a partial ה at the beginning of the word and nothing thereafter.) While I follow Yuditsky and Qimron's readings herein, I also devote a brief Appendix (see below) to some of Yardeni and Elizur's readings, if only for the sake of completeness.

3. In such cases, a superscript ʳ is placed after the line number.

4. For an excellent attempt to extract meaning from these words, see Yuditsky and Qimron, "Heʿarot ʿal ha-Ketovet," 138.

5. For an earlier treatment, see Bar-Asher, "ʿal ha-Lašon be-ʾHazon Gavriʾel,'" 196–99, though his data are based on the readings of Yardeni and Elizur.

6. I do not include here examples of the masculine plural ending, whether ים- or ין-, even though these include *yod*, since these are always written this way in *HazGab*. Some such forms are recorded here, though their inclusion in the list is due to the presence of another *mater lectionis*, either *waw* or *yod* earlier in the word. Nor do I include words that are always written *plene* in ancient Hebrew sources, such as ברית (18) and ברוך (23).

הַחֲסִידִין[וּ]	(16)
עוֹמֵד	(22)
מְקוֹמוֹ	(24)
קִיטוֹט	(24)
שׁוֹד	(27)
וּלְכוֹל	(28)
שְׁלוֹשָׁה	(30, 65, 70, 75, 79)
בְּטוּחִין	(66)
אוֹהֲבִין	(68)
נְבִיאִים	(70)
רוֹעִין	(70)
בְּכוֹחֲךָ	(73)
עוֹשֶׂה	(74)
רוֹעִין	(75)
קְדוֹשִׁין	(76)
אוֹתָךְ	(78)
רוֹעִים	(79)
שְׁלוֹשֶׁת	(80)

Forms with *defectiva* spellings—that is, where one would expect a *waw* or *yod* based on the usual orthography in BH and/or the preponderance of *plene* spellings in *HazGab* as revealed by the above list—occur as follows:

שְׁאָלַנִי	(11)
וָאֶגְדָּה	(12)
דֹּד	(16, 72)
לְפָנֶךָ	(17)
צְבָאֹת	(28ʳ, 68, 69) [line 28: צְֹבָֹ[אֹ]תֹ]
הָאֲהֲבִין	(28)

Notes:
- The active participle typically uses *waw* to represent the first /ō/ vowel, as in צֹֹבָֹאֹיֹם (14), עוֹמֵד (22), אוֹהֲבִין (68), עוֹשֶׂה (74), and in a noun derived from this grammatical form, that is, רוֹעִין (75), רוֹעִים (79).[7] In two instances, however, the form occurs without *waw*, viz., שְׁאָלַנִי (11) and הָאֲהֲבִין (28). Both of these are the result of what James Barr termed "affix effect," which is to say, the addition of morphological elements to a lexeme typically yields a *defectiva* orthography.[8] In the first case, the suffix pronoun -נִי serves as the catalyst, while in the second instance, the prefixed definite article -ה causes the resultant spelling.

---

7. In the Bible spelled always as רֹעִים (cstr. רֹעֵי).

8. James Barr, *The Variable Spellings of the Hebrew Bible* (Oxford: Oxford University Press, 1989), esp. 25–32.

- I have not included the many instances of the feminine plural ending וֹת- in the *plene* list above, since this is the standard usage, e.g., גדלות (12), המרכבות (26), and the many instances of צבאות (11, 18, 20, 26, 29, 58). The only feminine plural ending written *defectiva* is צבאת (28ʳ, 68, 69), most likely due to the scribe's desire to introduce variation into his orthography.[9]
- As expected, given both BH and QH orthography, the long /ī/ vowel of Hiphʿil forms is indicated throughout with *mater lectionis yod*—with one exception. Thus, one finds (and these are not included in the first list above) [הש]יֹבִ֗ני (17), ואגיד (21), מרעיש (24), תצילם (78), יצילו (78), versus only ואגדה (12) without *yod*. Again, I would explain this spelling (along with the presence of final *he*) as simply for the sake of variation; see further §2.5.9, first bullet.
- As expected, *matres lectionis* are used mainly for long vowels. In one sure instance, however, *yod* is used to represent a short /i/ vowel, viz., קיטוט, "trembling" (24).[10] For a parallel from the DSS, note 1QHᵃ 16:18 פיתאום, "suddenly."[11]
- The name "David" is spelled *defectiva*: דוד (16, 72). This spelling dominates in the Bible and in Ben Sira (5x), whereas the *plene* form דויד dominates in LBH (264x in Chronicles and Ezra-Nehemiah)[12] and in QH (19x [e.g., 1QM 11:2] vs. 1x without *yod* [CD 7:16 citing Amos 9:11[13]])[14]; see also Ben Sira 47:2, 49:4.
- An unusual spelling occurs with לפנך, "before you" (17),[15] a spelling attested once elsewhere in an ancient Hebrew source, viz., Mur.

---

9. For this underappreciated scribal technique, see Barr, *Variable Spellings of the Hebrew Bible*, 187, 194–95, though this approach goes back to Alfred Rahlfs, "Zur Setzung der Lesemütter im Alten Testament," *Nachrichten von der Königlichen Gesellschaft der Wissenschaften zu Göttingen,* Philologisch-historische Klasse (1916): 315–47, esp. 343–47 (cited by Barr on p. 186 n. 4).

10. On this word and its possible meanings and interpretations, see Rendsburg, "Linguistic and Stylistic Notes to the Hazon Gabriel Inscription," 108–10; Bar-Asher, "ʿal ha-Lašon be-ʾHazon Gavriʾel,'" 211–17; and Yuditsky and Qimron, "Heʿarot ʿal ha-Ketovet," 141.

11. See Rendsburg, "Linguistic and Stylistic Notes to the Hazon Gabriel Inscription," 110 and n. 11. To my mind, the attempt by Elisha Qimron (*Megillot Midbar Yehuda*, vol. 1, *ha-Ḥibburim ha-ʿIvriyim* [Jerusalem: Yad Ben-Zvi, 2010], 82–83) to read this form as פותאים, "simpletons," fails, given the context in 1QHᵃ 16:18.

12. For further details, see David Noel Freedman, "The Spelling of the Name 'David' in the Hebrew Bible," *HAR* 11 (1983): 89–104; reprinted in David Noel Freedman, *Divine Commitment and Human Obligation: Selected Writings of David Noel Freedman*, vol. 2, *Poetry and Orthography* (ed. John R. Huddleston; Grand Rapids: Eerdmans, 1997), 108–22.

13. Even though Amos 9:11 MT uses דָּוִיד.

14. In addition, 1QIsaᵃ always utilizes the longer spelling דויד, whereas Isaiah MT always has the shorter form דוד. See Edward Y. Kutscher, *ha-Lašon ve-ha-Reqaʿ ha-Lešoni šel Megillat Yešaʿyahu ha-Šelema mi-Megillot Yam ha-Melaḥ* (Jerusalem: Magnes, 1959), 5, 75; and Edward Y. Kutscher, *A History of the Hebrew Language* (Jerusalem: Magnes/Leiden: Brill, 1982), 94.

15. See already Bar-Asher, "ʿal ha-Lašon be-ʾHazon Gavriʾel,'" 197.

30:24.¹⁶ Note, by contrast, לְפָנֶיךָ 107x in the Bible, לפניך 15x and לפניכה 42 in the DSS, etc. Once more, one notes an attempt by our author to vary his text and orthography; cf. מן לפנך, "from before you" (17) and מלפניך, "from before you" (79).¹⁷

- On the spelling לכה, "to you" (21), see §2.1.2, first bullet.¹⁸

1.2. The Spelling of "Jerusalem"

HazGab evinces several different spellings of the city name "Jerusalem":

- ירושלם (12, 14, 27),¹⁹ without the second *yod*, as per BH (save for five examples, chiefly LBH)—see also Ben Sira 36:18; 47:11; ca. 10x in the DSS (e.g., 1QpHab 9:4, 12:7); three coins from Year 1 of the First Revolt; and four Bar-Kokhba coins.²⁰
- [י]רושלים (66), with the second *yod*, as per the dominant QH spelling (ca. 25x in the DSS [e.g., 1QM 1:3, 3:11]).²¹ See also 5x in BH (chiefly LBH); and seven coins from Years 2–4 of the First Revolt.²²
- [י]ֹרושלׄם (32), with the second *yod* hanging, no doubt added secondarily.

While one hesitates to summon the explanation of variable spelling as a stylistic aspect continually, such may be the best approach for the variant spellings of "Jerusalem" in *HazGab*. In analogous fashion, note that among the five passages in the Bible in which the "long" spelling occurs, two of the verses (2 Chr 25:1,

---

16. See Uri Mor, "Diqduq ha-ʿIvrit šel Teʿudot Midbar Yehuda ben ha-Mered ha-Gadol le-Mered Bar Kokhba" (Ph.D. diss., Ben-Gurion University, 2009), 41, 103, 199.

17. Variation in orthography is discussed above, with reference to the approach by Rahlfs and Barr (see n. 9 above). Variation in text (or wording) is mentioned here for the first time, though see further below, on several occasions.

18. See already Bar-Asher, "ʿal ha-Lašon be-'Ḥazon Gavriʾel,'" 199.

19. See also line 39, according to the reading of Yardeni and Elizur, even though that line is not included in the present treatment. For earlier discussions of the spelling of "Jerusalem" in *HazGab*, see Bar-Asher, "ʿal ha-Lašon be-'Ḥazon Gavriʾel,'" 198; and Yuditsky and Qimron, "Heʿarot ʿal ha-Ketovet," 142.

20. Data from *Maʾagarim*, except for the DSS data taken from *DSSEL*. This is also the sole spelling in the major Tannaitic works: Mishnah (14x), Tosefta (41x), Mekhilta (7x), Sifra (6x), Sifre BeMidbar (5x), Sifre Devarim (7x), with an occasional spelling with the second *yod* in a few other Tannaitic sources (see *Maʾagarim* for details). Of course, since our manuscripts are all early medieval and onward, the MH evidence may be less central to our discussion here. For discussion, see Shimʿon Sharvit, *Lešonah we-Signonah šel Masseket ʾAvot le-Doroteha* (Beersheva: Ben-Gurion University Press, 2006), 178–79; and Gabriel Birnbaum, *Lešon ha-Mišna bi-Genizat Qahir: Hege ve-Ṣurot* (Jerusalem: Academy of the Hebrew Language, 2008), 331–32 (with evidence for both the shorter and the longer spellings among the Geniza manuscripts).

21. See the brief comment in David Noel Freedman, "The Massoretic Text and the Qumran Scrolls: A Study in Orthography," *Textus* 2 (1962): 97–98; reprinted in Freedman, *Divine Commitment and Human Obligation*, 2:23.

22. Again, data from *Maʾagarim*, except for the DSS data taken from *DSSEL*.

32:9) witness the "short" spelling as well, while in a third instance (1 Chr 3:5) the previous verse bearing on the same subject includes the "short" spelling.[23]

1.3. Pronunciation of Various Consonants

Unusual or unexpected spellings reveal changes in the consonantal phonology represented in *HazGab*.

- The spelling גאים, "nations" (13) discloses the shift of intervocalic /y/ > /ʾ/. One assumes a pronunciation *gōʾîm*, as opposed to MT גּוֹיִם *gôyīm*; see further §2.3.1, first bullet.
- The spelling אלי, "God" (cstr.) (68) is most odd and apparently reflects something like אֱלֹי *ʾĕlōyê* (thus Yuditsky and Qimron), as opposed to MT אֱלֹהֵי *ʾĕlōhê*, with shift of intervocalic /h/ > /y/.
- The form נטוה, "outstretched" (74)[24] implies a pronunciation *nĕṭûwā*, as opposed to MT נְטוּיָה *nĕṭûyâ*, with shift of intervocalic /y/ > /w/. Alternatively, one could imagine the pronunciation *nĕṭûhā*, with the *waw* marking the /ū/ vowel and the *he* marking the consonant /h/, with a following /ā/ vowel unmarked in the orthography. If this were the case, then the consonantal shift would be intervocalic /y/ > /h/.
- These three unusual spellings demonstrate the weakening of intervocalic /y/ in particular, which presumably could be realized as either /ʾ/ (based on example 1) or /w/ (based on example 3, the first explanation), and perhaps /h/ as well (based on example 3, the second explanation). Though regardless of how one explains נטוה, "outstretched" (74), the shift of intervocalic /y/ to /h/ is independently suggested by what is presumably hypercorrection reflected in the second example, with intervocalic /h/ > /y/.
- On the other hand, none of the weakening of the laryngeals (e.g., /h/ > /ʾ/) and pharyngeals (e.g., /ḥ/ > /h/) inherent in QH and SH is evident in *HazGab*.[25] The spelling of תירה, "fear" (23) = MT תִּירָא is insufficient evidence to suggest any general weakening of this group of consonants.
- On the fluctuation between final *mem* and final *nun*, see §2.6.

1.4. Non-Assimilation of nun before Following Consonant

On this feature, see §2.2.4.

---

23. Does the author of Jer 26:18 utilize the "long" spelling, since the passage quotes Mic 3:12 with the "short" spelling?
24. See also the *ketiv* נטוות in Isa 3:16, with *qere* נְטוּיוֹת *nĕṭûyôt*.
25. For QH, see Kutscher, *ha-Lašon ve-ha-Reqaʿ ha-Lĕšoni šel Megillat Yešaʿyahu*, 398–400; idem, *History of the Hebrew Language*, 96; and Elisha Qimron, *The Hebrew of the Dead Sea Scrolls* (HSS 29; Atlanta: Scholars Press, 1986), 25–26. For SH, see Zeʾev Ben-Ḥayyim, ʿIvrit ve-ʾAramit Nusaḥ Šomron, vol. 5 (Jerusalem: Academy of the Hebrew Language, 1977), 20–37; Kutscher, *History of the Hebrew Language*, 109; and Zeʾev Ben-Ḥayyim, *A Grammar of Samaritan Hebrew* (Jerusalem: Magnes; Winona Lake: Eisenbrauns, 2000), 38–43.

2. Morphology

2.1. Pronouns

2.1.1. Independent Pronouns[26]

	Singular	Plural
1c	אני (17, 24, 77)	אנחנו (66)
2m	אתה (11, 22, 77)	---
2f	---	---
3m	הוא (22)	---
3f	היא (24)	---

Notes:
- The attested forms are exactly those of BH.
- According to Yardeni and Elizur, אנכי occurs in line 77, and indeed I discussed this word in a previous publication.[27] Yuditsky and Qimron, however, now read this word as אתה, so that only אני is listed in the chart above. As such the 1st com. sg. independent personal pronoun matches LBH especially.
- For the form מהו (31), a contraction of מה הוא, see below on the interrogative pronoun, §2.1.5.

2.1.2. Suffix Pronouns

	Singular	Plural
1c (with nouns)	־י (16, 18, 18, 70)	---
1c (with verbs)	־ני (11, 17, 21)	---
2m	־ך (17, 23, 66, 73, 78, 79)	---
	־כה (21)	
2f	---	---
3m	־ו (67)	־ם (76)
		־הן (76)
3f	---	---

---

26. For a recent comprehensive treatment of the subject, presenting the evidence from BH, QH, and MH (notwithstanding the title's spotlight on QH), see Moshe Morgenstern, "Maʿareket ha-Kinnuyim ha-Perudim be-Qumran: Le-Šeʾelat Toldot ha-ʿIvrit bi-Yme ha-Bayit ha-Šeni," in Šaʿare Lašon: Mehqarim ba-Lašon ha-ʿIvrit, ba-ʾAramit, u-ve-Balšanut ha-Yehudim Mugašim le-Moše Bar-ʾAšer, vol. 1 (ed. Aharon Maman, Steven Fassberg, and Yohanan Breuer; Jerusalem: Bialik, 2007), 44–63.

27. Rendsburg, "Linguistic and Stylistic Notes to the Hazon Gabriel Inscription," 111.

Notes:

- For the 2nd masc. sg. form, *HazGab* clearly prefers the shorter ך- to the longer כה-. This stands in contrast to the distribution of these two orthographic variants in the DSS, with about 900 of the latter and about 160 of the former.[28] The single instance of כה- in line 21 may be due to its use on the uniconsonantal preposition ל-, thereby giving the form לכה, "to you" greater "bulk" than would occur with לך.[29]

- I would explain the two alternative 3rd masc. pl. forms in line 76 as follows. The text reads: אם יש בהן אם יש בם, "if there is among [lit. 'in'] them, if there is among [lit. 'in'] them," repeating the same expression essentially, with שלושה רועין, "three shepherds" (75) or whatever is to be restored at the end of said line as the antecedent. Apparently the scribe wrote אם יש בהן first, but then realized that he had used an Aramaizing form instead of the proper Hebrew form.[30] Accordingly, he wrote the phrase again, this time using the proper Hebrew form. Perhaps, though, with a moment to consider his options at this point, our author selected the more archaic Hebrew form בם, instead of the later Hebrew form בהם.[31] Note that the form בם is the one that dominates in the DSS (בם 98x vs. בהם 33x; to select a single important text, note בם 9x vs. בהם 0x in 1QS), running against the trend of LBH continuance into QH.[32]

2.1.3. Demonstrative Pronouns

The masc. sg. form זה (= BH זֶה, the default form throughout the history of the Hebrew language) occurs in line 22, in the combination הצמח הרע הזה, "this evil plant," serving as a demonstrative adjective. The fem. sg. form זו occurs in line 67, in the combination זו המרכבה, "this is the chariot," where it serves in the nominative slot. The latter form, of course, is rare in the Bible (occurring as זו 2x and as זה 11x); it never occurs in QH; it appears twice in HJDD, both times with the definite article (Mur. 44:6 הזו, N.H. 49:7 הזוא), though note that הזות also appears 2x);[33] and then זו becomes the standard form in MH.

---

28. Qimron, *Hebrew of the Dead Sea Scrolls*, 58–59.

29. This practice would be in line with a general trend in the MT, as summarized by Barr, *Variable Spellings of the Hebrew Bible*, 118: "it seems as if there may be a certain tendency for the spelling with he to appear with *short* words such as particles, monosyllables."

30. בהן prevails in MH as well, occurring 215x in the Mishnah vs. 41 attestations of בהם (data according to Maʾagarim; the same situation obtains in the other Tannaitic texts).

31. On this issue, see Avi Hurvitz, *A Linguistic Study of the Relationship between the Priestly Source and the Book of Ezekiel: A New Approach to an Old Problem* (Paris: Gabalda, 1982), 24–27 (and the literature cited in his nn. 5 and 9).

32. Gary A. Rendsburg, "Qumran Hebrew (with a Trial Cut [1QS])," in *The Dead Sea Scrolls at 60: Scholarly Contributions of New York University Faculty and Alumni* (ed. Lawrence H. Schiffman and Shani Tzoref; STDJ 89; Leiden: Brill, 2010), 217–46.

33. Mor, "Diqduq ha-ʿIvrit," 116, 120–21.

2.1.4. Relative Pronoun

The form -ש occurs in line 71, prefixed to a finite verb, thus: שראיתי, "that I saw." The preceding vocable is חר[, which Yuditsky and Qimron restore as ו‍א[חר]. If their restoration is correct, we would have here the equivalent of a clause-connecting particle with temporal force, indeed one known from MH, e.g., *Mekhilta Kaspa* 20 אחר שלמדת, "after you taught." Though other options instead of the *waw* also are possible, such as *lamed* to create the particle ש- לאחר and *mem* to create the particle ש- מאחר, both of which are more common in MH. See *m. Ter.* 5:4; *m. Qidd.* 3:5; etc., for the former; and *m. Giṭ.* 8:4; *m. ʿEd.* 4:7; etc., for the latter.

A functional parallel, using the relative marker אשר instead of -ש, occurs once in BH and once in QH: Ezek 40:1 אַחַ֗ר אֲשֶׁ֛ר הֻכְּתָ֥ה הָעִ֖יר *ʾaḥar ʾăšer hukkĕtâ hāʿîr*, "after the city was defeated";[34] and 4Q227 (4QpsJub^c?) 2:1 אחר אשר למד'נוהו, "after we taught him."

On the genitive particle של, "of" (67), which incorporates the relative pronoun -ש, see §2.2.1.

2.1.5. Interrogative Pronouns

The interrogatives מה, "What?," and מי, "Who?," occur in lines 21 and 77, respectively—exactly as one would expect, since these forms occur in all varieties of Hebrew, ancient through modern.

In line 31, we encounter the form מהו, "What is it?," a contraction of מה הוא. The two-word phrase appears 3x in the Bible (Exod 16:15; Num 16:11; Esth 8:1),[35] while the one-word contraction appears in Mur. 46:9[36] and is characteristic of MH (*m. Moʿed Qaṭ.* 3:9; *m. Yad.* 4:8; *Mekhilta Pisḥa* 16–18; *Mekhilta Be-Shalaḥ* 1–3; etc.).[37]

2.2. Particles

2.2.1. Genitive Particle

The form של occurs in line 67 in the expression זו המרכבה של..., "this is the chariot of," though unfortunately one cannot be certain of what follows at this point, so caution is advised. Yardeni and Elizur read the full word שלהן here, though, as indicated, Yuditsky and Qimron are less confident. Assuming that the genitive

---

34. There are more examples with the longer form אַחֲרֵי אֲשֶׁר *ʾaḥărê ʾăšer*: Josh 7:8; 9:16; 23:1; 24:20; Judg 11:36; Judg 19:23; 2 Sam 19:31 (though in the last two the effect may be more causal than temporal).

35. The closest parallel in the Bible to a contraction of this sort is the *ketiv* מזה = *qere* מַה־זֶּה *mah zeh*, "What is this?," in Exod 4:2. Observe, however, the employment of this unique usage as a (chiefly) visual literary device to imitate and anticipate the word מַטֶּה *maṭṭeh*, "staff," three words later in the verse.

36. Mor, "Diqduq ha-ʿIvrit," 196.

37. Moshe Zvi Segal, *Diqduq Lešon ha-Mišna* (Tel-Aviv: Devir, 1936), 61; and Miguel Pérez Fernández, *An Introductory Grammar of Rabbinic Hebrew* (Leiden: Brill, 1999), 36.

particle של occurs in line 67 (regardless of what follows), we provide here the number of attestations in our other corpora: 7x in the Bible; 25x in 3Q15 Copper Scroll; one other attestation in QH, viz., 4Q385 (4QpsEzek*) 6:9 ואחד של אדם, "and one of a man"; 18x in the Bar Kokhba letters and associated documents[38]; and of course as a standard usage in MH.

2.2.2. Particle of Existence

יש, "there is, there are," occurs twice in line 76, though probably we have a scribal rewriting of the same phrase (see §2.1.2, second bullet). In any case, this particle is fully in use in all stages of ancient Hebrew, from BH through MH, and of course beyond.

2.2.3. Presentative Particle

The particle הנה, "behold," occurs twice: הִנֵּה כוֹל הַגּאִים צוֹבָאִ֔ים עַל יְרוּשָׁלַם, "behold, all the nations are besieging Jerusalem" (13[–14]), and הנה כבוד יהוה אֱלֹהִים צְבָאוֹת אלהי ישראל, "behold, the glory of YHWH, God of Hosts, God of Israel" (25[–26]). This form occurs throughout BH and is attested 17x in QH.[39] In MH, on the other hand, the presentative particle is הרי, serving in all contexts where BH/QH הנה would be expected.[40]

2.2.4. Prepositions

The following prepositions are attested in *HazGab*:

ב-	(12, 18, 73, 76, 76)
ל-	(19, 19, 21, 22, 28, 67, 68, 74, 75, 79, 80)
כ-	(32)
אל	(70, 71)
על	(66, 67)

Nothing about these occurrences requires comment.

For the forms of the preposition (מ(ן, "from," on the other hand, discussion is required, and thus we list here all the attestations, including the specific phrases:

מן לפני, "from before me"	(16)
מן לפנך, "from before you"	(17)
מִלְפֲנֵי הצדק, "from before the righteousness"	(21)

---

38. For the attestations, see Mor, "Diqduq ha-ʿIvrit," 58 (see also p. 200).

39. According to the *Maʾagarim* database. *DSSEL* lists many more attestations, though most of these either are fragmentary or are biblical citations embedded in DSS compositions (e.g., Exod 14:10 in 4Q365 [4QRPᶜ] 5:1).

40. Pérez Fernández, *Introductory Grammar of Rabbinic Hebrew*, 20, 54, 153, 173, 184, 187, 213–15, 226.

מִן מְקוֹמוֹ, "from its place"   (23–24)
מִלְפָנֶיךָ, "from before you"   (79)

Of the five attestations of the preposition (מִ(ן, "from," one is struck by several points. First, four of the five occur in the compound preposition מִלְפְנֵי, "from before." One is not sure what to make of this point, except to suggest that the usage is a favorite of the writer (for the record, this preposition occurs 73x in the biblical corpus and 40x in QH, including cases with pronominal suffixes).[41]

More strikingly, though, in three of the five instances the *nun* is not assimilated to the next consonant, as one would expect in Hebrew. One sees here the influence of Aramaic, exactly as one sees in LBH, with fifty-one examples in Chronicles and a few additional ones in Daniel and Nehemiah,[42] and in HJDD, with many such examples (e.g., Mur. 24.2:7 מִן קצת עפר, "a portion of land" [lit. "from some dust"]).[43]

Most remarkable is the example in lines 23–24, ברוך כבוד יהוה אלהים מִן מקומו, "blessed is the glory of YHWH God from its place," since it is based on Ezek 3:12 בָּרוּךְ כְּבוֹד־יְהוָה מִמְּקוֹמוֹ, *bārûk kĕbôd YHWH mimmĕqômô*, with the standard form מִמְּקוֹמוֹ, "from its place."

2.2.5. Conjunctions

For the sake of completeness, we mention here the standard conjunction -וְ, "and" (passim), and the conditional particle אם (76, where the word appears twice, though again see §2.1.2, second bullet, on the apparent rewriting of the same phrase).

The conjunction לְמַעַן occurs twice in *HazGab*, both times followed by nouns: לְמַעַן צִבְ[אֹ]ת [הַ]מַלְאָךְ מִיכָאֵל, "for the sake of the armies of the angel Michael" (27[–28], though the reading is uncertain), and לְמַ֫עַן דוד עבד יהוה, "for the sake of David, servant of YHWH" (72). This form is standard in BH, occurs 10x in Ben Sira, and ca. 70x in QH.[44] It is not a feature of MH, however.[45]

2.2.6. Adverbs

The temporal adverb עוֹד, "still" occurs in line 24, though the passage here is adapted from Hag 2:6. *HazGab* 24 reads עוֹד מעט קיטוט היא, while Hag 2:6 states עוֹד אַחַת מְעַט הִיא (with the continuation of each passage the same). Obviously, this adverb is common to all varieties of ancient Hebrew and beyond.

---

41. According to the counts of Avraham Even-Shoshan, *Qonqordansya Ḥadaša* (Jerusalem: Kiryat Sepher, 1993), 605–6; and *DSSEL*, respectively.
42. See Robert Polzin, *Late Biblical Hebrew: Toward an Historical Typology of Biblical Hebrew Prose* (HSM 12; Missoula, Mont.: Scholars Press, 1976), 66.
43. Mor, "Diqduq ha-ʿIvrit," 90.
44. Seventy-five times according to *DSSEL*, though some of these occur in fragmentary texts where considerable restoration is necessary.
45. See Pérez Fernández, *Introductory Grammar of Rabbinic Hebrew*, 160.

The second adverb that appears in *HazGab* is the logical marker כו/כה, "thus," spelled with *waw* in lines 11, 17, 19, 29, 57, 58 and with *he* in line 69, each time used to introduce variations of "thus says YHWH" statements.[46] This form is standard in BH, especially to introduce divine speech (153x in Jeremiah alone). It does not occur in QH and in effect not in MH either (see only *t. Soṭah* 5:13; *Sifra ʾAḥare Mot* 6:1).

2.2.7. Negative Marker

The negative marker אל occurs in the expression אל תירה, "do not fear," in line 23. This morpheme occurs throughout ancient Hebrew to express (one-time) prohibitions,[47] and thus its presence in *HazGab* is perfectly normal and expected.

If Yuditsky and Qimron are correct in their interpretation of לו in line 22 (Yardeni and Elizur read these letters the same) as a nonstandard spelling of BH לא, QH לוא,[48] then a second negative marker appears in our inscription.

2.3. Nouns

2.3.1. Common Nouns

With two exceptions (see the third and fourth bullets below), every noun in *HazGab* is a relatively common lexeme in ancient Hebrew. Here follows the list of common nouns (including construct forms) and their attestations:[49]

א(ו)הבין, "lovers"	28, 68 (written *defectiva* in line 28 and *plene* in line 68)
אות, "sign"	17, 80
אמרים, "sayings"	16
ארץ, "land"	25, 73
בית, "house"	12
בן, "son"	18
ברית, "covenant"	18
בשר, "flesh"	67
גאים, "nations"	13
גדולות, "great-things"	12
דם, "blood"	67
חסד, "fealty"	74

---

46. On these statements, see Rendsburg, "Linguistic and Stylistic Notes to the Hazon Gabriel Inscription," 114–16. Some of what I wrote there needs to be rephrased, in light of the readings by Yuditsky and Qimron, but the main point stands nonetheless.

47. If anything, its use increases in QH, on which see Qimron, *Hebrew of the Dead Sea Scrolls*, 80–81.

48. Yuditsky and Qimron, "Heʿarot ʿal ha-Ketovet," 138.

49. In both this list and the list of proper nouns below, I have not marked letters of uncertain reading with the dots or circles above.

חסידין, "pious-ones"	16
טבחי, "slaughters" (cstr. only)	57[50]
יד, "hand"	18
ימות, "days"	32
ימין, "days"	19, 80
כבוד, "glory"	23, 25
כוח, "strength"	73
כול, "all"	13, 28
מלאך, "angel"	22, 28, 31
מקום, "place"	24, 72
מרכבה, "chariot"	26, 67
נביא, "prophet"	78
נביאים/ן, "prophets"	15, 70, 79^r
עבד, "servant"	16, 72
עולם, "eternity"	32, 65
עם, "people"	70
עץ, "tree"	31
ערי, "cities" (cstr. only)	27
צבא(ו)ת, "armies"	11, 18, 20, 26, 28^r, 29, 57^r, 58, 68, 69 (written *defectiva* in lines 28, 68, 69; *plene* in the others)
צדק, "righteousness"	21
צמח, "plant"	21
קדושי(ן), "holy ones"	65 (cstr.), 76 (abs.)
קיטוט, "trembling"	24
רועה, "shepherd"	78
רועים/ן, "shepherds"	70, 75, 79
רע, "evil"	20 (see also §2.3.4. s.v.)
שבין, "elders"	15
שוד, "violence"	27
שמים, "heavens"	25, 73
שני, "years" (cstr. only)	32

Notes:

- גאים, "nations" (13), is never written this way in any ancient Hebrew text. The spelling גואים, with *mater lectionis waw* to mark the /ō/ vowel, appears 22 times in QH,[51] e.g., 1QM 12:14; 16:1; 11QT 56:13; 57:7; 60:21; 62:12; 64:10. In addition, the spelling גואין occurs in N.H. 51:6 (an extremely difficult text to read)—but the specific form גאים as attested in *HazGab* 13

---

50. On an alternative explanation for this word, see n. 70 below.
51. Data according to *DSSEL*, updating the 14 attestations mentioned by Qimron, *Hebrew of the Dead Sea Scrolls*, 31.

is unknown from elsewhere. Naturally, one would reconstruct the same pronunciation for גאים and גואים, viz., gōʾîm (see §1.3, first bullet), but the unique orthography is noteworthy nonetheless. In theory, the word גֵּאִים, "haughty ones," could be read here (cf. Pss 94:2; 140:6; Prov 15:25; 16:19), but the two passages in Isa 29:7–8 (כָּל־הַגּוֹיִם הַצֹּבְאִים עַל־אֲרִיאֵל, kol haggôyīm haṣṣōbĕʾîm ʿal ʾărîʾēl, "all the nations that besiege Ariel," and כָּל־הַגּוֹיִם הַצֹּבְאִים עַל־הַר צִיּוֹן, kol haggôyīm haṣṣōbĕʾîm ʿal har ṣiyyôn, "all the nations that besiege Mt. Zion") make this highly unlikely.

- *HazGab* 19 and 80 attest the expected plural form ימין, "days" (on the final *nun* in place of final *mem*, see §2.6). In *HazGab* 32, the atypical form ימות occurs in the expression יְמוֹת עוֹלָם, "days of eternity," clearly borrowed from Deut 32:7, יְמוֹת עוֹלָם yĕmôt ʿôlām.[52] One should note that this form is not attested in QH, though it continues to be productive in MH, as witnessed through an assortment of phrases: ימות המשיח, "days of the Messiah" (e.g., *m. Ber.* 1:5), ימות השנה, "days of the year" (e.g., *m. Šeqal.* 7:2; 8:1), ימות החג, "days of the festival" (e.g., *m. Sukkah* 3:13; 4:8), ימות החמה, "days of sun(shine)" (e.g., *m. B. Meṣiʿa* 8:6), ימות הגשמים, "days of rain" (ibid.), etc.—even if the phrase ימות עולם, "days of eternity," does not occur in the Tannaitic corpus.[53]

- The first rare word in the above list is קיטוט, "trembling" (24), treated in two earlier articles—by the present writer, with said definition, and by Bar-Asher, who would define the word as "just, only, little."[54] In either case, one notes that the form of the noun קיטוט is the verbal substantive *qiṭṭûl*, relatively rare in BH, but which appears more prominently in MH.[55]

- The second rare word in the above list is שבין, "elders" (15), an Aramaism in *HazGab*. In the Bible, the noun שָׂב, "old man," occurs in Job 15:10; the verb שַׂבְתִּי, "I am old/gray," appears in 1 Sam 12:2; and the unusual nominal form שֵׂיבוֹ, "his old age," occurs in 1 Kgs 14:4.[56] (I do not deal here with

---

52. The only other occurrence of ימות in the Bible is Ps 90:15. In Isa 63:9; 63:11, we encounter the expected phrase יְמֵי עוֹלָם.

53. The use of the plural construct ימות in Deut 32:7, Phoenician, and MH suggests that this form is an Israelian Hebrew (IH) feature (even if Ps 90:15 cannot be explained thereby). See further Gary A. Rendsburg, "The Galilean Background of Mishnaic Hebrew," in *The Galilee in Late Antiquity* (ed. Lee I. Levine; New York: Jewish Theological Seminary, 1992), 233.

54. Rendsburg, "Linguistic and Stylistic Notes to the Hazon Gabriel Inscription," 108–10; and Bar-Asher, "ʿal ha-Lašon be-'Ḥazon Gavriʾel,'" 211–17. See also Yuditsky and Qimron, "Heʿarot ʿal ha-Ketovet," 141.

55. See Kutscher, *History of the Hebrew Language*, 128; and Pérez Fernández, *Introductory Grammar of Rabbinic Hebrew*, 57. For the larger context, see Steven E. Fassberg, "The Movement from *Qal* to *Piʿʿel* in Hebrew and the Disappearance of the *Qal* Internal Passive," *Hebrew Studies* 42 (2001): 243–55.

56. This distribution suggests that the root is an IH feature, since in one passage the speaker is Samuel from the hill country of Ephraim, while in the other the setting is Shiloh. Its presence in Job 15:10 fits into the much larger picture of numerous Aramaisms in that book;

the standard noun שֵׂיבָה, "old age," which occurs 19x in the Bible.) This lexeme appears three times in Ben Sira (8:9; 32:3; 42:8),[57] again due to Aramaic influence on postbiblical Hebrew. The first occurrence (from MS A) is plural שבים; the latter two (from MS B) singular שב. Interestingly, the well-known Aramaic noun סב is spelled with *samek*,[58] while both *HazGab* and Ben Sira follow the biblical orthography in using *śin*.

- On the plural endings -ים vs. -ין, see §2.6.

2.3.2. Proper Nouns

The proper nouns (including the various forms meaning "God") attested in *HazGab* are the following:

אלה, "God"	26
אלהים, "God"	11, 20, 23, 25, 29
אלהי, "God" (cstr.)	13ʳ, 18, 20, 26, 29, 58, 58, 69
אלי, "God" (cstr.)	68
גבריאל, "Gabriel"	77, 80
דוד, "David"	16, 72
יהודה , "Judah"	27
יי, "YHWH"	11, 13, 18ʳ, 20, 23, 25, 29, 57, 58, 68, 69, 72
ירושלם, "Jerusalem"	12, 27, 32ʳ, 57, 66ʳ (line 32 with hanging *yod*, line 66 with *plene* spelling)
ישראל, "Israel"	12, 13, 18, 19, 20, 26, 30ʳ, 58, 59, 68, 69, 75
מיכאל, "Michael"	28

Notes:
- The shorter form אלה, "God," appears in line 26, in the expression אלה המרכבות, "God of the chariots." While one might be inclined to assume here the Masoretic Hebrew vocalization, viz., אֱלֹהַּ, *ʾĕlôah*, one should note that this word is almost always written *plene* in MT as אֱלוֹהַּ (55x), with only three instances of the *defectiva* orthography אֱלֹהַּ, each of which can be explained. In Deut 32:17, the expression לֹא אֱלֹהַּ, "non-god," creates a single unit, which leads to the non-use of *waw*; in Hab 1:11, the presence of the suffix pronoun explains the spelling לֵאלֹהוֹ, "to his god"; and in Dan

---

see Edward L. Greenstein, "The Language of Job and Its Poetic Function," *JBL* 122 (2003): 651–66.

57. Ben Sira 32:3, according to the numeration system of Pancratius C. Beentjes (*The Book of Ben Sira in Hebrew: A Text Edition of All Extant Hebrew Manuscripts and a Synopsis of All Parallel Hebrew Ben Sira Texts* [VTSup 68; Leiden: Brill, 2003], 58), as opposed to 35:3, according to the numeration system of *Sefer Ben Sira* (Jerusalem: Academy of the Hebrew Language, 5733), 31.

58. See, e.g., Michael Sokoloff, *A Dictionary of Jewish Palestinian Aramaic of the Byzantine Period* (Ramat-Gan: Bar-Ilan University Press, 1990), 364–65.

11:38, the use of וְלֶאֱלֹהַּ, "and to the god," allows for variation in light of וְלֶאֱלוֹהַּ, "and to the god," later in the verse. Given the propensity for *plene* spelling in *HazGab* (see §1.1), one wonders if אלה in line 26 should not be vocalized as in Aramaic, *viz.*, אֱלָהּ (Dan 2:28; etc.).

- On the construct form אלי in line 68 in the expression אלי ישראל, "God of Israel," presumably to be read as אֱלֵי (thus Yuditsky-Qimron), see §1.3, second bullet.

2.3.3. Construct Phrases

The following construct phrases are attested:

בית ישראל, "house of Israel"	(12)
גדלות ירושלם, "great things of Jerusalem"	(12)
כבוד יהוה, "glory of YHWH"	(23, 25)
אלה המרכבות, "God of the chariots"	(26)
שׁוֹד ירושלם, "violence of Jerusalem"	(27)
ערי יהודה, "cities of Judah"	(27)
צִבְ[אֹ]ת [ה]מלאךְ, "armies of the angel"	(28ʳ)
יְמוֹת עוֹלם, "days of eternity"	(32)
שני [ ], "years of [ ]"	(32)[59]
קדושי העולם, "holy-ones of eternity"	(65)
עבד יהוה, "servant of YHWH"	(72)

In addition to the above list, one finds the repeated expressions יהוה צבאות, "YHWH of armies" (traditionally "LORD of Hosts") and אלהי ישראל, "God of Israel" (with variant spellings and phrasings). Interestingly, we also encounter the following expressions, in which the absolute form אלהים, "God," is used:

אלהים צבאות	(11)
יהוה אלהים צבאות	(20, 25–26, 29)

These phrases are not original to *HazGab*, since they occur in the Bible: the former in Ps 80:8, 15; the latter in Pss 59:6; 80:5, 20; 84:9.[60]

2.3.4. Adjectives

Four adjectives are attested, in the following adjectival clauses:

בְּרִית חֲדָשָׁה, "new covenant"	(18–19)
הצמח הרע הזה, "this evil plant"	(21–22)

---

59. The construct of the numeral 2 is possible here, though given the presence of יְמוֹת עוֹלָם, "days of eternity," immediately preceding in line 32, one assumes that "years of [ ]" is the correct understanding (with Yuditsky and Qimron).

60. For more on these usages, see Rendsburg, "Linguistic and Stylistic Notes to the Hazon Gabriel Inscription," 115.

אוהבין רבים, "many lovers" (68)
הנטוה [ ], "outstretched [ ]" (74)[61]

2.3.5. Definite Article

The definite article -ה occurs in lines 13, 15, 15, 16, 17, 20, 21, 22, 22, 22, 25, 25, 26, 28, 64, 67, 72, 73, 73, 74, 80. It is used regularly and exhibits no peculiarities or departures from the grammatical norm of BH. Thus, for example, the definite article is attached to all three elements in the adjectival clause הַצֶּמח הרֹע הזה, "this evil plant" (21–22); it appears after each use of את (24–25, 73, even if both of these passages derive from biblical verses); etc.

2.4. Numerals

The following numerals are attested:

[א]חת	"one" (fem.)	15ʳ
אחד	"one" (masc.)	30
שתין	"two" (fem.)	15
שנין	"two" (masc.)	30
שלוש	"three" (fem.)	15
שלושה	"three" (masc.)	30, 65, 70, 75, 79, 79
של(ו)שת	"three" (masc. cstr.)	19, 80 (the form is written *defectiva* in line 19, *plene* in line 80)
ארבע	"four" (fem.)	15
ארבעה	"four (masc.)	30
חמשה	"five" (masc.)	30
ששה	"six" (masc.)	30
אלפים	"thousands"	74

Notes:
- In line 15, we have a simple counting of 1 through 4, using the feminine forms, even if it is not clear what is being enumerated here. The nouns that follow are all masculine: הַנביאין והֹשבין [ו]החסידין, "the prophets, and the elders, [and] the pious ones."
- In line 30, we have a simple counting of 1 through 6, using the masculine forms. In this instance, there are no nouns following, so again one must assume a basic enumeration.
- The fact that line 15 uses the feminine (that is, unmarked) forms, while line 30 uses the masculine (that is, marked) forms, should be ascribed to

---

61. Almost without a doubt the word ובזרועך, "and with your arm," is to be restored in the brackets representing the end of line 73, as per Yuditsky and Qimron.

stylistic variation.⁶² As an aside, one may observe that these two sequences of numerals represent the oldest simple counting in an ancient Hebrew text.⁶³
- Use of numerals beyond simple counting occurs in the following phrases:
  - שלושה קדושי העולם, "three holy-ones of eternity" (65)
  - שלושה רועין, "three shepherds" (70)
  - שלושה רועין, "three shepherds" (75)
  - שלושה רׄועׅים, "three shepherds" (79)
  - שלושה [נבי]אין, "three [pro]phets" (79r)
  - לשלשת ימין, "for three days" (19)
  - לשלושת ימין, "for three days" (80)
- One observes the use of the absolute form שלושה when counting individual items (holy ones, shepherds, prophets), but the use of the construct form של(ו)שת when counting items more naturally counted, such as "days." This pattern accords generally with the BH standard.⁶⁴ Note, for example, 27 occurrences of שְׁלֹשֶׁת יָמִים šĕlōšet yāmîm in the Bible vs. only 4 occurrences of שְׁלֹשָׁה יָמִים šĕlōšâ yāmîm.⁶⁵
- All seven instances above reflect the dominant order in SBH, QH, and MH, that is, with numeral preceding the item counted.⁶⁶

---

62. We have mentioned variant phraseology as a stylistic device several times above. For a convenient introduction to the subject, see Rendsburg, "Linguistic and Stylistic Notes to the Hazon Gabriel Inscription," 116. Such variations are legion in the Bible; see, e.g., Lev 11:27, טְמֵאִים הֵם לָכֶם, ṭĕmēʾîm hēm lākem, and Lev 11:28, טְמֵאִים הֵמָּה לָכֶם, ṭĕmēʾîm hēmmâ lākem, both meaning "they are impure to you." I plan to present a study of this stylistic device in the near future.

63. No such sequences occur in BH, QH, etc., though hardly anyone seems to have noticed this point. For a brief comment, see Saul Levin, "A Theory of Grammatical Gender, Suggested by the Anomalous Agreement of the Semitic Numerals," in *The Seventh LACUS Forum 1980* (ed. James E. Copeland and Philip W. Davis; Columbia, S.C.: Hornbeam, 1981), 297. For three later instances from the Tannaitic corpus, see *m. Bek.* 9:7, *t. Taʿan.* 2:2, and *Sifra Zavim* 5:2. All three of these passages use the masculine form, since days are being counted.

64. Paul Joüon and T. Muraoka, *A Grammar of Biblical Hebrew* (2 vols.; Subsidia Biblica 14; Rome: Pontificio Istituto Biblico, 1991), 526; and Bruce K. Waltke and M. O'Connor, *An Introduction to Biblical Hebrew Syntax* (Winona Lake, Ind.: Eisenbrauns, 1990), 278.

65. For the situation in MH, see Moshe Azar, *Taḥbir Lešon ha-Mišna* (Jerusalem: Academy of the Hebrew Language, 1995), 189–90. The author claims that the absolute forms of the numerals 3 to 10 are used when the counted item is unknown, and that the construct forms are used when the counted item is known—though measurements may take the construct forms regardless. At any rate, we note here that the MH standard for the specific phrase under discussion is שלשה ימים, with over 50 such examples, vs. only 3 instances of של(ו)שת ימים (*m. Šabb.* 1:9; *m. Moʿed Qaṭ.* 3:5; *m. Sanh.* 3:5).

66. For the situation in LBH, see Polzin, *Late Biblical Hebrew*, 58–60; though note the corrective presented in Gary A. Rendsburg, "Late Biblical Hebrew and the Date of 'P'," *JANES* 12 (1980): 71.

- The forms for 2, namely, שתין and שנין, both contain final *nun* instead of expected *mem*. The feminine form שתין is attested 3x in 3Q15 Copper Scroll (9:2; 10:9; 10:13) and once in the Judean Desert debt document, line 1.[67] See further §2.6, where these forms are integrated into the larger picture of final *mem/nun* usage.

2.5. Verbs

The following verbs are attested, presented here with root, specific form, gloss, and parsing.[68]

2.5.1. Suffix Conjugation (SC)

אמר	אמר, "he said" (11, 13, 17, 19, 29, 57, 58, 69)	Qal 3rd masc. sg. SC
בקש	בקש, "he requested" (16)	Piʿel 3rd masc. sg. SC
	בקשו, "they requested" (28)	Piʿel 3rd masc. pl. SC
יצא	יצאו, "they went out" (75)	Qal 3rd masc. pl. SC
ראה	ראיתי, "I saw" (71)	Qal 1st com. sg. SC
שוב	[הש]יבני, "he answered me" (17ʳ)	Hiphʿil 3rd masc. sg. SC + 1st com. sg. obj. pron.
שלח	שלחתי, "I sent" (70)	Qal 1st com. sg. SC
שמע	שמע, "he heard" (26)	Qal 3rd masc. sg. SC

2.5.2. Prefix Conjugation (PC)

ידע	תדע, "you will know" (19)	Qal 2nd masc. sg. PC
ירא	אל תירה, "do not fear" (23)	Qal 2nd masc. sg. PC (with neg. אל)
נגד	ואגדה, "and I will tell" (12)	Hiphʿil 1st com. sg. PC (long form) (with conj. -ו)
	ואגיד, "and I will tell" (21)	Hiphʿil 1st com. sg. PC (with conj. -ו)
נחם	ינחם, "he will console" (27)	Piʿel 3rd masc. sg. PC
נצל	תצילם, "you will save them" (78)	Hiphʿil 2nd masc. sg. PC + 3rd masc. pl. obj. pron.
	יצילו, "they will save" (78)	Hiphʿil 3rd masc. pl. PC

---

67. Magen Broshi and Elisha Qimron, "A Hebrew I.O.U. Note from the Second Year of the Bar Kokhba Revolt," *JJS* 45 (1994): 286–94, with discussion of שתין on pp. 288, 293. Otherwise HJDD uses forms with *mem*; see Mor, "Diqduq ha-ʿIvrit," 192.

68. As with the long list of nouns above, here too I omit dots or circles marking letters of uncertain reading.

2.5.3. *wayyiqtol* Forms (*wyqtl*)

אמר	ואמרה, "and I said" (31)	Qal 1st com. sg. *wyqtl* (long form)
ראה	ואראה, "and I saw" (32)	Qal 1st com. sg. *wyqtl* (long form)

2.5.4. Imperative (impv.)

שאל	שאלני, "ask me" (21)	Qal masc. sg. impv. + 1st com. sg. obj. pron.

2.5.5. Participle (ptc.)[69]

בקש	מבקש, "(I) request" (17)	Piʿel masc. sg. ptc.
עמד	עומד, "(you) stand" (22)	Qal masc. sg. ptc.
עשה	עושה, "(he) does" (74)	Qal masc. sg. ptc.
רעש	מרעיש, "(I) will shake" (24)	Hiphʿil masc. sg. ptc.
צבא	צובאים, "(they) besiege" (14)	Qal masc. pl. ptc.
שאל	שאלני, "(you) ask me" (11)	Qal masc. sg. ptc. + 1st com. sg. obj. pron.

2.5.6. Passive Participle (pass. ptc.)[70]

בטח	בטוחין, "(we) are certain" (66)	Qal masc. pl. pass. ptc.
ברך	ברוך, "(he) is blessed" (23)	Qal masc. sg. pass. ptc.

2.5.7. Infinitive Construct (inf. cstr.)

סמך	בסמכך, "in supporting you" (23)	Qal inf. cstr. + 2nd masc. sg. obj. pron.

2.5.8. Uncertain forms:

- נשבר (20). The Niphal of שבר, "break," though it is unclear whether the word to be read as a SC (= BH נִשְׁבַּר) or as a participle (= BH נִשְׁבָּר). Knohl rendered the phrase "the evil has been broken," suggesting the former.[71]

---

69. See also א(ו)הבין, "lovers" (28, 68), ו/רועים, "shepherds" (70, 75, 79), morphologically participles, though treated above under §2.3.1 Common Nouns.

70. See also הנטוה, "outstretched" (74), treated above under §2.3.4 Adjectives. Bar-Asher ("ʿal ha-Lašon be-'Ḥazon Gavriʾel,'" 198) would include טבחי (57) as well, equal to Masoretic טְבָחֵי, understanding דם טבחי ירושלם as "the blood of the slaughtered of Jerusalem." Thus also Knohl, "'By Three Days, Live,'" 151. But this usage is unknown in ancient Hebrew sources. Singular טָבוּחַ, "slaughtered," occurs in Deut 28:31 with reference to an ox/bull and in *b. Ketub.* 3b, 4a for meat that has been prepared, but not until the *ʾAvinu Malkenu* prayer (most likely from the Geonic period) does one read אבינו מלכנו עשה למען טבוחים על ייחודך, with the plural passive participle referring to Jews who have been killed. In light of this evidence, it is better to understand טבחי in line 57 as the plural construct of טֶבַח, "slaughter," used of humans in Isa 34:2; 65:12; etc. (though admittedly the specific form טְבָחֵי* is not attested in BH or in postbiblical sources).

71. Israel Knohl, "'Gabriel's Revelation' in English Translation," sidebar to Israel Knohl,

Yuditsky and Qimron would agree vis-à-vis the form, though they prefer to see the time reference as עתיד קרוב, that is, the imminent future.⁷²
- ‎‏[ ]קש (78). The root is clearly בקש, though one cannot be certain if the form is prefix conjugation or participle (suffix conjugation is less likely).

2.5.9. Suffixed ה- on 1st com. sg. PC and wayyiqtol Forms

- Two variant forms of "and I will tell you" occur in the inscription: ואגדה (12) and ואגיד (21). Unfortunately, the words preceding בית ישראל .... ואגדה בגדלות ירושלם, ".... house of Israel, and I will tell the great things of Jerusalem," cannot be read. Accordingly, one cannot determine if the verb here bears cohortative force or not.⁷³ I suspect not: to my mind a new statement begins here, in which case the cohortative preceded by conjunctive -ו would be unusual. Instead, we should see here the PC long form serving as the indicative, with no cohortative force. If this be the case, then the two forms in lines 12 and 21 are simply variants of one another, with no real distinction. Which is to say, once more we are dealing with the stylistic device of variation with repetition: in the first case the scribe used the long form ending in ה-, without internal *mater lectionis yod*; while in the second instance he used the standard form, with internal *mater lectionis yod*.⁷⁴
- Note further that the two 1st com. sg. *wayyiqtol* forms, ואמרה, "and I said" (31) and ואראה, "and I saw" (32) include the additional ה- ending. This usage is especially characteristic of LBH and QH.⁷⁵
- The trend visible in three of the aforementioned forms, to affix ה- to 1st com. sg. (and 1st com. pl.) PC verbs (both *wĕyiqtol* and *wayyiqtol*), which lack this ending in SBH, is a distinguishing feature of LBH (see the previous bullet), SH,⁷⁶ and QH (even if we cannot always distinguish the two in QH, given the lack of vocalization).⁷⁷

"The Messiah Son of Joseph: 'Gabriel's Revelation' and the Birth of a New Messianic Model," *BAR* 34 (2008): 62.

72. Yuditsky and Qimron, "Heʿarot ʿal ha-Ketovet," 138.

73. Though for an attempt to suggest such, see Yuditsky and Qimron, "Heʿarot ʿal ha-Ketovet," 137.

74. Note that Yuditsky and Qimron, "Heʿarot ʿal ha-Ketovet," 138, read both of these with final -*ā*.

75. Joüon and Muraoka, *Grammar of Biblical Hebrew*, 141; and Elisha Qimron, "The Type וְאָבְנֶה in the Hebrew of the Dead Sea Scrolls," in *Conservatism and Innovation in the Hebrew Language of the Hellenistic Period: Proceedings of a Fourth International Symposium on the Hebrew of the Dead Sea Scrolls and Ben Sira* (ed. Jan Joosten and Jean-Sébastien Rey; STDJ 73; Leiden: Brill, 2008), 149–54.

76. Ben-Ḥayyim, ʿIvrit ve-ʾAramit Nusaḥ Šomron, vol. 5, §2.9.10.

77. Qimron, *Hebrew of the Dead Sea Scrolls*, 44. For further details and analysis, consult Qimron's series of articles on the PC forms in their various manifestations in both BH and QH: "Consecutive and Conjunctive Imperfect: The Form of the Imperfect with *waw* in Biblical

2.6. Final mem/nun

With nouns, adjectives, numerals, and participles now presented, we may address the issue of the variant endings -ים and -ין.[78]

The following seven forms bear the -ים suffix:[79]

גאים	(13)
צובאים	(14)
אמרים	(16)
רבים	(68)
נביאים	(70)
אלפים	(74)
רועים	(79)

More dominant, however, is the -ין suffix, carried by eight different plural forms for a total of twelve attestations:

נביאין	(15, 79)[80]
שבין	(15)
חסידין	(16)
ימין	(19, 80)
א(ו)הבין	(28, 68)
בטוחין	(66)
רועין	(70, 75)
קדושין	(76)

In addition, the two forms of the numeral 2 bear the *nun* ending: שתין (15) and שנין (30). On the other hand, the common noun שמים, "heavens" (25, 73) retains the expected *mem*.

To my mind, no discernible pattern can be established for these data.[81] Clearly, *HazGab* does not cohere with BH, Ben Sira, and QH, in which forms with *mem*

Hebrew," *JQR* 77 (1986-87): 149–61; "A New Approach to the Use of Forms of the Imperfect without Personal Endings," in *The Hebrew of the Dead Sea Scrolls and Ben Sira: Proceedings of a Symposium held at Leiden University, 11–14 December 1995* (ed. T. Muraoka and John F. Elwolde; STDJ 26; Leiden: Brill, 1997), 174–81; and "Haṣaʿa Ḥadaša le-Feruš Ṣurot he-ʿAtid ba-ʿIvrit ha-Qeduma," *Lešonenu* 61 (5758): 31–43.

78. See the earlier treatment by Bar-Asher, "ʿal ha-Lašon be-'Ḥazon Gavriʾel,'" 199–200, though his data are based on the readings of Yardeni and Elizur.

79. I do not include here אלהים, "God," which always appears, not surprisingly, with final *mem*.

80. Again, in line 79, the reading is נבי[אין]. Even if another lexeme were to be read here (which is highly unlikely), the form ends with *nun* nonetheless.

81. See already Yuditsky and Qimron, "Heʿarot ʿal ha-Ketovet," 143: בכתובת לא נמצאו כללים אחידים לשימוש במ"ם או בנו"ן ("In the inscription there is no uniform principle governing the use of *mem* or *nun*.").

dominate, with a smattering of forms with *nun*. The two corpora in which the two endings occur with more or less equal frequency are MH and HJDD, but in these two cases at least some order is present. For MH, Shelomo Naeh established basic rules—dealing not only with the masculine plural ending but with personal pronouns and suffix pronouns as well—which interface with both phonology (depending on the nature of the preceding vowel) and morphology (depending on whether the form is a noun, adjective, or participle).[82] These rules are not operative in *HazGab*, however. Thus, for example, the masculine plural active participle occurs with both endings, viz., צובאים (14), א(ו)הבין (28, 68), and two common nouns, רועים/ן and נביאים/ן, appear with both endings (on which see further below). In the case of HJDD, Uri Mor determined that individual documents typically witness either *mem* or *nun*, indicating that individual scribes favored one ending over the other[83]—though naturally this issue is not relevant to our inscription, a single text written by a single scribe.

The only possible tendency that governs this issue in *HazGab* is dependency on the biblical text. This would explain the use of גאים (13) and צובאים (14) (cf. Isa 29:7 for both); אמרים (16) (assuming reliance on Prov 22:21);[84] and אלפים (74) (cf. Exod 20:6 // Deut 5:10). On נביאים (70) and רועים (79), see the next paragraph. This leaves only the adjective רבים (68) without a proper explanation. Though one must consider the possibility that the potential explanation offered here results merely from coincidence.

Finally, on the assumption that the last word in line 69 can be restored as [שלושה] (as per Yuditsky and Qimron), one observes the stylistic device of repetition with variation between the following two passages:

- [שלושה] נביאים . . . שלושה רועין, "[three] prophets . . . three shepherds" (69–70)
- שלושה רועים שלושה נבי[אין], "three shepherds, three [pro]phets" (79ʳ)

Note both (a) the order of "prophets > shepherds" in the first passage vs. "shepherds > prophets" in the second; and (b) how the first plural noun in each case ends in ־ים, while the second one ends in ־ין. This device yields attestations of both רועין / רועים and נבי[אין] / נביאים.

---

82. Shelomo Naeh, "Šte Sugyot Nedošot bi-Lšon Ḥazal," in *Qoveṣ Meḥqarim le-Talmud u-vi-Thumim Govlim Muqdaš le-Zikro šel Prof. ʾEliʿezer Šimšon Rosenthal* (ed. Moshe Bar-Asher and David Rosenthal; Jerusalem: Magnes, 5753) = *Meḥqare Talmud* 2 (5753): 369–92.

83. Mor, "Diqduq ha-ʿIvrit," 82–85.

84. Yuditsky and Qimron, "Heʿarot ʿal ha-Ketovet," 137.

3. Syntax

3.1. Object of the Verb

As can be seen above (in the various subsections in §2.5), the object of the verb is suffixed to the verb on four occasions:

[הש]יבני, "he answered me" (17)	Hiphʿil 3rd masc. sg. SC + 1st. com. sg. obj. pron.	
תצילם, "you will save them" (78)	Hiphʿil 2nd masc. sg. PC + 3rd masc. pl. obj. pron.	
שאלני, "ask me" (21)	Qal masc. sg. impv. + 1st com. sg. obj. pron.	
שאלני, "(you) ask me" (11)	Qal masc. sg. ptc. + 1st. com. sg. obj. pron.	

Coincidentally, each of the four principle parts of the verbs (SC, PC, imperative, and participle) is represented here.[85]

By contrast, there is only one instance of the object of the verb expressed via the independent morpheme, that is, אותך in the phrase יצִילוֹ אוֹתָךְ, "they will save you" (78).

This distribution accords with LBH, QH, HJDD, and MH, in which the former system prevails.[86] Once more we may invoke the stylistic device of variation to explain the lone counterexample in *HazGab*, as we observe how יצִילוֹ אוֹתָךְ, "they will save you," follows immediately upon תצילם, "you will save them," in line 78, with the same verb utilized in these two instances.[87]

3.2. Word Order

3.2.1. Word Order with Noun Subjects and Finite Verbs

In this section I treat verb clauses in which a noun serves as subject. I do not include the formulaic "thus says YHWH" clauses, in which the verb אמר always precedes the subject, due mainly to the presence of כו/כה, "thus," at the head of the clause.

---

85. One also notes the infinitive construct with object pronoun in the form בסמכך, "in supporting you" (23), though in this instance there is no alternative usage.

86. See Polzin, *Late Biblical Hebrew*, 28–31; Qimron, *Hebrew of the Dead Sea Scrolls*, 75–77; Mor, "Diqduq ha-ʿIvrit," 213; and Chaim E. Cohen, "ha-Šimmuš be-Kinnuy ha-Musaʾ ha-Davuq leʿumat ha-Šimmuš ʾet + kinnuy (ʾot-) bi-Lšon ha-Mišna," *Leshonenu* 47 (5743): 208–18.

87. For an instance of such in the Mishnah, see *m. Bek.* 9:7–8, with וּמוֹנֶן (9:7) followed by מוֹנֶה אוֹתָן (9:8), as noted by Cohen, "ha-Šimmuš be-Kinnuy ha-Musaʾ ha-Davuq," 211.

Subject–verb (SV) order occurs in the following:

- עבדי דוד בקש מן לפני, "my servant David requested from before me" (16)
- שלושה רועין יצאו לישראל, "three shepherds went out to Israel" (75)
- נבי[א ור]ועה יצילו אותך, "a prophet and a shepherd will save you" (78)

By contrast, *HazGab* includes only one example of verb–subject (VS) order, perhaps owing to the passive voice:

- נשבר הרע מלפני הצדק, "the evil is broken before the righteousness" (20–21)

The predominance of SV over VS in *HazGab* accords with the increased use of the former (compared to SBH) in LBH, QH, and MH.[88]

3.2.2. Word Order with Pronouns and Participles

HazGab includes four cases of pronoun + participle, with no instances of the reverse order. The relevant examples are:

- אתה שאלני, "you ask me" (11)
- אתה עומד, "you stand" (22)
- ואני מרעיש, "and I cause-to-quake" (24)
  (even if this passage is based on Hag 2:6)
- אנחנו בטוחין, "we are certain" (66)

I provide here information regarding the question of pronoun + participle vs. participle + pronoun throughout the varieties of ancient Hebrew. While I know of no study that presents the raw data for BH, according to Joüon-Muraoka, "The pronoun can precede or follow the verb, apparently without any difference in meaning; in most cases it precedes."[89] An exception would appear to be Qohelet, where the norm is participle + pronoun.[90] In QH, the more frequent order is

---

88. Steven E. Fassberg, "Shifts in Word Order in the Hebrew of the Second Temple Period" (paper delivered at the Twelfth International Orion Symposium, "Hebrew in the Second Temple Period: The Hebrew of the Dead Sea Scrolls and of Other Contemporary Sources," December 2008). I am grateful to Professor Fassberg for kindly sharing his unpublished paper with me.

89. Joüon and Muraoka, *Grammar of Biblical Hebrew*, 540. For a similar comment, see Samuel R. Driver, *A Treatise on the Use of the Tenses in Hebrew and Some Other Syntactical Questions* (3rd ed.; London: Oxford University Press, 1892; repr., Grand Rapids: Eerdmans, 1998), 169.

90. W. C. Delsman, "Zur Sprache des Buches Koheleth," in *Von Kanaan bis Kerala: Festschrift für Prof. Mag. Dr. J.P.M. van der Ploeg* (ed. W. C. Delsman; AOAT 211; Neukirchen-Vluyn: Neukirchener Verlag, 1982), 362; and Antoon Schoors, *The Preacher Sought to Find Pleasing Words: A Study on the Language of Qoheleth* (OLA 41; Leuven: Peeters, 1992), 184.

pronoun + participle.⁹¹ To cite one famous text, 4QMMT, one finds six instances of אנחנו, "we," preceding the participle (4Q394 4:5, 4Q396 1:3, 3:4–5, 4:2, 4Q397 1:7, 4:9) vs. only one case of אנחנו following the participle (4Q394 3:12). Most instances of the order participle + pronoun involve a performative act, most frequently with the passive participles ברוך, "blessed," and ארור, "cursed," e.g., 1QS 11:15: ברוך אתה, "blessed are you"; 1QS 2:7: ארור אתה, "cursed are you."⁹² In the second-century C.E. Judean Desert documents,⁹³ one finds the pronoun preceding the participle 3x (Mur. 174:5, N.H. 49:7, Yadin 49:3), and the pronoun following the participle 5x (Mur. 43:3, N.H. 6:1 [via restoration], Yadin 45:6, 46:3, Bet ʿEmer 4–5)—though four of these involve the verb ידה (H-stem), "thank," e.g., Yadin 45:6 מוֹדא אני לך הֹיום, "I thank you today," again a performative act. Nor do I know of a study that scrutinizes MH regarding this question, though apparently the more common usage is participle + pronoun.⁹⁴ In light of these data, *HazGab* fits with BH, QH, and HJDD, against the idiosyncratic Qohelet and MH.

4. Lexicon

4.1. Individual Nouns and Verbs

As the above lists of nouns and verbs indicate (see §§2.3.1; 2.5) most of the vocabulary in *HazGab* is basic Hebrew. Only a few items provide fodder for the LBH–QH–MH continuum of Second Temple period (and beyond) Hebrew, three of which (the nouns) have been discussed above already.

- The verbal noun קיטוט, "trembling" (24), occurs in the *qiṭṭūl* pattern, as treated elsewhere by the present author.⁹⁵
- The noun שבין, "elders" (15), occurs under Aramaic influence.
- The vocable אלה, "God" (26), may reflect the Aramaic, as opposed to the Hebrew, pronunciation.
- The verbal root בקש, "request," occurs 4x in *HazGab* (including the form in line 78, however it is to be restored). While this root appears in BH

---

91. Gregor Geiger, "ha-Benoni be-ʿIvrit šel Megillot Midbar Yehuda" (Ph.D. diss., Hebrew University, 2009), 189–92.
92. Ibid., 200–203.
93. Mor, "Diqduq ha-ʿIvrit," 208. See also his earlier study, U. Mor, "Seder ha-Millim bi-Štarot u-ve-ʾIggarot mi-Midbar Yehuda," *Meghillot* 7 (5769): 237–61.
94. Moses H. Segal, *A Grammar of Mishnaic Hebrew* (Oxford: Clarendon, 1927), 164; and Segal, *Diqduq Lešon ha-Mišna*, 182. Unfortunately, Azar (*Taḥbir Lešon ha-Mišna*, 29–61) is not as helpful as one would hope on this issue, since the material tends to be organized on a structural basis, without attention to the different parts of speech (noun vs. pronoun as subject; finite verb vs. participle as predicate).
95. Rendsburg, "Linguistic and Stylistic Notes to the Hazon Gabriel Inscription," 108–10.

texts of all periods, the verb becomes more common in LBH (e.g., 5x in Zechariah, 3x in Malachi, 10x in Ezra-Nehemiah, 9x in Esther, 7x in Qohelet),[96] a trend that continues into postbiblical times, as it occurs 15x in Ben Sira, 49x in QH,[97] and 200x in Tannaitic texts. The frequency of the verb בקש, "request," in *HazGab* dovetails well with this picture.

4.2. Phraseology

While not strictly belonging to a grammatical sketch, I take the opportunity to present here comments on two phrases in *HazGab* that reflect developments central to the Hebrew of Second Temple period sources.

In lines 23–24, ברוך כבוד יהוה אלהים מן מקומו, "blessed is the glory of YHWH God from his place," expands on Ezek 3:12, בָּרוּךְ כְּבוֹד־יְהוָה מִמְּקוֹמוֹ *bārûk kĕbôd YHWH mimmĕqômô*, "blessed is the glory of YHWH from his place." The inclusion of אלהים in the *HazGab* version reflects the growing trend in Second Temple sources toward less frequent use of the divine name יהוה, "YHWH," with a concomitant increase in the use of אלהים, "God." For example, in the Bible, יהוה occurs 6,828x,[98] while אֱלֹהִים (including construct אֱלֹהֵי, with suffixes, etc.) occurs ca. 2,500x.[99] In Samuel-Kings, the data are 1,007 and 346, respectively; that is, these books use YHWH about 75 percent of the time. In Ezra-Nehemiah, by con-

---

96. These numbers are more glaring when one realizes that the root בקש, "request," occurs but 8x in the entire Torah. I do not include here instances of the noun בַּקָּשָׁה, "request," which is a separate LBH feature; see Avi Hurvitz, "Observations on the Language of the Third Apocryphal Psalm from Qumran," *RevQ* 5 (1965): 226–27; idem, *Ben Lašon le-Lašon* (Jerusalem: Bialik, 1972), 59–60; and Ronald L. Bergey, "The Book of Esther: Its Place in the Linguistic Milieu of Post-Exilic Biblical Hebrew Prose: A Study in Late Biblical Hebrew" (Ph.D. diss., Dropsie College, 1983), 133–34, 168 (*non vide*).

97. Qimron (*Hebrew of the Dead Sea Scrolls*, 89) lists the combination בקש ש- as an element "mainly attested in the DSS and in the Late Biblical Books," based on a single attestation in each corpus: Dan 1:8, 4Q398 (4QMMTᵉ) frgs. 14–17 ii 4). As I indicate here, however, the increased use of the verb בקש, "request," by itself is an LBH trait.

98. This is the number presented by BibleWorks 7.0; Francis I. Andersen and A. Dean Forbes, *The Vocabulary of the Old Testament* (Rome: Pontificio Istituto Biblico, 1992), 330; and David J. A. Clines, *The Dictionary of Classical Hebrew*, (Sheffield: Sheffield Academic Press, 1993–), 4:122. Incongruously, Even-Shoshan (*Qonqordansya Ḥadaša*, 447) has the number 6,645 (6,639 plus the six additional attestations in the individual entries following).

99. BibleWorks 7.0 yields 2,602 occurrences. Clines (*Dictionary of Classical Hebrew*, 1: 277) and Even-Shoshan (*Qonqordansya Ḥadaša*, 74) have 2,603. From either of these numbers one needs to substract about 101 instances (according to my count, using the phrases presented in Even-Shoshan, *Qonqordansya Ḥadaša*, 69) where the reference is to foreign gods, e.g., אלהים אחרים, אלהי נכר , אלהי הגוים, etc. Quite oddly, Andersen and Forbes (*Vocabulary of the Old Testament*, 276) list only 1,073 occurrences, which apparently counts only אלהים and האלהים together (without the construct form אלהי), since BibleWorks 7.0 yields a count of 1,046 occurrences for these two forms—excluding instances of אלהים preceded by the uniconsonantal prepositions -ב, -כ, and -ל, which would add an additional 113 attestations.

trast, the data are 54 and 120, respectively, so that this material uses YHWH only about 31 percent of the time.[100] In the DSS, יהוה occurs 333x, while אלהים occurs 414x—though these occurrences are outweighed by the more frequent use of אל 694x.[101] Clearly, the author of *HazGab* could not simply delete יהוה in his paraphrase of Ezek 3:12, and thus the term remains in line 23. His inclusion of אלהים immediately thereafter, however, reflects the greater use of this divine term during the period of composition.

Yuditsky and Qimron have called attention to the idiom שבר, "break," + לפני, "before," as seen in lines 20–21 נשבר הרע מֹלפני הצדק, "the evil is broken before the righteousness." They cited two Qumran parallels: 4Q372 2:12 כי נשבר [לפניו], "for he was shattered before him"; and 4Q373 1:6 [כי שברו יהוה אלהינו לפני], "for YHWH our God shattered him before." A check of the latter (including the photograph), however, reveals that לפני is not visible before the break. Better to read [כי שברו יהוה אלהינו לפי], "for YHWH our God shattered him with the mouth of," with presumably the word חרב, "sword," following. Another potential parallel is forthcoming from 4Q393 2:7 נשברה מלפניך, "broken before you," though unfortunately little can be read with certainty before these words. Regardless, and more importantly, one will concur with Yuditsky and Qimron that the collocation derives from Aramaic, as per their noting *Tg. Onq.* Deut 20:3 ולא תיתברון מן קדמיהון to render וְאַל־תַּעַרְצוּ מִפְּנֵיהֶם, "and do not be in dread before them."[102]

5. Summary

5.1. Features shared by *HazGab* and BH

- Spelling of דוד
- Retention of laryngeals and pharyngeals
- Personal pronouns
- Suffix pronouns, especially use of בם
- Use of הנה
- Use of למען
- Use of כה
- Order of numeral + noun
- Use of שלו(ש)ת ימין, "three days"
- Order of pronoun + participle

---

100. I do not contrast Chronicles here, since much of the material parallels Samuel-Kings, including slavish copying of יהוה.
101. On this last divine name, see Rendsburg, "Qumran Hebrew," 238–39.
102. Yuditsky and Qimron, "Heʿarot ʿal ha-Ketovet," 138.

5.2. Features Shared by *HazGab* and LBH:[103]

- Retention of laryngeals and pharyngeals
- Personal pronouns
- Suffix pronouns, though not use of בם
- Relative pronoun -ש
- Use of הנה
- Non-assimilation of nun in the combination מן + following consonant
- Use of למען
- Use of כה
- 1st com. sg. verbs ending in -ה
- Object of the verb expressed through suffix pronoun attached to verb
- SV word order

5.3. Features Shared by *HazGab* and SH

- 1st com. sg. verbs ending in -ה

5.4. Features Shared by *HazGab* and Ben Sira

- Spelling of דוד
- Retention of laryngeals and pharyngeals
- Use of למען
- Use of שב

5.5. Features Shared by *HazGab* and QH

- Preponderance of *plene* spelling
- Pronunciation of גוים *gôyîm* > גאים *gōʾîm* (spelled גואים typically in DSS)
- Use of של (3Q15 Copper Scroll only; not general QH)
- Use of הנה
- Order of numeral + noun
- שתין (3Q15 Copper Scroll only; not general QH)
- 1st com. sg. verbs ending in -ה
- Object of the verb expressed through suffix pronoun attached to verb
- SV word order
- Order of pronoun + participle

---

103. Some of these features are not distinctive of LBH per se, but rather of BH as a whole; I include them here nonetheless. For an exceedingly long list of LBH traits identified by scholars in the last several decades (some of which are discussed herein), see the summary chart in Ian Young, Robert Rezetko, and Martin Ehrensvärd, *Linguistic Dating of Biblical Texts* (2 vols.; London: Equinox, 2008), 2:160–214—even if I disagree with the overall approach taken by the authors of this work. Incidentally, on p. 168, no. 32, the first word should be corrected from "decrease" to "increase."

5.6. Features shared by *HazGab* and HJDD

- The form לפנך
- Pronunciation of גוים *gôyīm* > גאים *gôʾîm* (spelled גואין 1x)
- Feminine singular demonstrative pronoun זו
- Use of מהו
- Use of של
- Non-assimilation of *nun* in the combination מן + following consonant
- Use of שתין
- Final *mem/nun* fluctuation (albeit with no apparent pattern in *HazGab*)
- Object of the verb expressed through suffix pronoun attached to verb
- Order of pronoun + participle

5.7. Features shared by *HazGab* and MH

- Feminine singular demonstrative pronoun זו
- Relative pronoun -ש
- Use of מהו
- Use of של
- *qiṭṭūl* formation, as in קיטוט
- Order of numeral + noun
- Final *mem/nun* fluctuation (albeit with no apparent pattern in *HazGab*)
- Object of the verb expressed through suffix pronoun attached to verb
- SV word order

Any ancient Hebrew text will share features with other Hebrew texts of the general period, especially large corpora such as those underlying QH and MH. The above digest demonstrates this point clearly, with many links between *Hazon Gabriel* and the two largest text groups of late antiquity: the Dead Sea Scrolls, on the one hand, and the Tannaitic literature, on the other. At the same time, however, *Hazon Gabriel* uses several forms that are lacking in one or the other of these corpora. For example, *HazGab* uses זו and מהו, which are lacking in QH but present in MH, while it uses למען and הנה, which are present in QH but lacking in MH—not to mention כה, which is wanting in both QH and MH.

In conclusion, I refrain from attempting to categorize the language of *HazGab* as closer to one variety of ancient Hebrew over another, though it is hoped that this grammatical sketch will serve researchers, especially as (*hoffentlich!*) more such texts come to light in the future.

6. Appendix

As indicated at the outset of this article, I follow the reading of *HazGab* provided by Yuditsky and Qimron. If the readings proffered by Yardeni and Elizur were followed, we would gain the following forms, not treated above.

כֹּה, "thus"	(11, 29, 58)
אַרְבָּעִין, "forty"	(15)
כִּי, "that"	(17, 19, 57)
מוֹשָׁבוֹ, "his seat"	(24)
שַׁעֲרֵי, "gates (of)"	(27)
מְלָאכָה, "work"	(28)
אַחֵרִין, "others"	(28)
מְלָאכָה, "work"	(31)
שֶׁלָּהֶן, "their"	(67)
כֹּהֵן, "priest"	(76)
בְּנֵי, "sons (of)"	(76)

All of these lexemes, once more, are part of the basic Hebrew vocabulary, spanning all of ancient Hebrew.

- The use of both כֹּה, "thus" (11, 29, 58), and כִּי, "that" (17, 19, 57), to introduce "thus says YHWH" statements would be, as Yuditsky and Qimron have stressed,[104] unusual—though it is hoped that the present author has provided a suitable explanation for their use,[105] should the reading(s) of Yardeni and Elizur be sustained.
- If the reading שֶׁלָּהֶן, "their," in line 67 is accepted, we would gain another attestation of the 3rd masc. pl. suffix pronoun הֶן-, seen also in the form בָּהֶן, "in them" (line 76), treated above, §2.1.2.

---

104. Yuditsky and Qimron, "Heʿarot ʿal ha-Ketovet," 137–39, s.v., lines 11, 17, 19, 29 (especially line 11).

105. Rendsburg, "Linguistic and Stylistic Notes to the Hazon Gabriel Inscription," 114–16.

SIX

RESPONSE TO ISRAEL KNOHL, *MESSIAHS AND RESURRECTION IN "THE GABRIEL REVELATION"*

Adela Yarbro Collins

In his book *The Messiah before Jesus*, published in 2000, and now in his new book on the *Gabriel Revelation* (2009), Israel Knohl has argued that what he calls the "catastrophic" type of messianism had already emerged in certain Jewish circles in the first century before the Common Era. The significance of this emergence is that Jesus may have been familiar with catastrophic messianism, and thus the "messianic secret" need not be an invention of his followers after his death. I would like to begin my response by saying that I strongly affirm Knohl's attempt to discern the afterlife of certain Jewish ideas, texts, and events in their effects on Jesus and his followers. To view the matter from the other direction, he attempts to interpret the self-understanding and teaching of Jesus in light of important facets of his Jewish context. This is an approach that must be taken by those of us who view Jesus as a Jew rather than as the first Christian.

In the introduction to his earlier book, Knohl states that the "main tendency of New Testament scholarship for over a hundred years" has been to deny that Jesus foresaw "his rejection, death, and resurrection" and to affirm that the predictions of these things "were only ascribed to him after his death."[1] This claim is true, on the whole, but I would like to point out an important exception.[2] In his first book, Dale Allison argued that Jesus "enjoined his followers to reckon seriously with the possibilities of suffering and death" because he, like some of

---

1. Israel Knohl, *The Messiah before Jesus: The Suffering Servant of the Dead Sea Scrolls* (trans. David Maisel; The S. Mark Taper Foundation Imprint in Jewish Studies; Berkeley: University of California Press, 2000), 2.

2. In this regard Knohl refers to an article by Helmut Koester that criticizes Bultmann's approach and offers a new one (ibid., 106 n. 8). Koester argues that Bultmann overemphasized the kerygma in studying the traditional formulae cited by Paul. Koester himself speaks rather about "the narrative of remembrance" of Jesus' suffering and death performed orally in the communities' ritual celebrations ("The Memory of Jesus' Death and the Worship of the Risen Lord" *HTR* 91, no.4 [1998]: 335–50, esp. 344 and n. 23, 350).

his Jewish contemporaries, expected a great tribulation before the coming of the new age. Allison argued further that Jesus "anticipated [his own] suffering and an untimely death," not alone but sharing the fate of "those around him."[3]

In *The Messiah before Jesus*, Knohl based his case for the emergence of "catastrophic messianism" on "certain hymns that were found among the Dead Sea Scrolls."[4] He refers to several versions of two hymns. One is usually referred to as "the Self-Glorification hymn" or "the Self-Exaltation hymn." The other seems to express realized eschatology; that is, it seems to celebrate the presence of the new age.

There is no consensus on the identity of the speaker of the self-glorification hymn. Knohl emphasizes several elements of this text. The speaker sits on "a throne of power in the angelic council" and is higher than all the angels ("Who is like me among the angels?" he asks). He also describes himself as "a friend of the king."[5] "King" here could be a reference to God, but Knohl takes it as "a king of flesh and blood." Some scholars have argued that the figure is the priestly Messiah. Knohl finds no priestly elements in the hymn, and so he concludes that he is the royal Messiah. Yet the speaker is portrayed as a teacher, a portrait more typical of other kinds of leaders in the Dead Sea Scrolls than the royal Messiah.[6]

Another aspect of the self-exaltation hymn is the speaker's self-understanding as the Suffering Servant of Isaiah 53. He says, "[Who] has been despised like [me? And who] has been rejected [of men] like me? [And who] compares to m[e in enduring] evil?" and "[W]ho has born[e all] afflictions like me?"[7] Knohl combines this element with the premise that the self-glorification hymn and the hymn with realized eschatology originally constituted a single hymn.[8] An aspect of the hymn that portrays the new age as present is the end of iniquity.[9] Knohl concluded that the combined hymn implies that a human Messiah has atoned for the sins of the community by his death.[10] A major problem with this hypothesis is that the hymn does not allude to the parts of Isaiah 53 that speak of vicarious suffering or bearing the sins of others.

Knohl then goes on to argue that the royal Messiah reflected in the hymn is Menahem the Essene, who is mentioned by Josephus. There are many problems with this identification, which I do not have time to discuss. Knohl explicitly states, in any case, that his argument about the historical identity of the figure

---

3. Dale C. Allison, Jr., *The End of the Ages Has Come: An Early Interpretation of the Passion and Resurrection of Jesus* (Philadelphia: Fortress, 1985), 116–17.
4. Knohl, *Messiah before Jesus*, 3.
5. Ibid., 17, 83.
6. Ibid., 18, 76.
7. Ibid., 17–18, 76–77.
8. Ibid., 20.
9. Ibid., 79, line 6.
10. Ibid., 24.

is not essential to his thesis that the combination of divinity and suffering in the hymns influenced the emergence of Christianity.

The *Gabriel Revelation*, however, has provided Knohl with new evidence for his hypothesis: it provides the basis for the messianic self-understanding of the historical Jesus.[11] Research on the stone, the script, and the language supports a date "around the end of the first century BCE."[12] Knohl interprets this text as reflecting the ideology of "an apocalyptic-messianic group" at the time of the crushing of the revolt of 4 B.C.E. A key claim is that the work provides evidence for "the killing of [the group's] messianic leader."[13] The text expresses "Catastrophic Messianism, according to which the defeat and death of the messianic leader and his resurrection 'by three days' form an essential part of the redemptive process. The blood of the slain messiah, expected to [rise] in three days, paves the way for the final salvation."[14] The place of origin of the stone itself has been identified as Transjordan. On the assumption that the inscribed text was also set up in that area, Knohl argues that Jesus learned about these ideas when he stayed with John the Baptist near the Jordan.

First a preliminary comment: there is much to be said for the view that scholars should not discuss texts that appear on the market without a known archaeological provenance.

Knohl's interpretation of this document depends primarily on two contested readings. The first is "Ephraim" in line 16. Yuditsky and Qimron read "those who say" instead of "Ephraim."[15] Even if "Ephraim" is the correct reading, Knohl's interpretation of it is dubious. Since Ephraim was the son of Joseph, he interprets the term as an allusion to "the Messiah son of Joseph."[16] This interpretation is problematic, since the earliest explicit reference to a Messiah son of Joseph is much later, in the Babylonian Talmud (*b. Sukkah* 52a). This figure was to come before the Messiah son of David and was to be killed. According to a seventh-century text, *Sefer Zerubbabel*, the Messiah son of Joseph would also rise from the dead. The first attestation of a messiah called "Ephraim" occurs in a medieval text, the *Pesiqta Rabbati*. This figure, however, is not explicitly called the son of Joseph. In fact, the figure could be the son of David.[17] In any case, a

---

11. Other appropriate titles of the text are *The Prophecy of Gabriel* and *The Vision of Gabriel*.

12. Israel Knohl, *Messiahs and Resurrection in 'The Gabriel Revelation'* (Kogod Library of Jewish Studies; London/New York: Continuum, 2009), xv.

13. Ibid., 95.

14. Ibid., 96.

15. Alexey (Eliyahu) Yuditsky and Elisha Qimron, "Notes on the Inscription 'The Vision of Gabriel'" (in Hebrew), *Cathedra* 133 (2009): 133–44.

16. Knohl, *Messiahs and Resurrection*, 10.

17. John J. Collins, "Excursus: Israel Knohl's *Messiah before Jesus*," in Collins, *The Scepter and the Star: The Messiahs of the Dead Sea Scrolls and Other Ancient Literature* (2nd ed.; Grand Rapids:: Eerdmans, 2010).

contemporary usage of the term "Ephraim" is in the Dead Sea Scrolls, where it refers to the Pharisees. Since the context of its occurrence in the *Gabriel Revelation* is so fragmentary, this usage cannot be ruled out. The term may, however, simply refer to Israel here.[18]

The other contested reading is "By three days, live" in line 80. Knohl reads this as Gabriel's command to the slain Messiah to rise from the dead in three days. Ronald Hendel has suggested that the word Knohl reads as "live" should be read as "sign."[19] Yuditsky and Qimron accept this suggestion.

The phrase "prince of the princes" occurs in line 81. Knohl takes this as a reference to the royal Messiah, but the context is so fragmentary that one cannot be sure.

The genre of the text cannot be established with any confidence, since it is not preserved to a sufficient degree. The inscription does, however, contain apocalyptic and eschatological elements. The angel Gabriel gives revelation to an apparently human recipient. The nations gather against Jerusalem, and God delivers his people. The phrase "my servant David" may refer to a royal Messiah, as Knohl argues. It seems, however, that the expected events are still future. In any case, there is no clear reference to the death of the Messiah.

So the existence of a "catastrophic" type of messianism before the public life of Jesus is doubtful. Even if such a messianic perspective had emerged by then, would its attestation support the argument that the messianic secret is historical? In other words, could it support a persuasive argument that the historical Jesus expected to die and be raised as part of the process of redemption?

First of all, one must recognize that the concept of a "messianic secret" in New Testament scholarship is complex, not simple. William Wrede coined the term in 1901 in order to explain a variety of features of the Gospel of Mark. These are the commands to demons and disciples not to reveal the identity of Jesus; the instructions to those who are healed by Jesus not to speak about their healing; the lack of understanding on the part of the disciples; other, individual features that betray a tendency against publicity; and the theory about why Jesus spoke in parables. Wrede argued that all of these features have their origin in the pre-Markan tradition. Followers of Jesus created these features in order to resolve the tension between the postresurrection affirmation that Jesus is the Messiah and the tradition about Jesus, which was thoroughly nonmessianic. Jesus acted and spoke like a prophet and a teacher. He did not exercise a royal or military role.

Beginning with Martin Dibelius, many scholars have interpreted the messianic secret as a device of the evangelist. Dibelius argued that the theory of secrecy had an apologetic function. It was intended to explain why, in spite of so many

---

18. See Knohl's remark that "Ephraim" is used in the Bible primarily for northern Israel (*Messiahs and Resurrection*, 10).

19. Ronald Hendel, "The Messiah Son of Joseph: Simply 'Sign,'" *BAR* 35 (2009): 8.

proofs of his supernatural power, Jesus was not recognized as the Messiah during his lifetime.[20]

Another way of interpreting the messianic secret in Mark is to view it as a *literary* device of the evangelist.[21] This device makes clear to the audience the importance of the things dealt with in the Gospel. It creates a dialectic of revelation and secrecy. It makes the Gospel of Mark, as Dibelius characterized it, a series of secret epiphanies. Finally, the various themes of secrecy in Mark may be viewed as literary devices created or adapted by the author of Mark to reinterpret the dominant, contemporary understanding of the royal Messiah. Jesus did not reign as king or wage victorious battle against the Romans because his suffering, death, and resurrection were part of the divine plan. This view is expressed succinctly in the first passion prediction. "And he began to teach them that the Son of Man *must* suffer much and be rejected by the elders and the chief priests and the scribes and be killed and rise after three days" (Mark 8:31). The idea that these things *must* happen comes from Daniel: there is a God in heaven revealing mysteries, who has made known to the king, Nebuchadnezzar, what *must take place* in the time of the last days (Dan 2:28 OG).

In his magisterial study of the historical Jesus, John P. Meier has concluded that Jesus presented himself as an eschatological prophet like Elijah.[22] In his multivolume work, Meier sifts the tradition about Jesus in a critical process of discerning what material belongs to the earliest recoverable period, some of which at least, goes back to the historical Jesus. The self-understanding or identity that is best supported by the earliest material is prophetic rather than messianic in the Davidic or royal sense. Thus, if Jesus anticipated his death, it was most probably in terms of the occupational hazard of a prophet or the collective trials and tribulations that were expected before the coming of the new age.

The argument that the *Gabriel Revelation* speaks of a royal Messiah who died and was expected to rise from the dead is tantalizingly ingenious but ultimately not persuasive. In spite of the ingenuity of Knohl's interpretation of the relevant hymns from Qumran and the *Gabriel Revelation*, most New Testament scholars would still agree with Bultmann's judgment that the creation of "the idea of a suffering, dying, rising Messiah or Son of Man" was "not done by Jesus himself but by" his followers "*ex eventu*," that is, after the fact of the crucifixion and the experiences of Jesus as risen.[23]

---

20. Martin Dibelius, *Die Formgeschichte des Evangeliums* (Tübingen: Mohr Siebeck, 1919; 2nd ed., 1933); Eng. trans. *From Tradition to Gospel* (New York: Charles Scribner's Sons, 1935), 233. For further examples, see Adela Yarbro Collins, *Mark: A Commentary* (Hermeneia; Minneapolis: Fortress, 2007), 170–71 and n. 85.

21. Yarbro Collins, *Mark*, 172.

22. John P. Meier, *A Marginal Jew: Rethinking the Historical Jesus* (4 vols.; Anchor Bible Reference Library; New York: Doubleday, 1991–2009).

23. Rudolf Bultmann, *Theology of the New Testament* (2 vols; trans. Kendrick Grobel; New York: Scribner, 1951, 1962), 1:31, cited by Knohl, *Messiah before Jesus*, 106 n. 6.

SEVEN

GABRIEL AND DAVID:
SOME REFLECTIONS ON AN ENIGMATIC TEXT

John J. Collins

Since its publication in 2007, the *Gabriel Revelation* has attracted a good deal of attention in the media.[1] "Ancient Tablet Ignites Debate on Messiah and Resurrection," announced the *New York Times* on July 6, 2008. On the following day, the *International Herald Tribune* asked, "Is 3-day resurrection an idea predating Jesus?" Similar articles appeared in Israeli newspapers, and a flurry of postings on the Internet followed.[2] Only a few scholars, however, have tried to engage the text on a scholarly level. We now have a new, although partial edition by Elisha Qimron and Alexey Yuditsky.[3] Moshe Bar-Asher and Gary Rendsburg have published studies of the language of the text.[4] Yuval Goren has published an analysis of the stone on which the inscription is written.[5] David Hamidović has published an independent reading of the text with some comments on genre and *Sitz im*

---

1. Ada Yardeni and Binyamin Elizur, "A Prophetic Text on Stone from the First Century BCE: First Publication" (in Hebrew), *Cathedra* 123 (2007): 155–66. See the English translation in this volume: "A Hebrew Prophetic Text on Stone from the Early Herodian Period: A Preliminary Report." See also Ada Yardeni, "A New Dead Sea Scroll on Stone? Bible-like Prophecy Was Mounted in a Wall 2,000 Years Ago," *BAR* 34, no. 1 (2008): 60–61.
2. E.g., Victor Sasson, "The Vision of Gabriel and Messiah in Mainstream Judaism and in Christianity: Textual, Philological, and Theological Comments," http://victorsasson.blogspot.com/2009/09/vision-of-gabriel-and-messiah-in.html. Despite its pretensions, Sasson's blog is an ill-informed rant against any deviation from "mainstream Judaism" and against Christianity. It contributes nothing to the understanding of the text.
3. Alexey (Eliyahu) Yuditsky and Elisha Qimron, "Notes on the Inscription, 'The Vision of Gabriel'" (in Hebrew), *Cathedra* 133 (2009): 133–44. See the English translation in this volume.
4. Moshe Bar-Asher, "On the Language of 'The Vision of Gabriel,'" *RevQ* 23(2008): 491–524; Gary A. Rendsburg, "Linguistic and Stylistic Notes to the Hazon Gabriel Inscription," *DSD* 16 (2009): 107–16.
5. Yuval Goren, "Micromorphologic Examination of the *Gabriel Revelation* Stone," *IEJ* 58 (2008): 220–29.

Leben.⁶ The most far-reaching attempt to make sense of the text and place it in a historical context, as of March 2010, is that Israel Knohl, who has discussed it at length in a monograph and several articles.⁷ Knohl deserves credit for his pioneering work on this text, and his interpretation is highly ingenious. It is also controversial and problematic, however, and calls for critical assessment.⁸

Since the circumstances of discovery remain unknown, there is inevitably some doubt about the authenticity of the inscription. Since the experts who have examined it are satisfied, however, we must proceed on the assumption that it is authentic until proven otherwise.⁹ Ada Yardeni and Binyamin Elizur identified the script as "typical of the Herodian period" and dated it to the late first century B.C.E. or early first century C.E. While the text may, in principle, be somewhat older than the inscription, it is in this general context that we must try to locate it.

Genre and Structure

Since the beginning of the text is missing, and we are not sure of its extent, it is difficult to determine the genre with any confidence. It is clear that the text is a revelation of some sort. David Hamidović identifies the genre as an apocalyptic vision.¹⁰ There is no report of a vision in the extant text, but there are questions in lines 31 and 77 that reflect a dialogue between the revealer and the recipient of the revelation. The question in line 31 asks about an object, variously identified as a frontlet or a tree, that may have been seen in a vision. It is apparent, in any case, that the revelation does not take the form of an extended symbolic vision, such as we find in Daniel 7 and 8, but is primarily a discourse, with elements of dialogue and perhaps visions of particular objects such as we find in Amos 7–8. Yardeni and Elizur suggest that it is "a collection of short prophecies dictated to a scribe, in a manner similar to prophecies appearing in the Hebrew Bible." Knohl interprets the text as unit. The main point of disjunction comes at line 77, where the speaker announces "I am Gabriel." Up to that point, the text appeared to be a speech of God, but a speech introduced by the formula "Thus says the Lord" can be spoken by a prophetic, or angelic mediator, and so it is possible that Gabriel is

---

6. David Hamidović, "La *Vision de Gabriel*," *RHPR* 89 (2009): 147–68.

7. Israel Knohl, *Messiahs and Resurrection in 'The Gabriel Revelation'* (Kogod Library of Judaic Studies; London/New York: Continuum, 2009). See also idem, "'By Three Days, Live': Messiahs, Resurrection and Ascent to Heaven in *Hazon Gabriel*," *JR* 88 (2008): 147–58; and idem, "The Messiah Son of Joseph: 'Gabriel's Revelation' and the Birth of a New Messianic Model," *BAR* 34, no. 5 (2008): 58–62.

8. I have already indicated the main lines of my critique in a short piece for nonspecialist readers, "The Vision of Gabriel," *Yale Alumni Magazine* (September/October 2008), 26–27.

9. Goren ("Micromorphological Examination," 228) finds "no indication of modern treatment of the surface of the stone," but he emphasizes that "by no means does this statement indicate that the entire inscription or parts of it were created in antiquity beyond any trace of doubt." Bar-Asher ("On the Language of 'The Vision of Gabriel,'" 517) accepts that the Hebrew dates from "the end of Second Temple times."

10. Hamidović, "La *Vision de Gabriel*," 159.

the speaker throughout. Knohl is probably right, nonetheless, that the identification of the angel marks a new, concluding section of the composition. A partial analogy for the genre of the text can be found in the discourse of the angel Gabriel in Daniel 10–12, but that discourse describes a much clearer historical and eschatological sequence than is the case here. One might also compare the discourses of the angel Uriel in 4 Ezra, which occur in the context of dialogues. There are hints of dialogue in the *Gabriel Revelation* insofar as the speaker occasionally addresses commands to the human recipient. The only passages that might be ascribed to the recipient are a response to a question in line 31 and the question about the revealer's identity in line 77. The *Gabriel Revelation* may well qualify as an apocalypse, insofar as it is a revelation mediated to a human recipient by an angel and is concerned with heavenly realities and eschatological events,[11] but this judgment must be qualified by the fragmentary nature of the available text.

Knohl further divides lines 1–76 into three subsections: lines 9–12, 13–42 and 56–76.[12] The first of these subsections is extremely fragmentary. It says something about someone asking questions of the Lord, and, as Knohl puts it, it "presumably served as an introduction to the revelation . . . that follows."[13] The other two sections are separated by text that is either barely intelligible or entirely unintelligible, but they are not marked off formally as distinct sections. There are several prophetic formulae ("thus says the Lord . . .") throughout the text (lines 13, 18, 20, 29, 57, 69), but these do not necessarily mark new units in the text.

An Eschatological Assault on Jerusalem

The revelation concerns an attack by the nations on Jerusalem (lines 13–14). This motif is familiar from the Psalms (2; 48), and from prophetic (Zechariah 14) and apocalyptic (*4 Ezra* 13) literature. Such a scenario could be inspired by an actual historical assault on Jerusalem, or it could be an eschatological fantasy, without historical basis.

According to Knohl, "lines 16–17 present the request from Ephraim to place the sign, probably portending the coming redemption, which is also announced by God's statement that His 'gardens' are ripe and ready for Israel (lines 18–19)."[14] In this, he is following the reading of Yardeni and Elizur in lines 16–17 ("My servant, David, asked from before Ephraim(?) 17. [to?] put the sign(?)"). They, however, leave blank the end of line 18, where Knohl finds the reference to gardens.[15]

Yuditsky and Qimron read these lines quite differently: "David, my servant, asked me: 'Answer me, I ask you for the sign.' Thus said YHWH, God of Hosts, the God of Israel: 'My son, I have a new testament for Israel.'"

---

11. On the definition of an apocalypse, see John J. Collins, ed., *Apocalypse. The Morphology of a Genre, Semeia* 14 (1979), especially p. 9.
12. Knohl, *Messiahs and Resurrection*, 31.
13. Ibid., 32.
14. Ibid.
15. Hamidović ("La *Vision de Gabriel*," 153) also reads the reference to "gardens."

Where Yardeni and Elizur read Ephraim, they read אמרים ("words," as in Prov 22:21). Instead of "my gardens" (גני) they read בני ("my son"), a reading that Knohl now accepts. Insofar as one can judge from the photos published in Knohl's book,[16] and his article in *BAR*,[17] it seems possible to read the second letter of the last word on line 16 as a *pe*, as in Ephraim, but Yuditsky and Qimron, working from new, digital photographs, say that it "can hardly be a *pe*." The reading must be considered doubtful. Knohl makes much of the supposed reference to Ephraim here, and we will return to his interpretation at the end of this article. For the present, it must suffice to note that it is uncertain whether the text refers to Ephraim at all.

The person addressed by God as "my son" is presumably David, the person who asked for the sign. The idea that the Davidic king, or Messiah, can be addressed by God as "son" is familiar from Psalm 2 and 2 Samuel 7, and it is also reflected in a number of texts from the Hellenistic and Roman periods.[18] The request for a sign is answered by an assurance "in three days you will know," and by a further prophetic announcement that "evil is broken before righteousness." Knohl translates this in the perfect tense, but it is presumably a prophetic perfect, and so Yuditsky and Qimron rightly take it as future. The point is that the nations besieging Jerusalem will be defeated. The assurance is offered in place of a sign, since the deliverance itself will be seen shortly.

An Evil Branch

After this, the addressee is encouraged to ask about the identity of an "evil branch" (צמח רע). The word צמח is a designation for the Messiah, derived from Jer 23:5 ("the days are coming, says the Lord, when I will raise up for David a righteous branch") and Jer 33:15, and is used in eschatological contexts in the Dead Sea Scrolls, notably in 4Q285, 4Q252, and 4QpIsaª.[19] A צמח רע is presumably a false messiah. Several messianic pretenders appeared in the first century of the Common Era, especially in connection with the revolt against Rome.[20] In the Gospel of Mark, Jesus warns his disciples: "And if anyone says to you at that time, 'Look! Here is the Messiah!' or 'Look! There he is!'—do not believe it. False messiahs and false prophets will appear and produce signs and omens, to lead

---

16. Knohl, *Messiahs and Resurrection*, 104.
17. "Knohl, "The Messiah Son of Joseph," 60.
18. See further Adela Yarbro Collins and John J. Collins, *King and Messiah as Son of God: Divine, Human, and Angelic Messianic Figures in Biblical and Related Literature* (Grand Rapids: Eerdmans, 2009), 48–74.
19. John J. Collins, *The Scepter and the Star: Messianism in Light of the Dead Sea Scrolls* (2nd ed.; Grand Rapids: Eerdmans, 2010), 61–73.
20. Richard A. Horsley and John S. Hanson, *Bandits, Prophets, and Messiahs: Popular Movements in the Time of Jesus* (New Voices in Biblical Studies; Minneapolis: Winston, 1985), 88–134; Collins, *Scepter and the Star*, 219–28.

astray, if possible, the elect" (Mark 13:21–22). Knohl asserts that "this evil messianic figure must be distinguished from the more conventional type of false messiah, who wishes to redeem Israel but cannot achieve this goal. Here, emphasis is laid upon the sheer wickedness of the would-be redeemer."[21] Instead, Knohl associates the evil branch with the Antichrist, as that figure appears in Christian literature, beginning with the book of Revelation. The Antichrist is "characteristically duplicitous, presenting himself as the Messiah and Redeemer while actually being the Devil's spawn, seeking to corrupt and lead astray."[22] In support of this interpretation, Knohl reads the next word as לובנסד, an expression otherwise unattested, which he renders as "plastered white." Yuditsky and Qimron do not venture a reading here.[23] Again, Knohl's bold interpretation has a dubious textual basis. The idea of an Antichrist who apes the Christ is not reliably attested before the book of Revelation and seems to be a distinctively Christian development.[24] The phrase צמח רע cannot bear the interpretive weight that Knohl lays on it.

Divine Deliverance

Shortly after this comes the promise of a theophany, formulated in the language of the prophet Haggai: "In a little while I shall shake heaven and earth" (lines 24–25). In line 26, Yardeni and Elizur, followed by Knohl and Hamidović, read: "these are the seven chariots." Yuditsky and Qimron, however, read "the God of chariots (parallel to "the Lord God of hosts") will listen to (the cry of Jerusalem)," reading שמע as a prophetic perfect, instead of שבע ("seven"). Knohl, following Yardeni and Elizur, locates the supposed seven chariots at the gate (שער) of Jerusalem and the gates (שערי) of Judah,[25] but Yuditsky and Qimron read that (God will listen to the cry of) the devastation (שוד) of Jerusalem and the cities (ערי) of Judah. Again, Knohl reads "three angels" in line 28,[26] where Yardeni and Elizur

---

21. Knohl, *Messiahs and Resurrection*, 12 n. 51.
22. Ibid., 12. See further Knohl, "On 'the Son of God,' Armilus and Messiah Son of Joseph" (in Hebrew), *Tarbiz* 68 (1998): 13–38. Cf. David Flusser, *Judaism and the Origins of Christianity* (Jerusalem: Magnes, 1988), 207–13, 433–53. Knohl takes the figure who is called "Son of God" in 4Q246 to be an Antichrist figure and identifies him with the Roman emperor Augustus (*Messiahs and Resurrection*, 52–84). That figure is more plausibly interpreted as the Davidic Messiah. See Yarbro Collins and Collins, *King and Messiah as Son of God*, 65–73.
23. Yardeni and Elizur allowed Knohl's reading as one of several possibilities but offered no translation.
24. On the Antichrist, see Gregory C. Jenks, *The Origins and Early Development of the Antichrist Myth* (BZNW 59; Berlin: de Gruyter, 1991); L. J. Lietaert Peerbolte, *The Antecedents of Antichrist: A Traditio-Historical Study of the Earliest Christian Views on Eschatological Opponents* (JSJSup 49; Leiden: Brill, 1996); Bernard McGinn, *Antichrist: Two Thousand Years of the Human Fascination with Evil* (San Francisco: HarperSanFrancisco, 1994), esp. 32–56 ("Christ's Alter Ego").
25. So also Hamidović.
26. So also Hamidović.

offer no reading and Yuditsky and Qimron read "the hosts" (צבאת). There is a reference to the angel Michael in line 28.

Readings diverge again in line 31, where Knohl followed the original reading of Yardeni and Elizur, הצץ "the frontlet",[27] but they now accept the correction of Yuditsky and Qimron, and read "the tree" (העץ). The two editions construe the tree in different ways. Yardeni and Elizur translate: "'What is it?' said the tree." Yuditsky and Qimron, more plausibly: "'What is it?' and I said, 'a tree.'" (Knohl has "he said, the frontlet"). In either case, there seems to be a vision implied. (Compare Amos's visions of a plumb line and a basket of summer fruit in Amos 7–8). Unfortunately, very little of this passage is legible. If Knohl's reading were accepted, we might speculate that the "frontlet" was intended as a crown for the Davidic figure. It is difficult to imagine what the significance of the tree might be. Yuditsky and Qimron offer no reconstruction of lines 33 to 63, although they offer some new readings in these lines. Yardeni and Elizur read only scattered words between lines 32 and 44 (Jerusalem is mentioned twice, and there is possible mention of exile in line 37) and declare lines 45 to 50 to be unintelligible. Knohl and Hamidović read "a sign from Jerusalem" in line 36 and "a sign of exile" in line 37. In line 40, Knohl reconstructs "that his mist will fill most of the moon" and in line 41 "blood that the northerner would become maggoty." Even apart from the difficulty of reading anything in those lines, the meaning of the reconstructed text is not clear. Knohl's translation of line 40 is admittedly conjectural. He suggests an analogy to the signs of the Day of the Lord in Joel 2. Yuditsky and Qimron are probably wise to leave those lines almost entirely blank.

Blood and Chariots

When legible text resumes, there is mention of "three days" in line 54, marked with a question mark by Yardeni and Elizur but without context. We have an intriguing reference to "the blood of the slaughters (?)/sacrifices (טבחי) of Jerusalem" in line 57 (so Yardeni and Qimron, who think it "more plausible to understand the word *ṭbḥy* as referring to the flesh of the sacrifices in the Jerusalem Temple" than to the slaughter on some occasion when Jerusalem was sacked). They also read the word סתום immediately before this phrase and comment: "the precise meaning of סתום in this context is obscure, either ending the preceding verse or perhaps referring to the interruption of the sacrifice-practice at the Jerusalem temple." Knohl construes the references as to "the blood of the slaughtered of Jerusalem," and reads סתום as "seal up." Compare Dan 8:26, where Gabriel tells Daniel to "seal up the vision, for it refers to many days from now." "Sealing" can be applied more easily to a revelation than to "blood," but perhaps the blood is to be kept as evidence or testimony for a coming judgment. Knohl's reading at

---

27. So also Hamidović.

line 60: "He will have pity... his mercy are [*sic*] near" departs from Yardeni and Elizur, who read only a vague reference to "spirit" or "wind."[28]

The text becomes a little clearer beginning with line 65. There we find mention of שלושה קדשי העולם, "the three holy ones of the world." Knohl asserts that "'holy ones' is used in the Hebrew Bible and early Jewish literature to designate both angels and human beings,"[29] but in fact the term is predominantly used to refer to angels.[30] He suggests that "holy ones of the world" must refer to "creatures of this world only" and suggests a reference to martyrs. This seems quite arbitrary. A reference to angels seems to me more likely, analogous, perhaps, to the angels who preside over the nations.[31] The Greek equivalent, *hagioi,* is used for martyred human beings in the book of Revelation (11:18; 13:10; 14:12; 16:6; 17:6; etc.), but they are not called "holy ones of the world," and the usage derives from their association with the angels after death.

In lines 66–67, Knohl, following Yardeni and Elizur, reads: "in you we trust... Announce him of blood (בשר לו על דם), this is their chariot."[32] This is scarcely intelligible. Knohl offers a highly imaginative interpretation:

> The good tidings are presumably connected to the fate of a group of people ("their chariot") killed by the enemies of Jerusalem. Through the recipient of the vision, God promises that the blood of the martyrs will serve as their chariot. The prophecy is probably based on the story in 2 Kings 2:11, in which Elijah goes up to heaven in a chariot of fire.[33]

Yuditsky and Qimron, however, take the word בשר not as a verb meaning "to preach good news," but as a noun meaning "flesh," which makes much better sense in conjunction with "blood." Their reconstruction also goes beyond their actual reading: "on you we rely [not on] flesh (and) not on blood. This is the chariot..." While this reconstruction is also speculative, it does not require nearly as great a flight of imagination as Knohl's transformation of the blood of the slain into the chariot of Elijah.

In line 70, Knohl and Yuditsky and Qimron agree against Yardeni and Elizur in reading "three shepherds." There is also mention of prophets at the beginning of the line, and Yuditsky and Qimron identify these with the shepherds. Knohl

---

28. Hamidović reads differently: "Dieu n'est [pas] profane [הלל] Ainsi is saisira c[es] biens..."

29. Knohl, *Messiahs and Resurrection*, 22.

30. See John J. Collins, *Daniel: A Commentary on the Book of Daniel* (Hermeneia: Minneapolis: Fortress, 1993), 313–17.

31. E.g., in Daniel 10. Compare also the seventy angelic shepherds in the Animal Apocalypse, in *1 Enoch* 89:59–90:19.

32. Hamidović reads the same words but construes slightly differently: "Informe-le au sujet du sang de ce char qui est à eux."

33. Knohl, *Messiahs and Resurrection*, 23.

sees the "three shepherds" as an allusion to Zech 11:8.[34] In the biblical passage, however, the three shepherds are bad rulers whom the Lord has to replace: "In one month I disposed of the three shepherds, for I had become impatient with them, and they also detested me." In the *Gabriel Revelation*, the three shepherds are sent by the Lord. They are mentioned again in line 75. There is no indication in the extant text of divine disapproval. The term "shepherds" usually represents rulers rather than prophets, so the prophets here are probably distinct emissaries. Hamidović does not find any reference to shepherds here, reading ואני instead of רועי. There is, in any case, an undisputed reference to "three shepherds" who went out to (ל) Israel in line 75.[35]

Line 72: "the place for the sake of David, the servant of the Lord," may be part of a divine assurance, or it may be part of a prayer, since two lines later we read "showing kindness to thousands." In any case, the line confirms the importance of David in this composition.

In line 76, Yardeni and Elizur, Knohl, and Hamidović all read כהן, "priest," but Yuditsky and Qimron read בהן, "among them," a variant of בם in the preceding phrase. Again, where Yardeni and Elizur, followed by Knohl and Hamidović, read בני קדושים, literally "sons of holy ones," Yuditsky and Qimron read בם קדושים. Even if בני קדושים should prove to be correct, however, it should be translated simply as "holy ones." Priests might be associated with angelic "holy ones," but it is uncertain whether there is any reference here to a priest at all.

The Concluding Section

Line 77 seems to mark a transition in the text, probably the beginning of the conclusion. The speaker is now identified as Gabriel, in a passage that implies a dialogue.[36] Someone is told, "you will rescue them" (line 78). Yuditsky and Qimron read the following statement as "A proph[et and a she]pherd will save you" and they reconstruct "three shepherds, three [pro]phets" in line 79. Yardeni and Elizur, Hamidović, and Knohl also recognize the word "three" in line 79, but they reconstruct the reference as "three signs." None of these readings, other than the word "three," is at all clear.

Knohl's reading of line 80 is the most controversial suggestion about this text to date. Yardeni and Elizur read only: "In three days . . . I, Gabriel . . ." Knohl read the word חאיה after "three days," and interpreted it as "live!" a command to rise from the dead.[37] Hence the headlines proclaiming "resurrection after three days before Jesus." The spelling, however, is anomalous. Knohl asserts that the

---

34. Ibid., 24.

35. Knohl construes the preposition as "for" Israel.

36. Yardeni and Elizur, Hamidović, and Knohl read "who am I?" Yuditsky and Qimron read "who are you?"

37. Hamidović ("La *Vision de Gabriel*," 155) reads the same word, but translates as an injunctive future: "on vivra." In his note, however, he suggests that it may be an infinitive

use of *aleph* as a vowel is quite common,[38] but he provides no instance of its use in the verb "to live." Moreover, as Moshe Bar-Asher has pointed out, an *aleph* is never used to represent a *hatef patah*; it is always a whole vowel, usually a long one.[39] The parallel cited by Knohl from Ezek 16:6 ("in your blood, live") does not envision resurrection from the dead. Ronald Hendel resolved the problem by suggesting that the word should be read as האות, "the sign," and this reading is now accepted by Yuditsky and Qimron.[40] There are other references to signs in the text, and the *aleph* is not problematic. The main pillar on which Knohl's controversial interpretation of the text rests has disappeared on inspection.

In line 81, Knohl follows Yardeni and Elizur in reading "the Prince of Princes." This title, as he notes, is found in Dan 8:25, where the "little horn," "a king of bold countenance," rises up against the Prince of Princes, who is also called "the prince of the host." Knohl argues that "if the 'host of heaven' represents the People of Israel, the 'prince of the host' represents their leader."[41] He then supposes that the author of the *Gabriel Revelation* read the prophecy of Daniel 8 to mean that the king of bold countenance will destroy Israel and attack, perhaps even kill, their leader—the "prince of princes." He concludes: "what our text adds to the original prophecy is that Gabriel will resurrect the executed leader."[42] But in Daniel, the host of heaven is clearly the angelic host, and the Prince of Princes is the Most High.[43] Daniel 8 is not describing an attack on a human leader at all. Moreover, even if the author of the *Gabriel Revelation* takes the title "Prince of Princes" from Daniel 8, it does not follow that he is offering an interpretation of the Danielic passage in which the phrase occurs. The *Gabriel Revelation* says nothing here of an attack on any human leader, much less his death or resurrection.

Line 83, "to me, from the three, the small one that I took," is too elliptic to make much sense. The "three" may well refer back to the three shepherds mentioned earlier. Knohl suggests that "it is possible that 'took' implies ascent to heaven," since the same verb is used for the taking of Enoch in Gen 5:24. But of course the word need not have that meaning at all. The attraction of Knohl's interpretation depends on his reading of line 80 as a reference to resurrection, which we have already rejected.

Knohl finds a final reference to resurrection in line 85, "then you will stand."

---

absolute and may be the equivalent of an imperative. He also notes, however, that the verb "to live" does not necessarily refer to resurrection (ibid., 161).

38. Knohl, *Messiahs and Resurrection*, 26.
39. Bar-Asher, "On the Language," 501.
40. Ronald Hendel, "The Messiah Son of Joseph. Simply 'Sign,'" *BAR* 35 (2009): 8.
41. Knohl, *Messiahs and Resurrection*, 28.
42. Ibid.
43. See Collins, *Daniel*, 333. Cf. Dan 11:36, where the upstart king offends "the God of gods." The archangel Michael has also been proposed as a possible identification for the prince of princes.

In this case, he has a plausible parallel in Dan 12:13, where the visionary is told: "you shall rise for your lot at the end of days." While the legible text in the *Gabriel Revelation* is far too elliptic to warrant confidence, it is not implausible that the revelation would end as Daniel's had. In that case, however, the reference is to the future resurrection of the visionary, whose death is not a subject of the revelation.

From this perusal of the reconstructions of the text that have been offered to date, it is clear that many of the readings are uncertain, and that only a very elliptic text is available to us. The text contains a revelation about an attack of the nations on Jerusalem. God, apparently speaking through the angel Gabriel, promises deliverance very soon. ("In three days" should not be taken literally). It is apparent that the Davidic Messiah has a role to play in this eschatological drama, and it would seem from line 72 that God delivers Jerusalem "for the sake of David, the servant of YHWH." Some other figures (prophets, shepherds) also have a role, but the text is too elliptic to allow us to fill in the details. There is also mention of a false messiah, "an evil branch," but there is nothing to indicate that this figure is an eschatological adversary of the Messiah like the Antichrist in Christian tradition, or the much later figure of Armilus in *Sefer Zerubbabel*.[44]

A Messiah of Ephraim?

Knohl has argued that the Davidic Messiah is not the only, or even the most important, messianic figure in this text. He also finds reference to the "Messiah son of Joseph," known from the Babylonian Talmud, or "Messiah of Ephraim," who is mentioned in the medieval *Pesiqta Rabbati*, and he claims that the *Gabriel Revelation* provides evidence that this figure was known already around the turn of the era. This claim is highly problematic.

As noted above, Yardeni and Elizur read the word "Ephraim" at the end of line 16 (with a question mark to indicate that the reading was uncertain). They translate: "my servant, David, asked from before Ephraim [to?] put the sign (?). I ask from you . . ." Knohl, reading the same text, translates the verb "ask" as an imperative: "My servant David, ask of Ephraim [that he] place the sign; (this) I ask of you." Yuditsky and Qimron reject the reading Ephraim and read: "David, my servant, asked me: Answer me, I ask you for the sign." Where Yardeni and Knohl read [ ]שים at the beginning of line 17, Yuditsky and Qimron read [הש]יבני, "answer me." It is not possible to decide between the readings on the basis of the published photos. If we accept the reading "Ephraim," however, it would be very odd to ask a human figure, even a messiah to "place the sign." In the entire biblical and Jewish tradition, one asks God for a sign (e.g., Isaiah 7) or asks what the

---

44. On Armilus, see Joseph Dan, "Armilus: The Jewish Antichrist and the Origins and Dating of the *Sefer Zerubbavel*," in *Toward the Millennium: Messianic Expectations from the Bible to Waco* (ed. Peter Schäfer and Mark Cohen; SHR 77; Leiden: Brill, 1998), 73–104.

signs will be (e.g., *4 Ezra* 5–6). The construal of the text proposed by Yuditsky and Qimron is much more plausible than the alternatives in this respect.

Knohl infers from his reading of this passage that the Messiah of Ephraim is superior in status to the Davidic Messiah: "the fact that David is sent by God to request Ephraim to place the sign may attest that Ephraim has superior rank. He, and not David, is the key person who is asked to place the sign; David is only the messenger!"[45] When the Messiah son of Joseph appears in the Talmud, however, the relationship is quite different. There, the Messiah son of Joseph precedes the Davidic Messiah and is killed:

> Our Rabbis taught: The Holy One, blessed be He, will say to the Messiah, the son of David (May he reveal himself speedily in our days!), "Ask of me anything, and I will give it to thee," as it is said, *"I will tell of the decree"* etc. *"this day have I begotten thee, ask of me and I will give the nations for thy inheritance."* But when he will see that the Messiah the son of Joseph is slain, he will say to Him, "Lord of the Universe, I ask of Thee only the gift of life," "As to life," He would answer him, "Your father David has already prophesied this concerning you," as it is said, *He asked of thee life, thou gavest him [even length of days for ever and ever]* (*b. Sukkah* 52a)[46]

Nowhere in Jewish tradition does the Messiah son of Joseph take precedence over the Davidic Messiah.[47] The Messiah son of Joseph is introduced in this talmudic passage (*Sukkah* 52a) in the context of a discussion of the referent of Zech 12:10 ("they will look on him whom they have pierced").[48] It is apparent that this figure was well known by talmudic times, but his origin is uncertain. The most plausible explanation remains that the idea of a dying messiah took hold after the defeat of Bar Kokhba, in the second century C.E. In the words of Joseph Heinemann, "we must look for a dramatic, even traumatic event to account for this transfiguration of the legend [i.e., of messianic expectation]; and no other would supply as likely a cause for the creation of the new version as the defeat and death of Bar Kokhba."[49] There is certainly no hint of the expectation of such a figure in the surviving Jewish literature from the period before Bar Kokhba.

Moreover, while Ephraim was certainly a son of Joseph, it is not certain that the Messiah who is called Ephraim in the medieval *Pesiqta Rabbati* should be

---

45. Knohl, "Messiah Son of Joseph," 60.

46. Trans. I. W. Slotki, the Traditional Press edition. The italicized passages are citations from Ps 2:7–8 and Ps 21:4.

47. On the Messiah son of Joseph, see Joseph Heinemann, "The Messiah of Ephraim and the Premature Exodus of the Tribe of Ephraim," *HTR* 68 (1975): 1–15, and the older literature cited there, especially in n. 1. In addition to the talmudic passages, the Messiah son of Joseph is mentioned in the Palestinian Targumim and in late medieval midrashim.

48. See George Foot Moore, *Judaism in the First Centuries of the Christian Era, the Age of the Tannaim* (2 vols.; 1927–30; repr., New York: Schocken, 1971), 370.

49. Heinemann, "Messiah of Ephraim," 8–9.

identified with the Messiah son of Joseph known from the Talmud. At least some parts of the relevant passage, *Pesiq. Rab.* 36, suggest rather that "Ephraim" is a name for the Davidic Messiah.[50]

The *Pisqa* begins with a consideration of Isa 60:1–2: "Arise, shine, for thy light is come." These words, we are told, are to be considered in the light of what David, king of Israel, was inspired to say: "For with thee is the fountain of life; in Thy light we see light" (Ps 36:10). The light is identified as "the light of the Messiah," and the verse is cited as proof that "the Holy One, blessed be he, contemplated the Messiah and his works before the world was created, and then under his throne of glory put away his messiah until the time of the generation in which he will appear." Satan then asks to see the Messiah. When he sees him, he is shaken, and he asks, "Who is this through whose power we are to be swallowed up? What is his name? What kind of being is he?" The Holy One replies: "He is the Messiah, and his name is Ephraim, my true Messiah, who will pull himself straight and will pull up straight his generation, and who will give light to the eyes of Israel and deliver his people; and no nation or people will be able to withstand him." The passage goes on to say that God tells the Messiah that he will have to suffer for a period of seven years for the sins of those who are put away with him under the throne. The Messiah responds: "Master of the universe, with joy in my soul and gladness in my heart I take this suffering upon myself, provided that not one person in Israel perish; that not only those who are alive be saved in my days, but also those who are dead, who died from the days of Adam up to the time of redemption."[51]

The *Pisqa* continues: "During the seven-year period preceding the coming of the son of David, iron beams will be brought and loaded upon his neck until the Messiah's body is bent low. . . . It was because of the ordeal of the son of David that David wept, saying My strength is dried up like a potsherd (Ps. 22:16). During the ordeal of the son of David, the Holy One, blessed be He, will say to him: Ephraim, my true Messiah, long ago, ever since the six days of creation, thou didst take this ordeal upon thyself."[52] In this passage, it is difficult to distinguish the Messiah named Ephraim from the son of David.

The following *Pisqa*, 37, also refers many times to the Messiah as Ephraim and cites Jer 31:20: "Is Ephraim my dear son?" It may be that the fact that Ephraim is said to be the son of God in Jeremiah (compare Hos 11:1, 8) gave rise to the assumption that Ephraim and the Messiah son of David were one and the same.[53]

If the reading proposed by Yuditsky and Qimron is correct, there is no refer-

---

50. This was suggested to me orally by Martha Himmelfarb.

51. Trans. William G. Braude, *Pesikta Rabbati: Discourses for Feasts, Fasts, and Special Sabbaths* (2 vols.; Yale Judaica Series 18; New Haven: Yale University Press, 1968), 2:678–79.

52. Ibid., 680.

53. Michael Fishbane notes correctly that there is only one messianic figure in this text and that he is the sufferer called Ephraim, but he argues that this is a polemical position and that "any other messianic figure, like David, is excluded." ("Midrash and Messianism: Some

ence here to Ephraim at all, and so the consideration of the Messiah of Ephraim loses its relevance to the discussion. But even if Knohl's reading is correct, it does not follow that Ephraim is a name for a messiah in this text. Ephraim is often used in the Bible as a metonym for Israel, and it could be so used here.[54] In short, Knohl's attempt to find the Messiah son of Joseph in the *Gabriel Revelation* is problematic on many counts.

In contrast to the supposed references to the Messiah son of Joseph, "my servant David" appears unambiguously in this text. In line 16, he is either said to ask God for a sign or is commanded to ask for one. He is most probably the person addressed by God as "my son" in line 18.[55] The question arises, then, whether "my servant David" is the addressee throughout or at least from line 18 forward? This is perhaps unlikely, since David is referred to in the third person again in line 72, where something happens "for the sake of David, the servant of YHWH." It is true that other figures, prophets, and shepherds play a role in this revelation, but it is clear that the primary agent of God is the Davidic Messiah.

The Setting

One of the many uncertainties about this text is whether it was inspired by a historical siege of Jerusalem or should rather be understood as an eschatological fantasy of the final attack of the gentiles on Jerusalem. The urgency of the request for a sign probably argues for a historical crisis. If Yardeni's dating of the paleography is correct, then the siege of Jerusalem during the first Jewish revolt may be too late. The siege under Pompey in 63 B.C.E. provides one possible occasion. The *Psalms of Solomon*, which reflect on that event, are also notable for their expectation of a Davidic Messiah.[56] Knohl's suggestion of the suppression of a revolt in Judea by Varus in 4 B.C.E. is also possible, but his attempt to fill out the events by using the passage in Revelation 11 about the death of two witnesses[57] is highly fanciful.[58]

Much remains unclear about this text, even in the elementary matter of the

---

Theologies of Suffering and Salvation," in Schäfer and Cohen, *Toward the Millennium*, 57–71, here 65). But then we must wonder why the *Pisqa* also refers to "the ordeal of the son of David".

54. See further Hamidović, "La *Vision de Gabriel*," 156 n.16. He concludes: "En contexte il demeure difficile de reconnaître la désignation d'un messie, fils de Joseph, à la lecture du nom Éphraïm" (ibid., 161).

55. As noted above, Ephraim is said to be the son of God also in Jeremiah 31 and Hosea 11.

56. See especially *Psalms of Solomon* 17; and Kenneth Atkinson, *I Cried to the Lord: A Study of the Psalms of Solomon's Historical Background and Social Setting* (JSJSup 84; Leiden: Brill, 2004).

57. Knohl, *Messiahs and Resurrection*, 66-71.

58. See John J. Collins, "An Essene Messiah? Comments on Israel Knohl, *The Messiah before Jesus*," in *Christian Beginnings and the Dead Sea Scrolls* (ed. John J. Collins and Craig Evans; Acadia Studies in Bible and Theology; Grand Rapids: Baker Academic, 2006), 37–44.

actual readings. Whatever the setting, however, the chief significance of this text is as a witness to the importance of the *Davidic* Messiah around the turn of the era. It is unfortunate that this simple fact has been obscured by speculation about a suffering and dying messiah who is simply not attested in the inscription, insofar as it can be deciphered.

EIGHT

Some Observations on the *Hazon Gabriel*

Matthias Henze

In April of 2007, the Israeli epigraphers Ada Yardeni and Binyamin Elizur published a hitherto unknown Hebrew inscription that had only recently come to light.¹ They named the text *Hazon Gabriel*, or the *Gabriel Vision*, since it appears to be a prophetic text, possibly an apocalyptic vision, in which the angel Gabriel is mentioned three times by name. The limestone stele that bears the inscription is owned by Dr. David Jeselsohn, a private antiquities collector from Zurich, Switzerland, who had purchased the stone about a decade earlier from an antiquities dealer named Ghassan Rihani in Jordan.² It was at Jeselsohn's invitation that Yardeni and Elizur worked on the text.

Not long after the publication of the *editio princeps*, the inscription caught the interest of scholars and the interested public alike. There are mainly two reasons why the text soon attracted attention. The first is the unusual nature of the inscription itself. The scribe, likely a trained professional, wrote the text in black ink directly onto the surface of the flat grayish limestone. The text is divided into two columns, much like a Hebrew text on a scroll. The letters are written below thin horizontal lines scratched into the surface of the stone that are clearly visible to the naked eye. Yardeni and Elizur describe the script as "a 'Jewish' formal hand, typical of the Herodian period," and date it "securely" to the late first century B.C.E. or the early first century C.E.³ Even though on paleographic grounds the *Hazon Gabriel* is related to the scripts of the Dead Sea Scrolls, there are good reasons why it is most unlikely that the *Hazon Gabriel* comes from the Qumran

---

I presented an earlier version of this paper at the Internationale Ökumenische Konferenz der Hebräisch-Dozenten/innen on May 1, 2010, at the University of Rostock, Germany, and would like to thank Professor Martin Rösel for the kind invitation and his valuable comments.

1. Ada Yardeni and Binyamin Elizur, "A Prophetic Text on Stone from the First Century BCE: First Publication" (in Hebrew), *Cathedra* 123 (2007): 155–66. An abbreviated English version of the article appears in this volume, "A Hebrew Prophetic Text on Stone from the Early Herodian Period: A Preliminary Report."

2. See Jeselsohn's article in this volume, "The *Jeselsohn Stone*: Discovery and Publication," in which he tells the story of the purchase and early work on the inscription.

3. Yardeni and Elizur, "Hebrew Prophetic Text," in this volume, p. 25.

community.⁴ These include the frequent use of the name of God and the absence of any explicitly sectarian language or motifs. Still, the obvious affinities with the Dead Sea fragments undoubtedly contributed to the text's appeal.

The second reason why the *Hazon Gabriel* attracted attention was the numerous publications of Israel Knohl of the Hebrew University in Jerusalem. Knohl was instrumental in starting the discussion on this difficult text. His work is in many respects ingenious, if at times controversial. In a series of publications, Knohl argued that the *Hazon Gabriel* is a messianic text in which a messianic figure dies and is resurrected on the third day. It was this idea, according to Knohl, that later inspired Jesus regarding his own death and resurrection. The following brief quotation from the introduction to Knohl's book *Messiahs and Resurrection in 'The Gabriel Revelation'* captures well the nature and scope of Knohl's original thesis.

> The discovery of *The Gabriel Revelation*, then, reveals far more than the messianic hope of the 4 BCE rebels; its unusual portrayal of the Messiah sheds new light on Jesus' act of self-sacrifice. It seems that Jesus did indeed possess a messianic secret. The son of Joseph the carpenter of Nazareth probably believed himself to be the embodiment of the Messiah the son of Joseph. Inspired by such secret texts as *The Gabriel Revelation*, Jesus followed the path of the tortured and killed Messiah, who was believed to be resurrected by Gabriel on the third day and to have placed the sign of the coming of redemption and salvation.⁵

It does not surprise that such recently rediscovered ancient text would attract some attention. This short paragraph already includes several of Knohl's hypotheses worth parsing. One is that the *Hazon Gabriel* is a "secret" text. Unfortunately, Knohl does not tell us why he thinks the text is secret, and the inscription does not make that clear either. A second hypothesis concerns the Messiah son of Joseph, to whom Knohl finds a reference at the end of line 16. He reads the word in question as אפרים, "Ephraim," for Knohl a designation of the suffering Messiah. However, the reading is contested (the word אפרים has to be reconstructed and is not attested anywhere else in the text), and even if the text had "Ephraim," it is not clear that the author of the *Hazon Gabriel* refers to the Messiah son of Joseph, as Knohl claims (we will return to this point below). A third hypothesis concerns the possible connection between the violent death of the Messiah son of Joseph and Jesus, who, according to Knohl, interpreted his own life and death in light of the Messiah who preceded him. There are several problems here. First, the Messiah son of Joseph is securely attested only in texts that are significantly

---

4. Ada Yardeni, "A New Dead Sea Scroll in Stone? Bible-like Prophecy Was Mounted in a Wall 2,000 Years Ago," *BAR* 34, no. 1 (2008): 60–61.

5. Israel Knohl, *Messiahs and Resurrection in 'The Gabriel Revelation'* (Kogod Library of Judaic Studies; London/New York: Continuum, 2009), xiii.

later than Jesus; second, it is notoriously difficult to distinguish between Jesus' self-perception and the ways in which his followers wrote about his life about a century after the *Hazon Gabriel* was written; and, third, we know nothing about the original context of the *Hazon Gabriel* or its reception history and therefore need to exercise the greatest caution when speculating about the possible influence the text may have had on its first readers. A fourth hypothesis, finally, is that Gabriel speaks in the *Hazon Gabriel* about the death and resurrection of the Messiah "on the third day." Here Knohl refers to line 80, in which Gabriel is the speaker. At first Knohl argued that the angel tells the Messiah that he will be resurrected on the third day. But as he clarifies in his essay in this volume, Knohl himself has since abandoned that reading and no longer maintains that Gabriel speaks about the resurrection on the third day.[6]

Since 2007, several scholars have investigated the stone and written on its inscription. Yuval Goren has submitted the rock to a microarchaeological examination and has confirmed the authenticity of the inscription.[7] Moshe Bar-Asher and Gary Rendsburg have produced detailed studies on the language of the text. They corroborated the initial hypothesis of Yardeni and Elizur that the text stems from the late Second Temple period.[8] Alexey Yuditsky and Elisha Qimron have produced their own edition of the text with many improved readings.[9] And David Hamidović has proposed that the *Hazon Gabriel* contains an apocalyptic vision about the final war and that it was written in a Jewish community in Transjordan, possibly in a community of Essenes.[10]

The reconstruction of the inscription, its paleography and lexicon have received a fair amount of scrutiny. Apart from Knohl's numerous publications, however, relatively little has been written on the actual content of the text and its meaning. The fact that the inscription is only partially preserved imposes some severe limits on what we can say about the *Hazon Gabriel* with any degree of confidence, but enough of the text survives for us to offer a few preliminary observations on its literary form, story line, and main motifs.

---

6. Israel Knohl, "The Apocalyptic and Messianic Dimensions of the *Gabriel Revelation* in Their Historical Context," p. 43 n. 12.

7. Yuval Goren, "Micromorphologic Examination of the *Gabriel Revelation* Stone," *IEJ* 58 (2008): 220–29.

8. Moshe Bar-Asher, "On the Language of 'The Vision of Gabriel,'" *RevQ* 23 (2008): 491–524; "On the Langue of 'The Vision of Gabriel'" (in Hebrew), in *Meghillot: Studies in the Dead Sea Scrolls 7* (2009)): 193–226; Gary A. Rendsburg, "Linguistic and Stylistic Notes to the Hazon Gabriel Inscription," *DSD* 16 (2009): 107–16.

9. Alexey (Eliyahu) Yuditsky and Elisha Qimron, "Notes on the Inscription 'The Vision of Gabriel'" (in Hebrew), *Cathedra* 133 (2009): 133–44. An abbreviated English version of the article appears in this volume, "Notes on the So-Called 'Gabriel Vision' Inscription."

10. David Hamidović, "La *Vision de Gabriel*," *RHPR* 89 (2009): 147–68.

The Hazon Gabriel: Story Line and Main Motifs

The first ten lines of the inscription unfortunately are illegible, and so Yuditsky and Qimron begin their edition with line 11.[11] In line 10, Yardeni and Elizur read the word שאלת, "you have asked." The verbal root שאל, "to ask," reappears in the next line, line 11, שאלני. The form could be a participle, "you are asking me," or, as in line 21 below, an imperative, "ask me!"[12] As the case may be, it appears that in its original form the *Hazon Gabriel* took the form of a dialogue—or of a sequence of conversations. A major difficulty in reading the preserved text portions is that it is often unclear who is talking to whom. Similarly, in line 11 we do not know who the speaker is, nor do we know the nature of the question. The grammatical form in line 10 (the second person masculine singular) makes it likely that this is an individual who enters into a conversation with God.

In the second half of line 11, the response to the question comes in the form of the messenger formula known from the biblical prophets, כו אמר אלהים צבאות, "Thus says the God of Hosts."[13] It is not God who answers the question. Instead, the answer is given by a respondent who claims to speak with divine authority. He could be a prophet, possibly associated with the temple in Jerusalem, since Jerusalem emerges as the main subject of the inscription. Alternatively the interlocutor speaking on God's behalf could be an angel, perhaps the angel Gabriel mentioned by name in lines 77, 80, and 83, but this is not clear. What is clear, however, is that the dialogue that runs through the *Hazon Gabriel* and gives it its literary form is of a revelatory nature. The dialogue between a divine and a human interlocutor has precedents in the Hebrew Bible, in wisdom literature (e.g., Job 3–27) and in the prophetic disputation. It is known from other texts of the late Second Temple period—e.g., Daniel 10–12 and the Pseudo-Ezekiel text from Qumran—and, from a slightly later period, *4 Ezra* and *2 Baruch*. All of these texts are eschatological in their outlook. In all of them a human individual receives instructions about the eschatological future, either directly from God or through an interpreting angel, and in all texts visions are a principal means of revealing the secret lore to a human recipient. In the surviving text fragments of

---

11. Bar-Asher, "On the Language," 491 n. 4: "Lines 1–10, 32–56, and 59–64 are almost entirely obliterated, and very little can be read within them. Lines 66–87 are damaged at their ends, and there are other smaller lacunae in other lines, as well."

12. Gary Rendsburg, "*Hazon Gabriel*: A Grammatical Sketch," in this volume, reads the word שאלני in line 11 as a participle. It is preceded by the personal pronoun of the second person masculine singular אתה, "you," which may corroborate that the form is a participle, "you are asking me," unless the pronoun refers to the *tetragrammaton* that precedes, "You are the Lord."

13. Note the unusual אלהים צבאות, "God of Hosts," repeated in *HazGab* 20, 25–26, 29. In the Hebrew Bible, the expression occurs only in the Psalms (Pss 59:6; 80:5, 8, 15, 20; 84:9). More common is the construct form, אלהי צבאות (2 Sam 5:10; 1 Kgs 19:10, 14; Jer 5:14; 15:16; 35:17; 38:17; Ps 89:9; etc.).

the *Hazon Gabriel*, no vision is mentioned, though we cannot exclude the possibility that the text began with a vision report or that the surviving stele is part of a longer composition that included a vision.

The main topic of the dialogue that unfolds, we learn in line 12, is Jerusalem. The respondent declares that he wants to speak of the great things that are happening to Jerusalem, ואגדה בגדלות ירושלם, "I will recount the greatness of Jerusalem." The language is reminiscent of Jer 33:3. There God bids the prophet Jeremiah to ask him about the future of Jerusalem and promises that he will reveal to him the city's future fate. "And I will tell you great and hidden things (ואגידה לך גדלות ובצרות) that you have not known."[14] The situation may well be similar in the *Hazon Gabriel*: God is about to reveal to the questioner the secrets regarding the eschatological fate of Jerusalem.

The impression is corroborated in the next two lines. Lines 13–14 begin once again with the messenger formula, [כו] אמר יהוה אלה[י] ישראל. Then Yuditsky and Qimron read, הנה כול הגאים צובאים על ירושלם, "Soon all the nations fight against Jerusalem."[15] The reading of צובאים, "they are storming/fighting," is disputed. Yardeni and Elizur leave a gap, yet Yuditsky and Qimron claim that the word "fits the traces and the size of the lacuna."[16] If they are right, then we have here a description of the event that marks the beginning of the "great things" (line 12) that will happen to Jerusalem at the end of days: the storm of the nations against Jerusalem. The motif is known from Zechariah 14 (cf. Joel 3), Psalm 2, and *4 Ezra* 13. The language in the *Hazon Gabriel* is again biblical. Isaiah 29, for example, speaks of a siege of Jerusalem, "the multitude of all the nations that fight against Ariel (כל הגוים הצבאים על אריאל)" (Isa 29:7), "the multitude of all the nations ... fight against Mount Zion (כל הגוים הצבאים על הר ציון)" (Isa 29.8). Zechariah 14 also speaks of the eschatological gathering of all the nations against Jerusalem. Verse 12 of that chapter gives a gruesome account of what will happen to Israel's enemies at the end of time, to "all the peoples that wage war against Jerusalem (כל העמים אשר צבאו על ירושלם)." The eschatological connotations, in the Zechariah passage and in *Hazon Gabriel*, are unmistakable.

The next lines of the inscription contain one of the most contested passages in the text. Qimron and Yuditsky translate lines 15–19 as follows. "The prophets and the elders [and] the pious ones. David, my servant, asked me: Answer me, I ask you for the sign. Thus said [Y]HWH of Hosts, the God of Israel: My son, I have a new testament for Israel." This short passage begins with a list of

---

14. In Deut 10:21; Pss 71:16, 106:21, גדלות, "great things," designates the great deeds of God; cf. Job 5:9; 9:10; 37:5.

15. The tense is unclear, since the Hebrew uses the participle. The storm of the nations may relate to an actual historical assault on Jerusalem at the time of the author, in which case we should translate in the present tense, or it may predict an eschatological event that is yet to occur, which would be more in line with the biblical texts on which the *Hazon Gabriel* is based.

16. Qimron and Yuditsky, "Notes on the So-Called 'Gabriel Vision' Inscription," in this volume, p. 34.

three groups, the prophets, the elders, and the pious, groups of some authority in the community, but who are not further identified in the text. Next it is God who is speaking, either directly or through an intermediary—this is not clear. God relates how David, whom he calls his "servant," had asked him for a sign and is now demanding an answer. The divine answer is again introduced by the messenger formula, כו אמר [י]הוה צבאות אלהי ישראל (lines 17–18). Now God addresses the figure of David directly, calls him "my son (בני)," and tells him that God has "a new testament" (ברית חדשה, lines 18–19; Jer 31:31) for Israel.[17]

In the Hebrew Bible, God addresses the king as his son in Ps 2:7 and 2 Sam 7:14. In 2 Sam 7:5, 8 God calls David his servant, the same language we find in *HazGab* 16 (עבדי דוד, "my servant David"). The figure of David in the *Hazon Gabriel* could therefore be a king of the line of David, or he could be the Davidic Messiah. The text itself does not make this clear, and both interpretations can be defended. The argument that David in the *Hazon Gabriel* is a royal rather than a messianic figure is supported by two observations. One is the absence of any messianic titles from the *Hazon Gabriel*, titles such as "Son of Man" that are characteristic of other messianic compositions of the time.[18] The other observations is that the figure of David remains entirely passive in our text. He does not get involved in the events of the end-time: rather than defeating Israel's enemies and sitting down to judge them, he turns to God and asks for a sign. The strongest argument in support of the hypothesis that David in the *Hazon Gabriel* is the Davidic Messiah is the unambiguously eschatological perspective that governs the text. In that case the author would have interpreted Psalm 2 and 2 Samuel 7 as messianic texts.

If we assume that the siege of Jerusalem from lines 13–14 is still the subject, then the situation that is here presumed becomes clearer. Of all the people who are besieged in Jerusalem—prophets, elders, and the pious—it is the Davidic king, or the Davidic Messiah, who approaches God on behalf of the others and asks God for a sign. The situation is reminiscent of Isaiah 7, where God prompts King Ahaz to ask for a sign in light of the approaching foe who will soon lay siege to Jerusalem. "Ask a sign (שאל לך אות) of the Lord your God" (Isa 7:11), a command Ahaz refuses to follow. If we are right in our reading, then *HazGab* 15–19 relates the duress of those who are besieged in the city and underscores the lead-

---

17. The reading of ברית חדשה, "new testament," in lines 18–19 is contested. Yardeni and Elizur have וכרי. קדשה, which they render "sanctity (?)/sanctify (/)." Knohl (*Messiahs and Resurrection*, 11) reads lines 18–19 differently, גני מבוכרים קדשה לישראל, "my gardens are ripe, My holy thing for Israel," though in his last rendition ("Apocalyptic and Messianic Dimension," in this volume), he reads ברית ח\קדשה, "I have a new/holy covenant for Israel."

18. Martin Hengel, "Christological Titles in Early Christianity," in *The Messiah: Developments in Earliest Judaism and Christianity. The First Princeton Symposium on Judaism and Christian Origins* (ed. James H. Charlesworth; Minneapolis: Fortress, 1992), 425–48. The only possible exception in the *Hazon Gabriel* is line 18, where Qimron and Yuditsky, followed by Knohl, read בני, "my son." The reference here clearly is to "my servant David" mentioned in line 16.

ing role of the one whom God calls "my servant David." He is about to receive the sign for which he had previously asked.[19]

The answer to the royal request for a sign then follows in lines 19–21. If we stay with Qimron and Yuditsky, the text reads as follows: "By three days you shall know. Thus says YHWH, God of Hosts, the God of Israel: Evil will be defeated by justice." In Isaiah 7, the sign given to Ahaz is the birth of a baby. By the time the baby can express her or his preferences the danger will be averted and the approaching enemy defeated. In essence, the sign is a measurement of time. Similarly in the *Hazon Gabriel*, the sign is the promise that already in three days the questioner will witness that evil will be broken before righteousness (נשבר הרע מלפני הצדק).[20] This is the assurance that the nations that are now storming Jerusalem will be defeated in only a few days.

Knohl reconstructs the passage rather differently. He reads the last word in line 16 as אפרים, "Ephraim," and the verb in line 16, בקש, as an imperative, "ask!" In his reconstruction, the beginning of line 17 reads ישׂ[ים], "[that he] place," so that the two lines together read, "My servant David, ask of Ephraim [that he] place the sign; (this) I ask of you." Knohl furthermore asserts that in the *Hazon Gabriel* Ephraim does not stand for the northern kingdom (as in the Hebrew Bible) or for the Pharisees (as in the Dead Sea Scrolls)[21] but for a messianic figure, the Messiah son of Joseph, of whom we read in the Talmud, in the *Pesiqta Rabbati*, and in the *Sefer Zerubbabel*. The *Hazon Gabriel* hence includes the oldest reference to this figure in Jewish literature. In other words, lines 16–17 refer to two messianic figures who are here interacting with each other, the Messiah son of David and the Messiah son of Joseph. Moreover, the former is subordinate to the latter, as God addresses David and asks him to request a sign from Ephraim.[22]

Knohl's interpretation of lines 16–17, which is crucial for his understanding of the text as a whole, is problematic for at least two reasons. First, the reading of the last word in line 16 is contested. Even though Knohl asserts, "in my view, the

---

19. A similar reference to a sign given by God to confirm an eschatological prophecy is found in the Book of Mysteries at Qumran (1Q27 1 i 5): וזה לכם האות, "and this will be for you the sign." See also 4Q387 2 iii 5–6; 4Q389 8 ii 5–6; *2 Bar.* 25:2–4; Exod 3:12; 1 Sam 14:10; 2 Kgs 19:29; 20:9. Menahem Kister, "Wisdom Literature and Its Relation to Other Genres: From Ben Sira to *Mysteries*," in *Sapiential Perspectives: Wisdom Literature in Light of the Dead Sea Scrolls. Proceedings of the Sixth International Symposium of the Orion Center for the Study of the Dead Sea Scrolls and Associated Literature, 20–22 May, 2001* (ed. John J. Collins, Gregory E. Sterling and Ruth A. Clements; STDJ 51; Leiden: Brill, 2004), 35–36.

20. On the expression נשבר הרע ("evil will be broken") as an expression of the crushing of the enemy, see Dan 8:8, "the great horn [Alexander] was broken (נשברה הקרן הגדולה)"; and Jer 22:20, "all your lovers are crushed (כי נשברו כל מאהביך)."

21. Hanan Eshel, "Ephraim and Manasseh," in *Encyclopedia of the Dead Sea Scrolls* (ed. Lawrence H. Schiffman and James C. VanderKam; 2 vols.; Oxford: Oxford University Press, 2000), 1:253–54.

22. Knohl, *Messiahs and Resurrection*, 10–11; and idem, "Apocalyptic and Messianic Dimensions," in this volume, pp. 40–44.

reading of the word as אפרים (Ephraim) is certain,"[23] Yardeni and Elizur place a question mark next to the word,[24] and Qimron and Yuditsky reconstruct the line based on Prov 22:21 (להשיב אמרים אמת, "so that you may give a true answer") and note, "the second letter in אמרים can hardly be *pe*."[25] And, second, even *if* the word read Ephraim, it is far from obvious that the author of the *Hazon Gabriel* is here referring to a messianic figure. As we noted, the Messiah son of Joseph is attested only in much later texts, and even there he is not commanding the Davidic Messiah.[26]

In lines 21–22 the dialogue continues in language that is already familiar from the previous lines, שאלני ואגיד לכה מה הצמח הרע הזה, "Ask me and I will tell you what this bad plant is." Similar to lines 11–12 above, the questioner is asked, presumably by God or by a revealing angel, to pose another question. He is promised that this, in turn, will lead to further revelations, in this case about the nature of "the bad plant (הצמח הרע)." The word for "plant," צמח, is taken from the prophets.[27] See, for example, Jer 23:5, "The days are surely coming, says the Lord, when I will raise up for David a righteous Branch (והקמתי לדוד צמח צדיק), and he shall reign as king and deal wisely," or Jer 33:15, "I will cause a branch of righteousness to spring up for David (אצמיח לדוד צמח צדקה)."[28] Early interpreters found here a reference to the Davidic Messiah. Note the prophecy for the tribe of Judah at the end of 4QCommentary on Genesis A (4Q252), "Until the Messiah of Righteousness comes, the Branch of David (עד בוא משיח הצדק צמח דויד)," or the messianic reference in the War Rule (4Q285), "A shoot will emerge from the stump of Jesse [...] the Branch of David ([...] ויצא חוטר מגזע ישי צמח דוד)."[29] In the *Hazon Gabriel*, however, the branch is evil, not good. Most likely this is a reference to a false king or messiah, who is about to be defeated. It may be that this is the leader of the troops who are storming towards Jerusalem, but the text does not make this clear.

---

23. Knohl, *Messiahs and Resurrection*, 10.
24. Yardeni and Elizur, "A Hebrew Prophetic Text on Stone," in this volume, p. 15.
25. Qimron and Yuditsky, "Notes on the So-Called 'Gabriel Vision' Inscription," in this volume, p. 34.
26. For a more detailed refutation, see the article by John J. Collins, "Gabriel and David: Some Reflections on an Enigmatic Text," in this volume.
27. See the brief overview by Loren T. Stuckenbruck, "The Plant Metaphor in Its Inner-Enochic and Early Jewish Context," in *Enoch and Qumran Origins: New Light on a Forgotten Connection* (ed. Gabriele Boccaccini; Grand Rapids: Eerdmans, 2005), 210–13.
28. Similarly Isa 60:21; 61:3; Zech 3:8; 6:12. Also *1 En.* 10:3, 16; 93:5, 10; *Jub.* 1:16; 16:26; 21:24; and 36:6.
29. Bilha Nitzan, "Benedictions and Instructions for the Eschatological Community (11QBer; 4Q285)," *RevQ* 16 (1993): 77–90; John J. Collins, "A Shoot from the Stump of Jesse," *The Scepter and the Star: Messianism in Light of the Dead Sea Scrolls* (2nd ed.; Grand Rapids: Eerdmans, 2010), 52–78; Loren T. Stuckenbruck, "Messianic Ideas in the Apocalyptic and Related Literature of Early Judaism," in *The Messiah in the Old and New Testaments* (ed. Stanley E. Porter; McMaster New Testament Studies; Grand Rapids: Eerdmans, 2007), 90–113.

Here, too, Knohl's interpretation differs significantly. For him, the enigmatic figure of the "evil branch" is "a precursor to what would subsequently be termed the Antichrist."[30] This figure pretends to be the Messiah and redeemer, while in effect his whole intention is to corrupt and to lead astray. Knohl bases much of his interpretation on the word in line 22 that immediately follows the reference to "this evil branch (הצמח הרע הזה)." Neither Yardeni and Elizur or Qimron and Yuditsky attempt to read the word but leave a gap in their editions and only read a few letters. Knohl reconstructs לובנסד, even though he readily admits that this "expression is not known elsewhere."[31] He then goes on to translate the mysterious word as "white plaster" (לובן סיד), or "plastered white" (לובן סוד), a phrase that connotes hypocrisy and for which Knohl finds analogies in the New Testament. However, Knohl's interpretation is not without problems. The New Testament passages that Knohl lists that refer to whitewashing as a form of hypocrisy (Matt 23:27; Acts 23:3) do not talk about the Antichrist. Moreover, there is nothing in the inscription itself to support Knohl's Antichrist hypothesis apart from the reference to the "evil branch" and the word that follows it. That word has to be reconstructed, however, and Knohl's hypothetical reading again relies on traditions, in this case about the Antichrist, that postdate the *Hazon Gabriel*.[32]

The next lines, *HazGab* 22–24, form a transition in the narrative from the description of the onslaught on Jerusalem to the announcement of the divine intervention. The individual who was just prompted to ask further questions is now encouraged to endure. He is told to remain standing, albeit with some physical support from the angel, in order to receive further revelations. "You stand, the angel supports you (אתה עומד המלאך הוא בסמכך)." This transitional scene is patterned after a similar transitional scene in Dan 8:15–19, with which it shares several features. Like the anonymous individual in the *Hazon Gabriel*, Daniel is in need of a revelatory interpretation of what will happen at "the appointed time of the end" (Dan 8:19). The interpreting angel in the book of Daniel is none other than the angel Gabriel (8:16). And before he offers his inspired interpretation, the angel strengthens the seer physically (8:18), just as the human interlocutor in the *Hazon Gabriel* is propped up by the angel (lines 22–23).

Next the seer is told not to be dismayed. We again follow the rendition by Qimron and Yuditsky. "Fear not! Blessed be (or: Bless ... !) the glory of the Lord God from his place (ברוך כבוד יהוה אלהים מן מקומו)." The language of the phrase

---

30. Knohl, *Messiahs and Resurrection*, 12, 74–83; idem, "On 'The Son of God,' Armilus, and Messiah Son of Joseph" (in Hebrew), *Tarbiz* 68 (1998): 13–38; John J. Collins, "A Messiah before Jesus?", and "An Essene Messiah? Comments on Israel Knohl, *The Messiah before Jesus*," in *Christian Beginnings and the Dead Sea Scrolls* (ed. John J. Collins and Craig A. Evans; Acadia Studies in Bible and Theology; Grand Rapids: Baker Academic, 2006), 15–35 and 37–44.

31. Knohl, *Messiahs and Resurrection*, 13.

32. Hamidović ("La *Vision de Gabriel*," 153) translates lines 21–22, "Réclame-moi et je te raconterai ce qu'est ce germe mauvais pour moi, fils du conseil."

is biblical.³³ The formula "Blessed be the glory of the Lord" already anticipates the divine action that is announced in the next sentence in lines 24-25. "In a short while there will be trembling,³⁴ and I will cause the heaven and the earth to quake." The divine intervention takes the form of a theophany of apocalyptic proportions: God is about to come to Jerusalem's rescue and will shake up heaven and earth (Zech 14:3-5). Here the author of the *Hazon Gabriel* inserts a quotation from Hag 2:6: "In a little while, I will shake the heavens and the earth (עוד אחת מעט היא ואני מרעיש את השמים ואת הארץ)." Similarly Joel 4:16: "The Lord roars from Zion, and utters his voice from Jerusalem, and the heavens and the earth shake (ורעשו שמים וארץ)." God leaves his heavenly abode to rescue beleaguered Jerusalem.

The glory of the Lord continues to be the subject in the next lines as well. The seer is consoled and learns more about the nature of the divine intervention. The reconstruction of lines 25-29 by Qimron and Yuditsky makes good sense, "Lo, the glory of the Lord, the God of Hosts, the God of Israel, the God of the chariots, has heard the cry of the devastation of Jerusalem. And the cities of Judah he will console for the sake of the Host of the angel Michael and for all the lovers who requested from you . . . ." According to this reading of the text, the passage begins with the glory of the Lord (כבוד יהוה; line 25), which the seer had just been asked to bless (ברוך כבוד יהוה; line 23). There follow three divine attributes: God is the God of Hosts (אלהים צבאות), the God of Israel (אלהי ישראל), and the God of the chariots (אלה המרכבות). God will intervene, we learn next, because he has heard (שמע, in the prophetic past) the outcry of Jerusalem and has seen her devastation.³⁵ When God comes, God will console not just Jerusalem but all the cities of Judah.³⁶ God will intervene for the sake of the angel Michael, together with the angelic host, and for "all the lovers" (ולכול האהבין).³⁷ In the book of Daniel, the angel Michael is fighting the heavenly battle on behalf of Israel (Dan

---

33. On the assurance "Fear not! (אל תירה)," see Dan 8:12, "Fear not, Daniel! (אל תירא דניאל)," and Dan 10:19, "Do not fear, greatly beloved! (אל תירא איש חמדות)." For the second half of the sentence, see Isa 26:21, "For the Lord comes out from his place (יהוה יצא ממקומו) to punish the inhabitants of the earth"; Ezek 3:12, "And blessed be the glory of the Lord from its place (ברוך כבוד יהוה ממקומו)"; and Mic 1:3, "For lo, the Lord is coming out of his place (כי הנה יהוה יצא ממקומו)" (quoted in 1QpMic 5.2).

34. The verbal noun קיטוט is not attested in Biblical Hebrew. Its meaning "trembling" can be deduced from the use of the root קטט in Job 8:14; so Gary A. Rendsburg, "Linguistic and Stylistic Notes to the Hazon Gabriel Inscription," *DSD* 16 (2009): 108-10.

35. The Hebrew expression קול שוד ירושלם in line 27 is reconstructed. The expression שוד ירושלם is not attested in the Hebrew Bible. On שוד, "devastation," see Isa 13:6; 51:19; 59:7; 60:18; Jer 6:7; 20:8; and Ezek 45:9.

36. On line 27, ואת ערי יהודה ינחם, "and the cities of Judah he will comfort," see Isa 40:1, "Comfort, comfort my people (נחמו נחמו עמי)."

37. See also line 68 below, אוהבין רבים ליהוה צבאות, "many lovers has the Lord of Hosts." Yardeni and Elizur and Knohl read in line 28 מיכאל ולכול האחרין, "Michael and all the others," likely a reference to the other angels (cf. Dan 10:13-14).

10:13, 21). He is "the great prince, the protector of your [Daniel's] people" (Dan 12:1; compare *1 En.* 9:1; 20:5; 71:9), and so his appearance at this moment in the *Hazon Gabriel* seems appropriate. It is not clear, however, who "the lovers" are. They could be the accompanying angels, or even the faithful in Jerusalem who love God. It is on their behalf, after all, that God appears.

Yardeni and Elizur and Knohl read this passage rather differently. The main difference starts in line 26 with the words אלה המרכבות, which Qimron and Yuditsky translate "God of the chariots" (cf. Deut 32:15, 17), but which Yardeni and Elizur render, "these are the chariots." And whereas Qimron and Yuditsky read the last word in line 26 as a verb, שמע, "he heard," Yardeni and Elizur read that word as the number seven, שבע. Hence, they reconstruct lines 26–27 as follows. "These are the chariots, seven, [un]to (?) the gate (?) of Jerusalem, and the gates of Judah . . ."[38] According to their reconstruction, God sends seven chariots to Jerusalem and other places throughout Judah. In either case, whether God is the God of chariots or whether God sends seven chariots, the passage marks the beginning of the divine intervention.[39]

The text continues in line 29 with another messenger formula, כו אמר יהוה אלהים צבאות, "Thus says the Lord God . . ." (cf. line 13). There follows in line 30 a list of numerals one through six (compare line 15 above). Unfortunately we do not know what is being counted here.

According to Qimron and Yuditsky, line 31 reads [ויש]אל מלאך ... מהו ואמרה עץ, "And the angel asked . . . 'What is this?' And I said, 'A tree . . . .'" The reading of the word עץ, "tree," seems certain, though without any context it is impossible to make much sense of this passage and to know which tree this is.[40] It appears, however, that the dialogue continues at this point. Only a few more words survive of the remainder of the first column. Jerusalem is mentioned again at least twice (in lines 36 and 39), which corroborates our earlier impression that the eschatological fate of the city is the main topic in the *Hazon Gabriel*.

Unfortunately, the opening lines of column B are only poorly preserved. Line 52 may include the word "angels" (ה[מ]לאכים), and line 54 refers again to the "three days" (שלשת ימין) familiar already from line 19 (לשלשת ימין). This means

---

38. Similarly Hamidović, "La *Vision de Gabriel*," 153, who translates, "Ce (sont) les sept chars [à] la porte de Jérusalem et aux portes de Juda." Later (p. 157) Hamidović explains, "La guerre eschatologique débute avec les sept chars qui circonscrivent le périmètre de Jérusalem, cf. *Targum des petits prophètes* Za 12,10; 1QM I, 3, et de Juda en s'installant aux portes. [...] Les sept chars transportent probablement les sept archanges."

39. See the discussion of the use of chariots in related literature by Kelley Coblentz Bautch, "Hosts, Holy Ones, and the Words of Gabriel: The Angelology of *Hazon Gabriel* in the Context of Second Temple and Late Antique Literature," in this volume.

40. Elsewhere in apocalyptic literature one finds references to the tree of life, e.g., *1 En.* 25:5; *3 En.* 23:18; *T. Levi* 18:10–11; *Apoc. Mos.* 28:4; *Apoc. Elijah* 5:6; and Rev 2:7; 22:2, 14, 19, but not enough of the *Hazon Gabriel* survives to argue that this is the reference here.

that language and motifs repeat themselves in the second column of the inscription, but we are lacking any context to be more precise.

According to Yardeni and Elizur, we are on safer ground beginning in line 57, which they reconstruct as follows: ... סתום דם טבחי ירושלם, "closed (?). The blood of the slaughters (?)/sacrifices (?) of Jerusalem."[41] In their annotations, Yardeni and Elizur further reflect on the meaning of דם טבחי ירושלם. The word טבח can either mean "slaughter" or "sacrifice." If the meaning is "slaughter," then it is conceivable that the *Hazon Gabriel* is here referring to a specific historical event. If the text was indeed composed during the first century B.C.E., then the allusion could be to the fall of Jerusalem to the Roman general Pompey in 63 B.C.E., or, as Knohl argues, to the uprising following the death of Herod in the year 4 B.C.E. In the end, however, Yardeni and Elizur dismiss the historical interpretation and opt for the latter meaning of טבח, "sacrifice." It is more likely, they conclude, that the phrase refers "to the flesh of the sacrifices in the Jerusalem Temple, i.e. to the feasts held in Jerusalem."[42] In that case the *Hazon Gabriel* describes the cessation of the sacrificial cult in Jerusalem.

Knohl, however, takes the other route. He finds in the phrase a description of the attack on the city's inhabitants and translates "the blood of the slaughtered of Jerusalem." Further, whereas for Yardeni and Elizur the first word in line 57, סתום, connotes the end of the sacrifices, Knohl prefers the meaning "to seal up." In support of his reading he points to Daniel 8, a text that is closely related to the *Hazon Gabriel*. There, in v. 26, Daniel is told to "seal up the vision" (ואתה סתם החזון), since the vision concerns events that lie in the eschatological future. By analogy, Knohl argues, "in *The Gabriel Revelation*, the recipient of the vision is asked to suppress his prophecy regarding those who will be slaughtered in Jerusalem."[43] But it is not clear that the two texts really are analogous. Daniel is asked to seal up the vision, whereas in the *Hazon Gabriel*, the word סתום is followed by the word "blood."[44] If anything, the seer is asked to "seal up the blood," which makes little sense.

The next lines are again illegible. The readable section resumes in line 65 with the phrase שלושה קדושי העולם, "the three holy ones of the world/of eternity." This is possibly a reference to three angelic figures (compare line 76 below).[45] The speakers of the following lines are an otherwise unidentified group who address

---

41. Qimron and Yuditsky do not comment on this line apart from noticing in their "Further New Readings" that are attached to their article "Notes on the So-Called 'Gabriel Vision' Inscription" in this volume that כי should be read כו, as already previously suggested for line 11. Hamidović ("La *Vision de Gabriel*," 154) translates, "Garde fermé le sang des massacres de Jérusalem."

42. Yardeni and Elizur, "Hebrew Prophetic Text on Stone," in this volume, p. 18.

43. Knohl, *Messiahs and Resurrection*, 22.

44. Similarly, see 4Q300 1 ii 2, כי חתום מכם [ח]תם החזון, "for sealed up has been from you [the s]eal of the vision."

45. Note also the designation of the two angels in Dan 8:13, whom Daniel overhears

God in the first person plural. Yardeni and Elizur leave a gap at the beginning of line 66 and read the second word as שלום, "peace," whereas Qimron and Yudtisky assert that the first word is [י]רושלים, "Jerusalem." In that case the we-group may well be the people who are enclosed in Jerusalem and who are now turning to God. More specifically, they are making a confessional statement. "On you we are relying, not on flesh, not on blood" (עליך אנחנו בטוחין [לו על] בשר לו על] דם). According to this reading, which is conjectural, the we-group affirms their loyalty to God. Underlying their statement is an opposition between reliance on God and reliance on human strength. The group declares that they trust in God alone and not in human strength made of flesh and blood.

The text continues in lines 67–68, "This is the chariot of . . . . Many are those who love the Lord of hosts, the God of Israel . . . (זו המרכבה של ... אוהבין רבים ליהוה צבאת אלי ישראל ...)." The motif of the chariots appeared already in line 26, where it is part of the divine epithet "the God of chariots (אלה המרכבות)." Here those who are beleaguered in Jerusalem use the same epithet to profess that their only hope comes from God, who will act as a divine warrior on their behalf. The we-group then continues to affirm that those who are loyal to their God are many (אוהבין רבים ליהוה; see line 28). Lines 66–68 appear to inject a note of confidence into the text, in which an anonymous group professes their dependence on and allegiance to God who alone can come to their aid.

Yardeni and Elizur, again followed by Knohl, propose a different reading. For them the first word in line 67, בשר, is not the noun meaning "flesh" (which fits well with the word דם, "blood," in the same line); they treat it as a verbal imperative, meaning "bear tidings!" Hence they translate, "Inform him of the blood of this chariot of them (בשר לו על דם זו המרכבה שלהן)." It is not clear, however, what the phrase "blood of this chariot" (דם זו המרכבה) means, or who is to be informed of the blood. This is where Knohl comes in. He proposes that the blood is the blood of those who were killed in Jerusalem (compare his reading of line 57). The image of the chariot, Knohl continues to argue, is taken from 2 Kgs 2:11, the chariot in which Elijah ascends into heaven. In the *Hazon Gabriel*, the blood of those who were slain effectively becomes their chariot. "Through the recipient of the vision, God promises that the blood of the martyrs will serve as their chariot. [. . .] I assume that the speaker of the previous line is one of those slain, and that his words 'in you we trust' express the hope of the martyrs for ascension."[46] Maybe. It remains rather unclear, however, what exactly the alleged connection is between the *Hazon Gabriel* and 2 Kings 2. The term in 2 Kgs 2:11 is רכב אש, "chariot of fire," not המרכבה, "chariot," as in *HazGab* 67, and there are no martyrs involved in the ascension story of Elijah. Even if we stay with

---

discussing the meaning of the vision, "Then I heard a holy one speaking (ואשמעה אחד קדוש מדבר) . . . ." The Aramaic equivalent is found in Dan 4:10, 20, "a holy watcher" (עיר וקדיש).

46. Knohl, *Messiahs and Resurrection*, 23–24.

the *Hazon Gabriel*, it is not clear how the blood of the martyrs could become a chariot that supposedly transports them heavenward.

In line 69, the *Hazon Gabriel* uses once again the messenger formula, כה אמר יהוה צבאת אלהי ישראל, "Thus says the Lord of Hosts, the God of Israel," to introduce the divine response to the profession of the we-group. Qimron and Yuditsky read lines 69–71 as follows, "[Three] prophets have I sent to my people, three shepherds. And after that I saw . . . ." The three shepherds reappear again in line 75, שלושה רועין יצאו לישראל, "three shepherds went out to Israel," and in line 79, [אני מב]קש מלפניך שלושה רועים, "[I as]k from You three shepherds." It is not clear who these shepherds are. Knohl suggests that the motif is taken from Zech 11:8, "I disposed of the three shepherds (שלשת הרעים) in one month." This may be, since Zechariah clearly stands in the background of the *Hazon Gabriel*, though it should be noted that in Zechariah God has become impatient with the three shepherds who, in turn, detest God, whereas in the *Hazon Gabriel* the shepherds were sent to Israel by God, presumably to support or to defend Israel.[47]

The text continues in lines 71–72. God is still the speaker: "[I returned them] to the place for the sake of David, the servant of the Lord." God continues to comfort Jerusalem. The "place" (המקום) may well be Jerusalem (compare lines 23–24), but whom God is returning there we do not know. God acts "for the sake of David, the servant of the Lord (למען דוד עבד יהוה)." The motif of God's defense of Jerusalem for the sake of David is found in Isa 37:35, where it is expressed in language that is strikingly similar to *HazGab* 72, "For I will defend this city to save it, for my own sake and for the sake of my servant David (למעני ולמען דוד עבדי)."[48]

The speaker in the next few lines is not identified. According to the reconstruction of Qimron and Yuditsky, the speaker changes, and an unidentified individual says to God, [הנה] א[תה עשית] את השמים ואת הארץ בכוחך [הגדול ובזרועך] הנטוה עושה חסד לאלפים מ[...], "Y[ou made] heaven and earth with your great [might and outstretched] arm. You show kindness to the thousandth generation. . . ." In support of their reconstruction, Qimron and Yuditsky claim that the author of the *Hazon Gabriel* inserts here a quotation from Jer 32:17–18: "Ah Lord God! It is you who made the heavens and the earth by your great power and by your outstretched arm! Nothing is too hard for you. You show steadfast love to the thousandth generation. . . ." In any case, *HazGab* 72–74 injects into the text

---

47. Knohl, *Messiahs and Resurrection*, 46–49, makes much of the reference to the three shepherds in lines 70, 75 and finds here a hint about the text's original historical context. Following the death of Herod in the year 4 B.C.E. and the accession of his son Archelaus, Josephus reports (*J.W.* 2.1.1–2.2.1 §§4–15) that a Jewish insurrection broke out in Jerusalem, which spread quickly until it was quelled by Varus, governor of Syria. The revolt was led by three men. Knohl asserts that these three men are the three shepherds in the *Hazon Gabriel* and that the text stems from a follower of one of the leaders, a certain Simon. "I assume that this text was composed and written within a group of followers of the messianic leader Simon, who was killed in Transjordan in 4 BCE" (p. 49).

48. Also 1 Kgs 11:12, 13, 34; 15:4; 2 Kgs 8:19; 19:34; 20:6.

another expression of confidence in God, the creator of heaven and earth, who is merciful to the thousandth generation (Exod 34:5–7).

Line 77 marks the beginning of a new section, the only section in the text in which Gabriel is mentioned by name. The passage begins with a question, מי אתה, "Who are you?," according to Qimron and Yuditsky, or מי אנכי, "Who am I?," according to Yardeni and Elizur and Knohl. In either case, the answer that immediately follows is the same, אני גבריאל, "I am Gabriel." This is the first time that Gabriel introduces himself. But does this also mean that Gabriel enters the text only now? If Gabriel has indeed been absent thus far, then the title for the inscription, the *Hazon Gabriel*, may well be a misnomer, as Gabriel would be only one among several angelic figures and the revelation would hardly be his. But it is also possible, and perhaps even likely, that Gabriel has been the revealing angel all along who only now introduces himself by name, in which case the title of the text is justified.

The end of line 77 is, unfortunately, not preserved. In the next lines (78–79), Gabriel addresses his interlocutor directly. Qimron and Yuditsky read as follows, תצילם נבי[א ור]ועה יצילו אותך [אני מב]קש מלפניך שלושה רועים שלושה [נבי]אין, "you shall save them. A proph[et and a she]pherd will save you. [I as]k from You three shepherds. Three [pro]phets." The restoration is based on some earlier lines (mostly lines 16, 17, and 82). Several motifs are repeated here, the three shepherds (שלושה רועים) and the three prophets (שלושה [נבי]אין). If we assume that the storming of Jerusalem still stands in the background, then Gabriel is here referring to the deliverance of the city, during which "a prophet and a shepherd" will play a central role.

Soon after the *editio princeps* of the *Hazon Gabriel* was published, line 80 became the most debated line in the composition. Up until recently, Knohl maintained that the line speaks about the resurrection of the Messiah. In a number of publications Knohl maintained that the text was to be read, לשלושת ימין חאיה, "By three days, live!" He furthermore maintained that the angel is here speaking to a slain Messiah whom he commands to live, that is, to be resurrected, on the third day. Since the *Hazon Gabriel* stems from the late first century B.C.E., this for Knohl was proof that the concept of a Messiah who dies and is resurrected on the third day predates Christianity and that it was from texts such as the *Hazon Gabriel* that Jesus himself learned of the concept. "It emerges that Jesus of Nazareth identified with the figure of the tortured and slain messiah that he had learned of from traditions in the vein of *The Gabriel Revelation*."[49] It was this claim, it should be recalled, that guaranteed our text a front-page article in the *New York Times* and propelled it to notoriety.

However, critics soon noticed the problems with Knohl's reading. First, it is not at all clear that Gabriel addresses a messianic figure, let alone that this Messiah is slain in the *Hazon Gabriel*. Second, it is equally unclear whether

---

49. Knohl, *Messiahs and Resurrection*, 87.

"live" does indeed mean "be resurrected," as there is no other early Jewish text in which an angel commands the Messiah to be resurrected. But it was the third objection that proved most troublesome, the fact that Knohl's proposed reading was immediately contested. Moshe Bar-Asher demonstrated that Knohl's reconstruction of the word, חאיה, "live!," would not work on grammatical grounds. While for Knohl the letter *aleph* was a *mater lectionis*, Bar-Asher observed that the *aleph* is never used to represent a *hatef patah*.[50] Ronald Hendel proposed reading the word in question as האות, "the sign."[51] The entire passage in *HazGab* 77-84 includes several motifs that we have seen in previous lines, and "the sign" may well be one of them (compare line 18 above).[52] This reading of line 80 is not entirely satisfactory either, however, if only because the sentence לשלושת ימין האות אני גבריאל, "In three days, the sign, I am Gabriel," does not make very good sense. And still, Hendel's suggestion has since been adopted by Qimron and Yuditsky and now also by Knohl himself.[53]

Not much of the remainder of the text survives. Line 81 begins with "the prince of princes (שר השרין)." The expression is taken from Dan 8:25, where it is an epithet of God.[54] In the *Hazon Gabriel*, the prince may be God as well, or the expression may designate an angel. Unfortunately the remainder of the line is illegible. In line 83, Gabriel continues to speak in the first person, אני גבריאל, "I, Gabriel." In line 85, finally, Yardeni and Elizur read אז תעמדו, "Then you will stand . . . ." Knohl sees here a parallel with Ezek 37:10 and Dan 12:13 and asserts that "it is possible that this line reiterates the concept of resurrection mentioned in line 80."[55] Since Knohl no longer maintains that line 80 refers to the resurrection, however, and since there is no unambiguous reference to the resurrection anywhere else in the *Hazon Gabriel*, that interpretation, too, is now called into question.

Some Concluding Thoughts

Undoubtedly the most striking feature of the *Hazon Gabriel* is its close reliance on the Jewish Bible in both language and thought. The author writes in the biblical idiom, leaning heavily on the prophets. Biblical pericopes of particular

---

50. Bar-Asher, "On the Language," 501.
51. Ronald Hendel, "The Messiah Son of Joseph: Simply 'Sign,'" *BAR* 35 (2009): 8.
52. Yardeni and Elizur propose that line 79 may include the words שלושה הא[ת]ות, "the three si[gn]s (?)," but the reading is contested. Knohl leaves a lacuna.
53. Qimron and Yuditsky, "Notes on the So-Called 'Gabriel Vision' Inscription," in this volume, p. 37; and Knohl, "Apocalyptic and Messianic Dimensions," also in this volume, p. 43 n. 12.
54. James A. Montgomery, *A Critical and Exegetical Commentary on the Book of Daniel* (ICC; 1927; repr., Edinburgh: T&T Clark, 1989), 351, "The 'Prince of princes' is 'the Prince of the host,' v. 11, *i.e.*, God."
55. Knohl, *Messiahs and Resurrection*, 30.

importance include Daniel 8 and 10–12, Haggai 2, and Zechariah 14, all texts with a pronounced eschatological orientation. Other biblical texts are Isaiah 7 and Jeremiah 31–32.

The nature of the biblical base texts fits in well with another feature of the *Hazon Gabriel*, the presence of angels and divine messengers in the text. Michael is mentioned by name in line 28, Gabriel in lines 77–83; other angelic figures appear in lines 22, 31, 65 and 76, and the "prince of princes" in line 81 could also be an angel. All these suggest that the *Hazon Gabriel* is an eschatological, and specifically an apocalyptic, composition. God shakes heaven and earth, and evil will be broken before righteousness. Regardless of whether we assume that the *Hazon Gabriel* was composed in direct response to a concrete historical event, it seems clear that the events that are here described are part of the end-time drama.

Texts such as Haggai and Zechariah have been called "proto-apocalyptic." The implication is that their depiction of the end is still fairly general and not as developed as in the early Enochic materials such as the Apocalypse of Weeks or the Book of the Watchers. The same holds true for the *Hazon Gabriel*, which resembles the biblical prophets much more than it resembles any of the Enochic apocalypses. *Hazon Garbiel* forms a direct extension to these biblical books; it adopts their language and continues their story line.

The dominant genre in the *Hazon Gabriel* is that of the revelatory dialogue (*Offenbarungsdialog*). The interlocutors change constantly, and so we should perhaps better speak of a sequence of dialogues. Among the principal participants are an individual who speaks on behalf of God, as indicated by the frequent use of the messenger formula, who is possibly an *angelus interpres*, and another individual, who is encouraged repeatedly to pose more questions. At some point God speaks directly; at another point a we-group confirms their reliance on God. The revelatory dialogue, we observed, is a well-established genre in apocalyptic writings composed during the turn of the era and shortly thereafter, and with the *Hazon Gabriel* we now have another example. The main theme of the inscription is the fate of Jerusalem at the end of time. The author writes of the great events that will unfold in Jerusalem: the nations will mount an attack on Jerusalem, but God will protect the city, for the sake of his servant David. Like Isaiah 7, the *Hazon Gabriel* speaks of a sign that suggests that God will very soon avert the threat. Nothing is said of a heavenly ascent. Instead, the *Hazon Gabriel* is concerned with the fate of Jerusalem in the end of time, and so it can perhaps be classified as an apocalypse of the historical type.[56] Even though the end is not preserved, we may assume that the *Hazon Gabriel* ended with the victory of God in Jerusalem.

---

56. There is another peculiarity of the *Hazon Gabriel* that is still in need of a good explanation, the author's predilection for numbers. In lines 15 and 30, for example, the author is simply counting (what, however, we do not know), and the number 3 occurs no fewer than twelve times in the text (lines 15, 19, 30, 33, 54, 65, 69, 70, 75, 79, 80, and 83).

NINE

Hosts, Holy Ones, and Words of Gabriel

The Angelology of *Hazon Gabriel*
in the Context of Second Temple
and Late Antique Literature

Kelley Coblentz Bautch

Hazon Gabriel (*HazGab*), an enigmatic composition inked on stone, is equally elusive in its angelology. The several possible allusions to otherworldly beings and what they suggest about the text's angelology and provenance are the subject of this essay. Forms of מלאך likely denote heavenly beings, and references to Michael and Gabriel would seem to indicate two named angels familiar from other Jewish (and Christian) texts of antiquity. On the other hand, expressions such as קדושין might intend subordinate divine persons, but such a determination is hampered ultimately by the limitations posed by a composition that is no longer fully extant. After considering the language in *Hazon Gabriel* that is evocative of heavenly beings (such as מלאך, צבאות, and מרכבות) and the roles assumed by otherworldly beings (for example, as interpreters or mediators of revelation, as actors in apocalyptic contexts), I take up how this text is like and unlike other writings of the Second Temple period and late antiquity in its depictions of otherworldly beings. Though so much about the composition is unknown or yet unclear, preliminary study of the depiction of otherworldly beings in *Hazon Gabriel* highlights the perspectives shared with late prophetic writings, such as Zechariah, as well as with some of the apocalyptic traditions found in Daniel. Features of the angelology anticipate aspects of *hekhalot* and *merkabah* traditions but more strongly reflect prior trends.

Certain challenges to the task at hand complicate study of *Hazon Gabriel* and the angelology of the composition in particular. Most notably, many portions of the text relevant to our study are unclear or are frustratingly no longer extant.[1] Further, the Second Temple period and late antiquity attest to developing

---

My appreciation to Matthias Henze, April DeConick, and Israel Knohl for their comments and our conversations, which have benefited my work on this subject. I am especially indebted to Angela Kim Harkins for reading and commenting on a draft of this paper; her keen insights and helpful suggestions have enriched this article and my approach to the *Hazon Gabriel*.

1. Pertinent are the remarks of Moshe Bar-Asher, "On the Language of 'The Vision of

views of otherworldly beings, and various texts offer glimpses of this diversity.² Moreover, though studies of the language, orthography, phonology, and morphology are helpful in terms of narrowing down the provenance of the inscription, the date and origin of *Hazon Gabriel*, finally, are unknown.³ Thus, for such a study, one must cast one's net widely to identify analogous traditions that might help to reconstruct, locate, or better understand the angelology in this text.

Hazon Gabriel includes at least one allusion to a biblical text or a motif common to or inspired by it—lines 24–25a strongly resemble Hag 2:6—and features expressions that are quite like and are possible allusions to other prophetic texts.⁴

Gabriel,'" *RevQ* 23 (2008): 491–524, esp. 491 n. 4: "Lines 1–10, 32–56, and 59–64 are almost entirely obliterated, and very little can be read within them. (Lines) 66–87 are damaged at their ends, and there are other smaller lacunae in other lines, as well." See also his "On the Language of 'The Vision of Gabriel'" (in Hebrew), *Meghillot* 7 (2009): 193–226, here 193. I wish to express my gratitude to Professor Bar-Asher for making this article available to me; his scholarship and generosity are very much appreciated.

2. Recent studies indicating such diversity include Michael Mach, *Entwicklungsstadien des jüdischen Engelglaubens in vorrabbinischer Zeit* (TSAJ 34; Tübingen: Mohr Siebeck, 1992), esp. 114–300; Ruth M. M. Tuschling, *Angels and Orthodoxy: A Study in their Development in Syria and Palestine from the Qumran Texts to Ephrem the Syrian* (Studien und Texte zu Antike und Christentum 40; Tübingen: Mohr Siebeck, 2007), 13–113; and Kevin Sullivan, *Wrestling with Angels: A Study of the Relationship between Angels and Humans in Ancient Jewish Literature and the New Testament* (AGJU 55; Leiden: Brill, 2004), esp. 7 and 227. Sullivan (*Wrestling with Angels*, 7), following Mach (*Entwicklungsstadien des jüdischen Engelglaubens*), emphasizes that there is not a coherent set of beliefs and, in light of a wide variety of views, not one systematic doctrine concerning angels that emerges from the Hebrew Bible; it is more accurate, Sullivan urges, to speak of angelologies than of *an* angelology. Tuschling's observation (*Angels and Orthodoxy*, 109) that "[t]here is no uniform angelogogy in the first to fourth centuries" is valid also for views of otherworldly beings prior to the start of the Common Era. See also Carol A. Newsom, "Angels," *ABD* 1:248–53, esp. 252.

3. Most helpful are the extensive studies that include transcriptions and discussions of the text's paleography, such as Ada Yardeni and Binyamin Elizur, "A Prophetic Text on Stone from the First Century BCE: First Publication" (in Hebrew), *Cathedra* 123 (2007): 155–66, and "A Hebrew Prophetic Text on Stone from the Early Herodian Period: A Preliminary Report," in this volume, as well as linguistic examinations by Elisha Qimron and Alexey (Eliyahu) Yuditsky, "Notes on the Inscription 'The Vision of Gabriel'" (in Hebrew), *Cathedra* 133 (2009): 133–44, and "Notes on the So-Called 'Gabriel Vision' Inscription," in this volume; Bar-Asher, "On the Language of 'The Vision of Gabriel'"; and Gary A. Rendsburg, "Linguistic and Stylistic Notes to the Hazon Gabriel Inscription," *DSD* 16 (2009): 107–16. With regard to dating, Yardeni and Elizur ("Hebrew Prophetic Text on Stone") consider the text to be from the late first century B.C.E.; Israel Knohl ("'By Three Days, Live': Messiahs, Resurrection, and Ascent to Heaven in *Hazon Gabriel*," *JR* 88 [2008]: 147–58, esp. 147), from the late first century B.C.E. or early C.E.; and Bar-Asher ("On the Language of 'The Vision of Gabriel,'" 517) from the end of the Second Temple era. Bar-Asher also notes, "Since the paleography points to a date in the first century BCE, it is possible that the view of the first editors that the text was copied not long after its composition is to be accepted." See also p. 219 in the Hebrew version of the article.

4. For example, Yardeni and Elizur ("Hebrew Prophetic Text on Stone") and Knohl ("Apocalyptic and Messianic Dimensions") both in this volume, note the citation of Hag 2:6

For this reason, one might wonder about the extent to which the work is a pastiche drawn from preexisting texts and traditions, which, in turn, would color its references to angels.[5] The fact that so much of the text and its context are uncertain (i.e., the provenance of the text; whether the text was continued on stones or another medium preceding and/or following the Gabriel inscription; whether the original setting could have further clarified the intended sense of the text; the many illegible and unsure readings) might caution us against being overconfident in determinations of genre. Nonetheless, from what is perceptible, as others have noted, the text shares much with prophetic (especially postexilic) literature and proto-apocalyptic texts.[6] Having addressed these issues, I consider briefly some of the expressions that relate to the text's depiction of otherworldly beings.

Angels, Hosts, and Holy Ones

A study of angelology in the composition might best begin with an overview of the language suggestive of heavenly beings, and here I offer some preliminary observations and an assessment of varying transcriptions and translations. We begin with מלאך and related forms. While מלאך can refer to a human "messenger" (see, e.g., 1 Sam 23:27; also in reference to a prophet [Hag 1:13] or priest [Mal 2:7]),[7] there is good reason in the context of *Hazon Gabriel* for understanding the lexeme in lines 22, 28, and 31 as otherworldly messengers. The same assessment can be made for the references to Michael and Gabriel in lines 28, 77, 80, and 83.[8] The strongest grounds for considering the referents as otherworldly beings

---

and find allusions to Deut 5:10 and Jer 32:17–18 as well as expressions from Zechariah and Daniel. Rendsburg ("Linguistic and Stylistic Notes," 111) also thinks that the author of the composition borrows the expression מי אנכי from Exod 3:11; 1 Sam 18:18; and 2 Sam 7:18 consciously in order to archaize.

5. In his detailed study of the language of the composition, Bar-Asher calls attention to the fact that צבאות appears six times with a *plene* spelling and then three times with a defective spelling (צבאת) ("On the Language of 'The Vision of Gabriel,'" 495 n. 27; "On the Language" [Hebrew], 197). Bar-Asher raises the question whether this might be evidence that a copyist worked from two different copies, written by different scribes. The observation and question posed by Bar-Asher are important; the inconsistencies might also lead one to reflect further on the use of sources with distinctive spellings retained. For another perspective on the defective spelling of צבאות, see Rendsburg, "Linguistic and Stylistic Notes," 116, and below.

6. See, e.g., Ada Yardeni, "A New Dead Sea Scroll in Stone? Bible-like Prophecy Was Mounted in a Wall 2,000 Years Ago," *BAR* 34, no. 1 (2008): 60–61.

7. In light of our text, we note that Israel Knohl, who emphasizes the messianic themes in the composition, understands David to be a messenger, conferring a sign (of salvation?) upon Ephraim—although I do not think that he has in mind that David is portrayed here as a heavenly messenger; see Knohl, "The Messiah Son of Joseph: 'Gabriel's Revelation' and the Birth of a New Messianic Model," *BAR* 34, no. 5 (2008): 58–62, 78, esp. 60; and idem, "'By Three Days, Live,'" 155.

8. Though "Michael" is also a personal name attested in a number of biblical texts (see Num 13:13; Ezra 8:8; 1 Chr 5:13–14; 6:40; 7:3; 8:16; 12:20; 27:18; 2 Chr 21:2), it appears

are, admittedly, contextual. Were only a word or two of this composition extant, there would be a greater burden of proof for reading מלאך in this manner. Given the multiple references to the divine and the celestial entourage (see below), and motifs that recall the revelatory context of apocalyptic literature and late prophetic texts, in which subordinate divine persons are so prominent, there is no compelling reason for doubting that otherworldly beings are intended by מלאך.[9] Another expression that occurs in *Hazon Gabriel* is צבאות, or "hosts," used most likely in the sense of "heavenly armies"; here צבאות is featured in a variety of titles for the divine (see lines 11, 18, 20, 26, 29, 40, 57, 58, 68, 69, 84). Two other expressions, קדושין ("holy ones"; lines 65, 76) and מרכבות/מרכבה ("chariot[s]"; lines 26, 67) may connote heavenly beings. I discuss these cases as well, though the evidence for reading them in this light is hardly decisive.

מלאך AND INTERPRETING ANGELS

מלאך and related forms appear three times in *Hazon Gabriel* (lines 22–23, 28, and 31); yet the contexts, which would aid in determining how the lexeme is used, are no longer extant. I begin with lines 22–23, noting diverse readings of the text. The transcriptions of Qimron and Yuditsky and of Yardeni and Elizur for line 22b are the same, though their translations differ; the readings and translations offered by both teams for line 23a diverge (cf. their respective translations in this volume).[10] Qimron and Yuditsky's translation is as follows: (line 22b) "You exist, (but)

---

in numerous Second Temple and late antique works in reference to the angel. Yardeni ("New Dead Sea Scroll in Stone?" 60–61), Yardeni and Elizur ("Hebrew Prophetic Text on Stone"), and Knohl ("Messiah Son of Joseph," 60–61; "'By Three Days, Live,'" 147–48, 151) also identify Michael and Gabriel in the composition as angelic figures. For helpful studies on מלאך, see Tuschling, *Angels and Orthodoxy*, 81–84.

9. While some assert the clear distinction between celestial beings and humans in Second Temple literature, more recently scholars have explored the notion of angelomorphic humans (individuals who are angelic in status or in nature). See, e.g., Crispin H. T. Fletcher-Louis, "Some Reflections on Angelomorphic Humanity Texts among the Dead Sea Scrolls," *DSD* 7 (2000): 292–312, esp. 292, 295–305. Fletcher-Louis argues that in such literature not only might humans be in community with angels (see, e.g., Björn Frennesson, *"In a Common Rejoicing": Liturgical Communion with Angels in Qumran* [Acta Universitatis Upsaliensis, Studia Semitica Upsaliensia 14; Uppsala: University of Uppsala, 1999]; and Angela Kim Harkins, "A New Proposal for Thinking about 1QH[A] Sixty Years after Its Discovery," in *Texts from Cave 1 Revisited: Texts from Cave 1 Sixty Years after Their Discovery. Proceedings of the Sixth Meeting of the IOQS in Ljubljana* [ed. Daniel K. Falk, Sarianna Metso, Donald W. Parry, and Eibert J.C. Tigchelaar; STDJ 91; Leiden: Brill, 2010], 101–34, esp. 110–19), but they also might become like angels (cf. *1 En.* 89:1) or share their fate (cf. 1QH[a] 11:20–24; 14:14). Sadly, given the state of our text, there are not enough contextual clues to warrant a study of so-called flexible theological anthropology (so Fletcher-Louis, "Some Reflections," 297) or to take up angelomorphy in the *Gabriel Revelation*. It may well be a feature of this text, though I am not inclined to argue in that direction in light of what is extant.

10. Qimron and Yuditsky transcribe lines 22–23 as: אתה עמד המלאך הוא בסמכך אל

the angel (line 23a) supports you; do not fear!" Yardeni and Elizur read instead: ^(line 22b) "You are standing, the messenger/angel. He ^(line 23a) . ... (= will ordain you?) to Torah(?)." Knohl's translation is a combination of these two: "You are standing, the angel is supporting you. Do not fear."[11] The conjectural reading of Yardeni and Elizur for line 23a is the more novel; they acknowledge that they do not have a firm sense of the meaning of the proposed reading "ordaining you to the Torah," noting that סמך can be rendered "ordained" in talmudic Hebrew.[12] In spite of the principle of *lectio difficilior*, the suggested reading of Yardeni and Elizur seems less probable in contrast to that of Knohl and Qimron and Yuditsky for 23a. The latter point to a similar expression in Daniel (10:19), occurring in an analogous context: a discussion between the seer and Gabriel. In fact, we might see a fitting parallel to Knohl's translation ("you are standing, the angel is supporting you. Do not fear") in the Book of the Watchers, in the course of the patriarch Enoch's encountering the divine. As Enoch enters the heavenly temple, sees the throne of God, and is prostrate, an angel—here "one of the holy ones"—stands him on his feet as God exhorts him not to fear (see *1 En.* 14:25).[13] Encounters with the divine or otherworldly beings described in prophetic or Second Temple texts often result in the seer being fearful (e.g., Dan 8:17; 10:8) and overwhelmed, expressed as a collapse, wherein the angelic being assists by offering physical support. In this light, the reading proposed by Knohl and Qimron and Yuditsky has merit. As long as Qimron and Yuditsky's transcription is correct—note the less common spelling of ירא [14]—lines 22 and 23 most likely describe a messenger in the sense of an otherworldly being who steadies and bolsters a visionary.

Other references to angels appear in lines 28, 31, and 52, but these are especially enigmatic because the surrounding context cannot be deciphered. Such is the case with line 52 which would seem to read ה[מ]לאכים, while little else can

---

תירה; the transcription of Knohl is almost identical. Yardeni and Elizur read: אתה עמד המלאך הוא כסמכך אל תורה.

11. See Knohl, "Messiah Son of Joseph," 62.

12. See Yardeni and Elizur, "Hebrew Prophetic Text on Stone," in this volume, n. 16.

13. My thanks to Angela Kim Harkins for pointing out this very relevant parallel. See also George W. E. Nickelsburg, *1 Enoch 1: A Commentary on the Book of 1 Enoch, Chapters 1–36; 81–108* (Hermeneia; Minneapolis: Fortress, 2001), 270, who observes that Enoch's collapse as a response to an epiphany is to be expected and prepares the reader for the reassurance or restoration. "The seer must be rehabilitated and accepted into the divine presence before he can receive his commission. Restoration by an angel becomes a typical feature in visions, where, however it is the angel whose appearance causes the collapse." See also Ezek 1:29–2:2, Rev 1:12–17, *4 Ezra* 10:29–30; *2 En.* 21:2–6. The exhortation not to fear recalls the assurance given by other mediating figures to seers. In addition to Dan 10:12, 19, see also Judg 6:23 and Luke 1:13, 30.

14. See Qimron and Yuditsky, "Notes on the So-Called 'Gabriel Vision' Inscription," in this volume; and also Bar-Asher, "On the Language of 'The Vision of Gabriel,'" 497, and "On the Language" [Hebrew], 199), who follows Knohl in accepting the spelling of תירה for תירא, pointing to evidence in the composition for ה over א in marking final vowels.

be discerned.[15] I turn, therefore, to the other examples of the lexeme, where more discussion is possible. Line 28 has been read variously as referring to three angels or to a host of angels that bear some relationship to Michael. While Knohl and Bar-Asher argue that the composition refers to "three angels, Michael and the others,"[16] Yardeni and Elizur prefer: "His(?) angel, Michael, and to all the others(?)," and Qimron and Yuditsky read "The Hosts of Michael [the] angel and for all the lovers." Tied to the translations is how scholars make sense of the distinctive spelling of מלאכה, which is explained variously.[17] Qimron and Yuditsky suggest that their own reading ("the Hosts of Michael") is doubtful; even so, we consider this possible reading later in light of the reference to Michael. The reading of Yardeni and Elizur, "His(?) angel, Michael," requires little explanation; not disputed at this point in transcriptions of line 28 is the reference to Michael. That Michael is named in this context and is distinguished in some manner accords with the prominent role enjoyed by this angel in the Second Temple period, which we consider below.

The reading of Knohl and Bar-Asher for line 28a ("three angels and Michael") is interesting because three is a key number in *Hazon Gabriel*. We also read, for example, about three holy ones (line 65), three prophets (line 70), and three shepherds (line 75). Reference to three angels in close proximity to Michael makes sense from another perspective as well. Traditions of four archangels, as a particular class of angels, are well known from the Second Temple period (see, e.g., *1 Enoch* 9–10; 40:10; 1QM ix.14–16; *Pirqe R. El.* 4), and, though the named angels among the four vary, Michael is typically present as one of the core members of this group.[18] Thus, the reading of Knohl and Bar-Asher that juxtaposes three angels and Michael would find precedent in Second Temple traditions of angels.

---

15. See, e.g., Yardeni and Elizur, "Hebrew Prophetic Text on Stone."

16. Knohl remarks with his transcription for line 28a, שלושה מלאכה מיכאל..., that the letters of the first word are doubtful. See "Apocalyptic and Messianic Dimensions of the Gabriel Revelation in Their Historical Context," in this volume. Yardeni and Elizur attempt to identify only a ל from the first word.

17. Yardeni and Elizur ("Hebrew Prophetic Text on Stone," in this volume), translating מלאכה as "angel" (possibly "his angel"), wonder whether the spelling reflects Aramaic tendencies (for example, the Aramaic article or possessive suffix). See, e.g., Dan 3:28 and 6:23. Bar-Asher ("On the Language of 'The Vision of Gabriel,'" 502–3; and "On the Language" [Hebrew], 205) challenges the idea that מלאכה features the Aramaic article and is in apposition to "Michael." While noting that a possessive suffix would be possible, Bar-Asher wonders why the Hebrew composition would here adopt Aramaic. Bar-Asher ("On the Language of 'The Vision of Gabriel,'" 503; and "On the Language" [Hebrew], 205) reads מלאכה as a plural and suggests that the orthography is that of a Hebrew absolute plural form. See also below. We note also that the composition elsewhere seems to have adopted some Aramaic forms.

18. The tradition of four angels that surround the throne of God may derive from four living creatures (חיות; the cherubim in Ezek 10:15) that support the divine throne in Ezekiel 1. Zechariah also describes four spirits or winds of heaven (רחות השמים), which inspect or patrol each direction of the earth (Zech 6:1–7; cf. also LXX 1:8–11). See my "Putting Angels in

HOSTS, HOLY ONES, AND WORDS OF GABRIEL   137

Line 31, partially reconstructed by Qimron and Yuditsky as [...ויש]אל מֹלאךָ
מהו ואמרה .... suggests the context of an interpreting angel and, as Qimron and
Yuditsky indicate, the object of the vision would have preceded מהו.[19] Presumably the interpretation of the vision followed the form of אמר; the nature of the
response I leave for others to consider. The reading of Qimron and Yuditsky
requires little explanation on our part, as there are few difficulties in making
sense of the composition here per their transcription.

The transcription of Knohl and Yardeni and Elizur for line 31, שב[עה אל
מלאכה .... מה זו אמר, is more challenging, although their reading still suggests
the context of an interpreting angel. Their translations, which differ, present
some interpretative issues. Yardeni and Elizur tentatively propose reading line
31a as: "[se]ven, these (?) are(?) His (?) angel"; Knohl, taking אל as the preposition, translates: "[se]ven for my angels." In favor of their reconstruction of שבעה
is the series of numbers given in line 30, which could be continued ostensibly in
line 31; Knohl and Yardeni and Elitzur also read "seven" in line 26 in reference to
"chariots," which they could adduce as another example of this symbolic number
in the text.[20] Yet the relationship of the numbers, with or without a reconstructed
שבעה, vis-à-vis the מלאך (or מלאכה), is not clear, especially if preceded by the
preposition אל. What is being enumerated?

If מלאך (or מלאכה) is preceded by the preposition אל ("seven for [or "to"]
angels"?), the sense of the expression now eludes us. Bar-Asher, following the
transcription of Yardeni and Elizur, offers a very different reading. He argues
that מלאכה is an absolute plural and reads אל as a demonstrative pronoun.[21] Thus,
his proposed translation for line 31 is: "these seven are the/my messengers."[22]

Their Place: Developments in Second Temple Angelology," in *"With Wisdom as a Robe": Qumran and Other Jewish Studies in Honour of Ida Fröhlich* (ed. Miklós Kőszeghy, Gábor Buzási, Károly Dobos; Sheffield: Sheffield Phoenix Press, 2009), 174–88; and also Christoph Berner, "The Four (or Seven) Archangels in the First Book of Enoch and Early Jewish Writings of the Second Temple Period," in *Angels: The Concept of Celestial Beings. Origins, Development and Reception* (ed. Friedrich V. Reiterer, Tobias Nicklas, Karin Schöpflin; Deuterocanonical and Cognate Literature Yearbook 2007; Berlin: de Gruyter, 2007), 395–411, esp. 397–98. See also Nickelsburg, *1 Enoch 1*, 207; and Jan Willem van Henten, "Archangel," *DDD*, 2nd ed., 80–82.

19. See Qimron and Yuditsky, "Notes on the So-Called 'Gabriel Vision' Inscription," in this volume. On their reconstruction, see ibid., and also "Notes on the Inscription" (Hebrew), 136.

20. The composition's fascination with numbers (see, e.g., lines 15, 19, 54, 65, 70, 75, 80, 83) recalls proto-apocalyptic works such as Zechariah (2:10; 3:9; 4:2–3, 10–11; 6:1–5) and apocalypses (e.g., *1 En.* 18:6, 13; 21:3; 24:2–3; Rev 1:4, 12, 16, 20; 2:1; 3:1; 4:4–10; 5:5–8; 7:1–8; 8:6); see below. On seven as a symbolic number in Revelation, see David E. Aune, *Revelation 1–5* (WBC 52A; Waco: Word, 1997), 114–15.

21. Bar-Asher, "On the Language of 'The Vision of Gabriel,'" 502–6; and "On the Language" (Hebrew), 205–8.

22. Bar-Asher, "On the Language of 'The Vision of Gabriel,'" 506; and "On the Language" (Hebrew), 208.

Recommending the reading of Bar-Asher for line 31 is that, in addition to four angels (typically thought to be archangels) as one group or level of hierarchy, seven angels are distinguished also in many Second Temple works, perhaps inspired by reference to the seven eyes of God in Zech 4:10.[23]

If one does not favor the reading of מלאכה nor understand the final consonant as signaling a plural, then it is more likely that a suggested reference to seven derives from a larger motif of the work—for example, a stock expression of the culture and of these writings—and is not principally bound to the description of the angel mentioned in line 31. For example, in calling attention to the number 3 (see above), *Hazon Gabriel* is not unlike other prophetic and Second Temple texts that emphasize that number (for instance, three days [Jonah 1:17; 3:3], three kings [*4 Ezra* 12:23], three shepherds [Zech 11:8], three angels [Rev 8:13]). Knohl and Yardeni and Elizur have also read "seven" in line 26, possibly in reference to chariots. If lines 30–31 also list seven numbers (resembling line 15 in counting), then seven may have been a structural device as we find in other texts, for example, the Book of the Watchers, *Songs of the Sabbath Sacrifice*, and Revelation.[24]

Though there is much uncertainty in our reading of line 31, in view of the role of angels in Second Temple and late antique apocalypses, the setting suggests a seer making an inquiry of an angel (Zech 1:9; 2:2) or an angel posing a question to the seer (see, e.g., *1 En.* 25:1; cf. also Rev 7:13). It is also possible that in line 31 an angel asks about a vision and Gabriel then provides an answer. There are instances of otherworldly figures such as angels and giants making inquiries, sometimes concerning visions. This is the case in the *Book of Giants* (4Q530), in which the sons of the fallen watchers ask about the interpretation of a disturbing dream. Second Temple literature also features angels explaining visions to other angels. Thus, in "Michael's Words" (4Q529), Michael shares with other angels what seems to be a vision of mountains; though the text is fragmentary, it would seem that Michael then shows (perhaps explains?) a vision to Gabriel. Thus, the role of the *angelus interpres* is well known, especially in apocalypses, and the notion of otherworldly figures serving as recipients of visions and interpretations is not unprecedented. It is interesting to note, however, that many of the texts

---

23. See my "Putting Angels in Their Place," 179–81. One might think also of the tradition in Ezek 9:2–11, in which six men appear as executioners and are joined by a man in white linen who serves as scribe. So also Berner, "Four (or Seven) Archangels," 398. References to seven angels, described by Greek *1 Enoch* 20 as "angels of the powers," occur in *1 En.* 90:21 (Book of Dreams), *T. Levi* 8:1–2; 18:2, and in some manuscripts of *1 En.* 81:5 (Astronomical Book). In these instances, the seven are often tending to the maintenance of the cosmos (see *1 Enoch* 20) and serving before the Glory of the Lord (see Tob 12:15). See also 4QShirShab and *3 Enoch* 18.

24. On the use of seven as a structuring device in the *Songs of the Sabbath Sacrifice*, see Carol A. Newsom, *Songs of the Sabbath Sacrifice: A Critical Edition* (HSS 27; Atlanta: Scholars Press, 1985), 12.

among the Qumran scrolls do not present heavenly beings as mediators of revelation; exceptions include Aramaic texts such as "Michael's Words" and the texts associated with Enoch, which do tend to depict angels in this manner.[25]

Hosts

צבאות, or "hosts," occur in a number of divine epithets given in *Hazon Gabriel*.[26] For example, we read about "the Lord of Hosts" (line 11); "YHWH of hosts" (lines 18, 39–40), "YHWH the Lord of Hosts, the Lord of Israel" (lines 20, 25–26, 29–30), and "YHWH of Hosts, the Lord of Israel" (lines 57–59; 68, 69, 84). The term "hosts" typically refers to the heavenly legion that accompanies the divine and is typically invoked in epithets for the deity.

With regard to the history of associating the divine with צבאות, Tryggve N. D. Mettinger observes that there is a link between the designation YHWH of hosts and the temple, as well as Zion, in a number of texts.[27] The formula appears to be celebrating the divine as enthroned in majesty on the cherubim in the Solomonic temple. Mettinger thinks that the epithet is preexilic and that it enjoyed a renaissance in postexilic writings such as Haggai (where it appears fourteen times), Zechariah (fifty-three times), and Malachi (twenty-four times). Though צבא ("host") is attested among the scrolls (see, e.g., 1QH 11:23, 36; or 1QM 12:1), Mettinger observes that divine epithets with צבאות do not occur at all in Ben Sira and are found only once in the texts of Qumran.[28] Given other associations with the postexilic Haggai and Zechariah, we should not be surprised that *Hazon Gabriel* also makes heavy use of a title or form of the title employed by these writings. Moreover, following Mettinger's observation that the title calls to mind the temple and Zion, the use of the epithet in *Hazon Gabriel* fits well with several references to Jerusalem (see, e.g., lines 12, 14, 27, 33, 36, 39, 57).

---

25. So Cecilia Wassen, "Angels in the Dead Sea Scrolls," in Reiterer, *Angels: The Concept of Celestial Beings*, 499–520, esp. 511–12, 519; and Maxwell Davidson, *Angels at Qumran: A Comparative Study of 1 Enoch 1–36, 72–108 and Sectarian Writings from Qumran* (JSPSup 11; Sheffield: Sheffield Academic Press, 1992), 309–13.

26. Rendsburg ("Linguistic and Stylistic Notes," 115–16) calls attention to the variations in epithet, including the expression אלהים צבאות and יהוה צבאות, and in spelling צבאת (lines 68, 69, 84) and צבאות (e.g., lines 11,18, 20). Rendsburg associates both with the technique of variation for the sake of variation, a stylistic device utilized as well in writings of the Hebrew Bible (see James Barr, *The Variable Spellings of the Hebrew Bible* [Schweich Lectures 1986; Oxford: Oxford University Press, 1989]).

27. Tryggve N. D. Mettinger, "Yahweh Zebaoth," *DDD*, 2nd ed., 920–24, here 922. See also his *The Dethronement of Sabaoth: Studies in the Shem and Kabod Theologies* (ConBOT 18; Lund: Gleerup, 1982).

28. Mettinger, "Yahweh Zebaoth," 924.

Holy Ones

קדושין, or "holy ones," occurs in lines 65 and 76. Both contexts require greater clarification than what the extant composition makes available in order to know whether the referents are pious humans ("saints") or otherworldly figures. Knohl and Yardeni and Elizur transcribe and translate line 65 as follows: שלושה קדושי העולם מן ...; "the three holy ones (or saints) of the world (or eternity) from (or of)...." Qimron and Yuditsky prefer to translate העולם as "past generations." Line 76 is transcribed variously. Knohl and Yardeni and Elizur transcribe the line thus: אם יש כהן אם יש בני קדושים...ה..; their translations are also similar: "if there is a priest, if there are sons of holy ones (or saints)." The transcription of Qimron and Yuditsky differs (אם יש בהן אם יש בם קדושין ...) as does their translation ("if there are [pious ones] among them, if there are holy ones among them").

The substantival use of "holy ones" (קדשים; Greek ἅγιοι) is especially restricted to divine or heavenly beings prior to the second century B.C.E.[29] Thereafter, the title seems to be used in reference to humans as well.[30] Yet what is intended by the title and the extent to which it blurs lines between humanity and divinity are disputed. For example, Ruth M. M. Tuschling notes that the title implies "a certain degree of divinization and participation in the heavenly reality."[31] Though a number of Second Temple texts refer unambiguously to celestial beings as "holy ones" (see *1 En.* 9:1; 14:25; Dan 8:13), other references make clear the uncertainty of the title, just as examples from Qumran demonstrate fluidity in categories like מלאך and קדשים.[32] Moreover, as noted above, many of the writings among the scrolls suggest that some Second Temple Jews understood themselves to enjoy a special relationship with angels, by which they were able to enter into fellowship with the congregation of angels or would fight alongside such heavenly beings.[33] If more of *Hazon Gabriel* were available, the composition could prove to be a useful datum in our attempts to clarify the meaning of this lexeme in Second Temple and late antique angelology.

---

29. See John J. Collins, *Daniel: A Commentary on the Book of Daniel* (Hermeneia; Minneapolis: Fortress, 1993), 313–17, esp. 313; and idem, "Saints of the Most High קדישי עליונין," *DDD*, 2nd ed., 720–22; and Chris H. W. Brekelmans, "The Saints of the Most High and Their Kingdom," *OTS* 14 (1965): 305–29.

30. See, e.g., *1 En.* 48:4, 7 (the use of the title in the Parables is distinct from other early Enochic writings, which use the title for celestial beings); 1 Cor 14:33; Phil 1:1. Collins ("Saints of the Most High," 721) rightly suggests that the use of the title for humans may be to call to mind the "affinity between the righteous and holy on earth and the angels in heaven" and to anticipate an eschatological communion between the two groups.

31. Tuschling, *Angels and Orthodoxy*, 84–87. See also Devorah Dimant, "Men as Angels: The Self-Image of the Qumran Community," in *Religion and Politics in the Ancient Near East* (ed. Adele Berlin; Bethesda: University Press of Maryland, 1996), 93–103.

32. Consider, e.g., 4Q511frg. 35.2–4; see also Collins, *Daniel*, 314–15.

33. See, e.g., 1QH 11:21–23; see also Tuschling, *Angels and Orthodoxy*, 115–37; Davidson, *Angels at Qumran*, 229–32; and Sullivan, *Wrestling with Angels*, 145–78.

We can offer some relevant observations that do not ultimately settle the use of the title in *Hazon Gabriel*. The distinction of three "holy ones" in line 65 anticipates שלושה רועין, or "three shepherds," in line 75 (and possibly line 70). Qimron and Yuditsky's reconstruction for line 64 suggests additional references to שלושה and העולם. The references to prophets (line 70), shepherds (line 75), David, the servant of YHWH (line 72), and possibly to priests (line 75) suggest human agents of God.[34] We do note, however, that Knohl detects an earlier reference to three angels in line 28, a reconstruction not shared by Qimron and Yuditsky or Yardeni and Elizur, creating a precedent in *Hazon Gabriel* for three distinctive heavenly beings.[35] Line 75 elicits a similar reaction. While Qimron and Yuditsky's transcription and translation for the line do not allow for a sharp adjudication, the transcriptions of Knohl and Yardeni and Elizur, which include the reading of כהן ("priest") and of בני ("sons of"), would seem to keep the focus of the composition on this-worldly actors.[36] Still, we note the ambiguity of קדושים, which is perhaps deliberate, so as to enhance the status of particular individuals. Of course, it is possible that heavenly beings are intended by *Hazon Gabriel*, so as to intimate that the leaders of the community enjoyed the company or status of angels.

Chariots

It seems less probable that the references to מרכבות/מרכבה ("chariot"/"chariots") in lines 26 and 67 can be taken as candidates for otherworldly beings, although, given the reverberations of Ezekiel's chariot throne vision in apocalyptic literature and *hekhalot* and *merkabah* traditions, we would be remiss not to consider the lexeme in a study of angelology. The vivid description of the chariot throne of God of Ezekiel 1 and 10 was influential in the Second Temple period and late antiquity, and one finds extensions of this tradition in a variety of texts, especially those that are apocalyptic and/or present visions of otherworldly realities. In these later incarnations, features of the chariot come to be understood as types of otherworldly beings in their own right, and thus we read about both *ophan-*

---

34. See Rev 11:18, which links prophets, holy ones, and those who fear the name of God as servants to be recompensed.
35. On traditions of three angels, see *1 En.* 87:2–3 and also Rev 14:6–9.
36. It is also true that some Second Temple texts present angels as priests in a heavenly temple, worshiping God; see, e.g., *Songs of the Sabbath Sacrifice* (4Q403 1 ii 22; 4Q405 frg. 7 lines 7, 8; 4Q405 frgs. 8–9 line 6) and *2 Enoch*. See Wassen, "Angels in the Dead Sea Scrolls," 505–8, Newsom, "'He Has Established for Himself Priests': Human and Angelic Priesthood in the Qumran Sabbath Shirot," in *Archaeology and History in the Dead Sea Scrolls: The New York University Conference in Memory of Yigael Yadin* (ed. Lawrence H. Schiffman; JSJSup 8; Sheffield: JSOT Press, 1990), 101–20; and Newsom, *Songs of the Sabbath Sacrifice*, 42. Expressions such as בני אל (11QMelch 2:14) or בני השמים (1QS 4:22; 1QH 11:23; 11QMelch 2:5) also indicate heavenly beings. Cf. Ps 29:1; see also Wassen, "Angels in the Dead Sea Scrolls," 500.

nim ("wheels"; *1 En.* 61:10; 71:7; *2 En.* 20:1) and *thrones* as veritable classes of angels (*T. Levi* 3:8; Col 1:16; *2 En.* 20:1 [J]).[37] Chariots are also personified and presented as a class of angels already in *Songs of the Sabbath Sacrifice* (4Q403 1 ii); the notion of heavenly worship likewise is attested in apocalyptic literature (see, e.g., *1 Enoch* 39–40; Revelation 4–5), and the animation of and praise by phenomena within the heavenly temple, like the wheels, flourishes in later *hekhalot* and *merkabah* mysticism (see, e.g., *3 Enoch* 30). The reference to "chariots" in line 26 could spring from such a trajectory, and the possibility that seven chariots are being indicated, per the transcription and translation of Yardeni and Elizur, is intriguing because of the importance of the number seven in *Songs of the Sabbath Sacrifice*.[38] As heavenly beings, chariots are typically presented in the context of ascents, where seers observe the chariots, along with other animated architectural structures, worshiping the divine in the context of a supernal temple.[39] That sort of otherworldly setting or ascent is lacking in *Hazon Gabriel*, and the fuller context of each lexeme, at least in terms of what is extant, does not support a comparable picture of מרכבות/מרכבה.

Line 67 makes reference to a single chariot, and while it could refer to God's chariot throne, if one follows Qimron and Yuditsky's transcription and translation ("this is the chariot . . ."), there is little else to suggest a type of heavenly being. The reference to chariots in line 26 is a more ambiguous case. For example, four spirits or winds (רחות השמים), identified with chariots (מרכבות) in Zech 6:1–6, patrol the earth (6:7), safeguarding various regions. To the extent that רחות intends heavenly beings here, it is possible that this imagery, which is either taken from Zechariah or mutually appropriated from another source, may illumine the reference to chariots in *HazGab* 26, suggesting particular beings. Yet, at the same time, the visions of Zechariah include other imagery associated with divine agents who patrol the earth or act on God's behalf (see Zech 1:8–11, four horses; 2:3–4, four blacksmiths).

We consider, thus, other ways of understanding "chariots" in line 26. Chariots are also suggestive of military action and, in reference to the deity, are evocative of divine might, which can overcome enemies. Qimron and Yuditsky, reading line 26 in light of line 27, may arrive at such a meaning for "chariots"

---

37. See Saul M. Olyan, *A Thousand Thousands Served Him: Exegesis and the Naming of Angels in Ancient Judaism* (TSAJ 36; Tübingen: Mohr, 1993), 34–42, 61–65. Olyan speculates that the latter class of divine being derived from the thrones mentioned in Dan 7:9.

38. See Newsom, *Songs of the Sabbath Sacrifice*, 12; and Hanan Eshel, מתי נהגו לומר את "שירות עולת השבת", *Meghillot* 4 (2003): 3–12; and see above.

39. See also Ra'anan S. Boustan, "Angels in the Architecture: Temple Art and the Poetics of Praise in the *Songs of the Sabbath Sacrifice*," in *Heavenly Realms and Earthly Realities in Late Antique Religions* (ed. Ra'anan S. Boustan and Annette Yoshiko Reed; New York: Cambridge University Press, 2004), 195–212, esp. 204–5. For another reference in the Qumran Scrolls to "chariots" in the context of the temple, see 4Q286 frg.1.

here. Their transcription for lines 26b–27 is as follows: אלה המרכבות שמֹעַ [קוֹ]ל֯ שׁוֹד֯ ירושלם ואת ערי יהודה ינחם למען ("the God of chariots will listen to the [cry] of Jerusalem and will console the cities of Judah for the sake of"). The language of this reading recalls Ps 68:18, which praises the Almighty from whom kings scatter, as it envisages God coming from Sinai with mighty chariotry (רכב אלהים; LXX: τὸ ἅρμα). Similarly, heavenly armies calling to mind rumbling chariots could indicate in *Hazon Gabriel* the divine taking action on behalf of Jerusalem and Israel (lines 13–14, 24–25, 57). The reference to the "glory of YHWH" in the preceding line (line 25; הנה כבוד יהוה אלהים) suggests God decisively acting on his people's behalf, defending Jerusalem against the attack of the nations, as one finds in Zechariah 14 (see also Joel 3).

The transcription and translation of Knohl and Yardeni and Elizur for lines 26b–27 differ and evoke another scenario: אלה המרכבות שבע [ע]ל֯ שׁעֹר֯ ירושלם ושׁעֲרי יהודה ינחו֯ למען ("These are the chariots, seven, [un]to(?) the gate(?) of Jerusalem, and the gates of Judah, and … for the sake of"). With this reading, one could understand the chariots in association with Zion or the temple and its environs. The references to David (lines 16, 72), the glory of the Lord that reigns from his seat (מקום or מושב as an allusion to the temple; lines 23–24), the gate of Jerusalem and the gates of Judah (line 27) and the several notable references to Jerusalem (lines 12, 14, 33, 36, 39, 57) provide another framework for "chariots." Such imagery could recall, for example, the ten bronze stands (המכנות עשר נחשת) described with wheels like those of chariots (כמעשה אופן המרכבה; cf. 1 Kgs 7:27–37, esp. 7:33), the chariots of the sun (מרכבות השמש, 2 Kgs 23:11) or the golden chariot of the cherubim (המרכבה הכרובים זהב, 1 Chr 28:18) associated with the ark of the covenant, which were located in the temple or the temple complex. Hence, there are many different ways in which "chariots" could be understood in this work apart from the matrix of angelology. While the language might suggest a heavenly cohort with chariotry—the "hosts" that accompany God in defending Jerusalem, for example—there is little to suggest that מרכבות here are the animated chariots engaged in worship of the divine, as they appear in later mystical writings.[40]

---

40. I would agree with David Hamidović ("La *Vision de Gabriel*," *RHPR* 89 [2009]: 147–68, esp. 157) that the reference to chariots occurs in the context of an eschatological battle. I would disagree, however, with his move to associate the chariots with either the seven angels distinguished in Second Temple tradition (see above) or with seven chariots of the seven heavens as presented in *Reʾuyyot Yeḥezqeʾl*. There is no reason to assume such a cosmology for *Hazon Gabriel*. Multiple heavens with different classes of beings predominate in literature with ascents and heavenly journeys (such as *2 Enoch*), which are lacking in this composition.

Michael and Gabriel

While much of the angelology of *Hazon Gabriel* recalls language from postexilic prophetic writings such as Zechariah, references to Michael (line 28) and Gabriel (lines 77, 80, 83) point the reader toward apocalypses and apocalyptic literature. As noted above, although the reading of line 28 is disputed, it would appear that Michael is mentioned in association with other angels (whether with three angels or "hosts" [צבאות]), and the lines that follow, 29–32, suggest the explanation of a vision. As noted above, the reading of Knohl and Bar-Asher for line 28 has merit in light of traditions about four prominent angels; we also consider briefly two other possible contexts for the reference to Michael in *Hazon Gabriel*.

On the one hand, this section of *Hazon Gabriel*, in light of lines 29–32, is evocative of a stock scene of the visionary (whether human or divine; see above) and an interpreting angel; such accounts flourished in the Second Temple and late antique periods (see, e.g., Zech 1:7–11; 2:1–6; 4:1–7; 6:1–8; *1 En.* 22:8–13; 27:1–4; Dan 7:15–27; 8:13–26; 12:5–13). In addition, there are other contemporaneous texts in which Michael serves as an interpreting angel. Distinguished in *1 Enoch* 20 as the angel placed over the good ones of humankind,[41] Michael explains to Enoch a vision of seven extraordinary mountains, one of which serves as the throne of God, and a tree reserved for the righteous and pious (*1 En.* 24:2–25:6). In "Michael's Words" (4Q529), Michael again is featured in the context of a vision of mountains, facilitating and perhaps interpreting a vision of Gabriel. There are, of course, other angels accorded the role of *angelus interpres* in the Second Temple period, from the unnamed angels in Zechariah to Gabriel in Daniel. With regard to the early Enoch literature, for example, Michael is not accorded a unique role as an interpreting angel; both unnamed angels, as in Zechariah 1–6, and other prominent angels like Gabriel, Sariel (or Uriel; see Astronomical Book and *4 Ezra*), Raphael (see also Tob 6:6–8) serve in that capacity as well.[42]

On the other hand, Michael does appear prominently in a number of texts in various contexts; his role has often been characterized as that of a celestial warrior, and he has been associated with eschatological themes. This understanding of Michael offers another possible reconstruction of the scene in line 28 and what precedes and follows. If we follow the tentative reading of Qimron and Yuditsky ("The Hosts of Michael [the] angel and for all the lovers") for line 28, צבאות suggests a heavenly legion with Michael as the leader of an angelic brigade. This scenario could be strengthened by what precedes in lines 24–26, which are indebted to Hag 2:6 and suggest that God will act decisively and on a grand scale on behalf of his people. The reference to chariots in line 26 could likewise fit a scenario of the divine executing judgment (see Isa 66:15–16; also Hag 2:21–22).

---

41. On the reading of *1 En.* 20:5, see Nickelsburg, *1 Enoch 1*, 294. Michael is presented here as patron of either the people of Israel or of the righteous (see *1 En.* 25:4–5).

42. See Nickelsburg, *1 Enoch 1*, 294–95.

Such a setting recalls characterizations of Michael as a celestial warrior. Michael is presented, for example, as one of the chief princes (Dan 10:13) or as the great prince who stands over the people (Dan 10:21; 12:1). Because Michael appears in a number of texts as ἀρχιστράτηγος, the title might bear some connection to the "commander of the Lord's host" (שר־צבא־יהוה) from Josh 5:14 (see also LXX).[43] While the characterization of Michael as a warring angel (cf. Rev 12:7-9) has been challenged by some scholars who assert that Michael is tied rather to eschatological contexts (cf., e.g., *T. Ab.* A 7-8; *T. Isaac* 2:1; *T. Jac.* 1:6; Jude 9, where Michael serves as psychopompos),[44] either view of Michael could be accommodated in the reading proposed by Qimron and Yuditsky. As Mach, who rejects a unique association of military functions with Michael, notes, military help is associated also with eschatological salvation.[45] What is significant is that Michael is distinguished in some manner in *Hazon Gabriel*. Although Michael is frequently mentioned as one of four angels in Second Temple texts (see, e.g., *1 Enoch* 9–11), here he, like Gabriel, is highlighted. Amid numerous Second Temple and late antique texts that refer to angels, named and unnamed, some may focus exclusively on Michael (4Q470 fragment mentioning Zedekiah[46]), on Michael and Gabriel (Dan 8:16; 9:21; 10:13, 21; 12:1; 4Q529; cf. also 4Q285 frg. 10.3 [though some conjecture that the names of two other angels would have followed], *Gk. Apoc. Ezra* 2:1; 4:7) or may privilege Michael (1QM 17:6–8; *1 En.* 69:14–15; 71:3; Rev 12:7-9).[47] Here, what has been preserved of *Hazon Gabriel* seems most like Daniel and what is preserved of 4Q529.[48]

---

43. See Michael Mach, "Michael," *DDD*, 2nd ed., 569-72, esp. 570. Mach also calls attention to the unnamed "prince of the army" of Dan 8:11, which might allude to Michael as well. Line 81 would also seem to feature the expression שר השרין. Could this be an allusion to Michael as a supreme "prince" or "commander"? Perhaps, though the context of the expression does not make such an interpretation clear.

44. See, e.g., Mach, "Michael," 570-71.

45. Ibid., 570.

46. See Erik Larson, "4Q470 and the Angelic Rehabilitation of King Zedekiah," *DSD* 1 (1994): 210-28.

47. On the prominent role of Michael in the magical papyri, see Thomas Kraus, "Angels in the Magical Papyri: The Classical Example of Michael, the Archangel," in Reiterer, *Angels: The Concept of Celestial Beings*, 611-27.

48. In addition to many certain references to Michael in Second Temple texts and the Qumran Scrolls, there are many instances where scholars suggest that a particular angelic figure in a text may be identified with Michael, even if Michael is not explicitly named. Thus, some associate Michael with "the one like a human being" in Dan 7:13 (see Collins, *Daniel*, 310), the "Prince of Light" in the *War Scroll* (1QM 13:10-11; Davidson, *Angels at Qumran*, 147-49), Melchizedek (11Q13; Adam van der Woude, "Melchisedek als himmlische Erlösergestalt in den neugefundenen eschatologischen Midraschim aus Qumran Höhle XI," *OTS* 14 [1965]: 354-73), and the speaker of the Self-Glorification Hymn (4Q491; Morton Smith, "Ascent to the Heavens and Deification in 4QMᵃ," in Schiffman, *Archaeology and History in the Dead Sea Scrolls*, 181-88). On Michael and Gabriel paired in an Aramaic incantation, see Hamidović, "La *Vision de Gabriel*," 157.

The angel Gabriel also appears in *Hazon Gabriel* in at least three lines (77, 80, and 83). In these contexts, Gabriel presents himself, perhaps to a seer or visionary; the contexts for such presentations are, sadly, obscure in the current state of the composition. The transcriptions for the first part of line 77 are comparable, though not much at the end of the line is extant; Yardeni and Elizur, Qimron and Yuditsky, and Knohl read: מי אנכי אני גבריאל. The first part of line 80 would seem to refer to a sign (האות) being manifest within three days, a topic on which we will not linger;[49] the second half of the line presents Gabriel again as the speaker: אני גבריאל ("I am Gabriel"), an expression that appears again at the end of line 83. One curiosity is the use of different forms for the first person in these expressions. Why use אנכי in line 77 and אני elsewhere? Rendsburg suggests that in line 77 *Hazon Gabriel* utilizes the expression מי אנכי from Exod 3:11; 1 Sam 18:18; and 2 Sam 7:18 for the purpose of archaizing.[50]

Like Michael, Gabriel is a well-known angel from Second Temple and late antique literature. In fact, of the named angels to emerge from this period, Michael and Gabriel are two of the leading heavenly beings. Early references to them both occur in the Book of the Watchers, where they appear alongside two other angels, Raphael and Sariel.[51] In this context they reside in the heavenly sanctuary, oversee affairs on earth, and are given the task of binding and punishing the rebellious angels and their offspring and of restoring the earth (cf. *1 Enoch* 9–11). The same four named angels, which the Byzantine chronographer George Synkellos (Syncellus) designated οἱ τέσσαρες μεγάλοι ἀρχάγγελοι ("the four great archangels"), are included as well in the *War Scroll* (1QM 9:14–16) and distinguished in other texts. Though they continue to be known in this group of four, both Gabriel and Michael appear together in Daniel and also in 4Q529, "Michael's Words" (see above).

Gabriel, like Michael, plays a distinctive role in many texts as well. Some scholars associate Gabriel with revelation, calling attention to Gabriel in Dan 8:15–26 and 9:21–27 and to the depiction of the angel in Luke 1:19 and 26 (cf. also

---

49. The transcription and translation of Qimron and Yuditsky and Knohl for the first part of line 77 ("by three days the sign") is comparable to that of Yardeni and Elitzur, though they do not include האות in their transcription, following ימין. Knohl argued for a different transcription for line 77 previously but has been persuaded of the reading of האות now, following an initial suggestion from Ron Hendel, *BAR* 35 (2009): 8 (see also the contribution of Knohl, this volume).

50. Rendsburg, "Linguistic and Stylistic Notes," 111; and above.

51. While the four are presented as Michael, Sariel, Raphael, and Gabriel in the Aramaic (cf. 4QEn^a 1 iv and 4QEn^b 1 iii), the extant Greek manuscripts of the Book of the Watchers feature Uriel (Codex Panopolitanus and Syncellus) or Istrael (Codex Panopolitanus) in place of Sariel (*1 En.* 40:10). In the first century B.C.E. or C.E. Book of the Parables (*1 En.* 40:2–10), four angels designated as "presences" (*1 En.* 40:10)—here Michael, Gabriel, Raphael and Phanuel—are situated around the sides of the divine throne. *Pirqe R. El.* 4 has a similar arrangement featuring Uriel instead of Phanuel.

Sib. Or. 8:459–63).[52] David Hamidović has suggested, based on descriptions in Daniel 10, the *War Scroll*, and *1 Enoch,* that Gabriel was associated also with a militant role.[53] The name of the angel, perhaps "man of God" or "God is my warrior," may have lent itself to a view of Gabriel as a warring angel. While it is true that as one of a group of four angels (the archangels), Gabriel also is presented as executing God's judgment (see, e.g., *1 Enoch* 9–11), and the roles of interpreting angel, archangel, and celestial warrior need not be mutually exclusive,[54] in *Hazon Gabriel* the picture of Gabriel that emerges is primarily that of a revealer. In what is preserved of the inscription, Gabriel converses and discloses. This depiction of the angel recalls the otherworldly messengers of Second Temple and late antique apocalypses.

Hazon Gabriel in Light of Second Temple and Late Antique Angelologies

How do the depictions of angels in the *Gabriel Revelation* compare to those from other Second Temple or late antique texts? A challenge to making any sort of comparison is that *Hazon Gabriel* no longer presents us with a complete composition. Thus, when considering what the inscription lacks in relation to other texts, one necessarily crafts arguments from silence; moreover, we do not know how the composition was used—that is, the context in which it was read and what other texts or traditions might have complemented it. Even so, the text that remains offers a useful place for beginning a conversation and from this we can observe aspects of *Hazon Gabriel* that are distinctive. Otherworldly beings do not figure as prominently as in some pseudepigraphical writings, or among some of the nonbiblical texts of Qumran scrolls, and later *hekhalot* or *merkabah* texts. Further, the diverse expressions used for otherworldly beings and demonic counterparts, notable especially in many of nonbiblical texts of the scrolls, are lacking in *Hazon Gabriel*. The angelology of the *Gabriel Revelation* recalls especially that of the highly stylized visions in Zechariah and the interpreting (and named) angels of Daniel and 4Q529.

To provide a context for such an assertion, we consider briefly some aspects of Second Temple and late antique angelologies, including distinctive terms used to represent such beings as well as the emergence of special classes of beings and hierarchies. Several designations employed for divine beings in Second Temple and late antique texts are lacking in *Hazon Gabriel*. Missing are references to

---

52. Hamidović ("La *Vision de Gabriel*," 159) observes that Gabriel is presented as an angel of revelation also in the Qur'an, Sura 2, 91–92.

53. David Hamidović, "More Traditions about the Angel Gabriel in the Dead Sea Scrolls," paper presented at the Society of Biblical Literature International Meeting in Tartu, Estonia, July 29, 2010.

54. On the name of Gabriel, see, e.g., John J. Collins, "Gabriel," *DDD*, 2nd ed., 338–39, esp. 338; and idem, *Daniel*, 336.

עיר/עירין ("watcher"/"watchers"), a name for a type of otherworldly being familiar from Enochic literature (4QEn^e 1 xxii; *1 En.* 22:6; translated in Greek as ἐγρήγοροι; see Greek *1 En.* 10:7), Daniel 4 (MT 4:10, 14, 20), and several texts from Qumran (CD 2:18; 1QapGen 2:1, 16; 4Q543 8).[55] Further, one does not see in the extant portions of *Hazon Gabriel* some of the more distinctive terms for otherworldly beings that appear in many of the texts discovered at Qumran.[56] That rich vocabulary includes אלים ("godlike beings"; e.g., 1QH 15:31; 18:10; 23:23; 1QM 1:10, 11; 4Q181 frg.1.4), רוחות ("spirits," as in "spirits of truth" [רוחי אמת, 1QS 4:23; 1QM 13:10]; "spirits of knowledge" [רוחות דעת, 1QH 11:23]; and "spirits of his lot" [רוחי גורלו, 1QS 3:24; 1QM 13:2, 4; 11QMelch 2:12]), אלוהי אורים ("godlike beings of light," 4Q405 frg. 46.2), and other titles combined with אלוהי and אלי, הרמים ("lofty ones," 4Q403 1 i 30), and כרובים (cherubim, 4Q403 1 ii 15; 11QShirShab frgs. 3–4:4).

The diversity of terms is matched by a growing interest in classifying or systematizing angelic beings by the first century of the Common Era, already assisted by—perhaps anticipated by—the appearance of the seraphim (Isa 6:2–6), cherubim (Gen 3:24; 2 Sam 22:11; Ezek 10:1–22: Ps 18:11), and living beings (חיות; Ezek 1:5–15) in the Hebrew Bible.[57] The chariot throne of Ezekiel 1 and 10 seems to have been the impetus for speculation on additional types of otherworldly beings, such as אופנים ("wheels"; cf. Ezek 1:16), גלגל ("wheelworks"; cf. Ezek 10:13) and "thrones" (cf. *T. Levi* 3; Col 1:16). An example of such speculation on different classes of angels is to be found in the Parables, from the first century B.C.E. or C.E.; the Parables, preserved only in Geʿez, make reference to *cherubin, seraphin, ophannin*, angels of the power and angels of the principalities (*1 En.* 61:10). Also from the first century, *T. Levi* 3:1–8 enumerates the powers of the hosts, thrones and authorities, angels, and angels of the presence of the Lord. First-century Christians including Paul, who is also apocalyptic in orientation, make reference to classes of otherworldly beings such as ἀρχαί ("rulers"; Rom 8:38), ἐξουσία ("authority"; e.g., 1 Cor 15:24), and δυνάμις ("power": Rom 8:38; 1 Cor 15:24). Such interest in the types of angels and where one might encounter these in heavenly strata is especially pronounced in *hekhalot* and *merkabah* lit-

---

55. On the use of this title, see also *T. Reu.* 5:6–7, *T. Naph.* 3:5, and *2 En.* 18:1 (the "Grigori" derive from the Greek ἐγρήγοροι). The name of this particular class of angels may derive from the idea that these otherworldly beings remain alert and do not sleep (see *1 En.* 71:7), guarding over the deeds of humankind (see *1 En.* 20:1). See also Robert Murray, "The Origin of Aramaic ʿir, Angel," *Or* 53 (1984): 303–17; and Nickelsburg, *1 Enoch 1*, 140.

56. On the use of these expressions to denote celestial forces, see David E. Aune, "Archai," *DDD*, 2nd ed., 77–80; and Hans Dieter Betz, "Authorities," *DDD*, 2nd ed., 124–25. Betz calls attention to parallels in *T. Levi* 3:8; *1 En.* 61:10 ("the angels of the power"); *2 En.*20:1 (J); and *Ascen. Isa.* 1:4.

57. Bill Rebiger, "Angels in Rabbinic Literature," in Reiterer, *Angels: The Concept of Celestial Beings*, 629–44, esp. 633–34; see also Olyan (*Thousand Thousands Served Him*, 32–50), who suggests that numerous names and classes of angels derive from exegesis of the Hebrew Bible.

erature. Even in works like *Hekhalot Rabbati* that lack systematic angelelogies, meditations on heavenly beings such as the חיות ("living creatures"; see above), praising or worshiping the divine, as well as lists of various types of angels (e.g., *3 Enoch*), are common in these visionary texts.[58]

Perhaps this more extensive speculation on heavenly beings is absent from *Hazon Gabriel* because the composition is decidedly this-worldly in orientation. In contrast to so many apocalypses that take up the heavenly realms and the angels that populate these (e.g., *2 Enoch*), *Hazon Gabriel* concerns events transpiring on earth, specifically a siege of Jerusalem. In that respect, the *Gabriel Revelation* shares with Ezekiel 38–39, Zechariah 14, and Rev 20:8–9 a motif of the nations attacking Israel or Jerusalem, to be defended ultimately by God; thus, the locus of activity is earth. Moreover, the extant content does not suggest that selections of *Hazon Gabriel* now lost to us offered speculation about angels in a heavenly temple or in various levels of heaven, akin to what one finds in *2 Enoch* and *hekhalot* and *merkabah* traditions.

Moreover, the available text of the inscription does not take up as extensively as many pseudepigraphical texts (e.g., the early Enoch literature) particular roles and functions for the angels, especially those distinguished as archangels (see, e.g., *1 Enoch* 20; 40:2–10). Unless mention of מרכבות in *Hazon Gabriel* refers to a class of otherworldly beings (as in the *Songs of the Sabbath Sacrifice* [4Q403 1 ii 15] and *merkabah* literature), it would seem that the inscription does not assume the same rich vocabulary for and speculation concerning angels that is employed especially in late Second Temple and late antique texts.

At the same time, *Hazon Gabriel* does not exhibit an interest in demons or feature the sort of demonology that emerges in early Enoch literature and at Qumran.[59] The theme of rebellious angels who descend to earth, as especially articulated in *1 Enoch* 6–16, not only is found in many texts associated with the patriarch Enoch (e.g., Animal Apocalypse; Parables; *2 Enoch*) but was known widely in antiquity as well (see CD 2:18; *Jubilees*; Jude 6; 2 Pet 2:4; Justin Martyr).[60]

---

58. See comments on angelology in Peter Schäfer, *The Hidden and Manifest God: Some Major Themes in Early Jewish Mysticism* (SUNY Series in Judaica; Albany: State University of New York Press, 1992), 21–36, 62–66, 81–86, 103–7, 129–34.

59. On evil spirits, fallen angels, and demons in Enoch literature and among the scrolls, see, respectively, Archie T. Wright, *The Origin of Evil Spirits: The Reception of Genesis 6.1–4 in Early Jewish Literature* (WUNT 2/198; Tübingen: Mohr Siebeck, 2005), 138–65; and Philip A. Alexander, "The Demonology of the Dead Sea Scrolls," in *The Dead Sea Scrolls after Fifty Years: A Comprehensive Assessment* (ed. Peter W. Flint and James C. VanderKam; 2 vols; Leiden: Brill, 1999), 2:331–53, esp. 331, where he observes: "Belief in demons was central to [the Qumran sect's] worldview."

60. James C. VanderKam offers a helpful survey of ancient Christian texts that know and refer to the tradition of the rebellious watchers: "1 Enoch, Enochic Motifs, and Enoch in Early Christian Literature," in *The Jewish Apocalyptic Heritage in Early Christianity* (ed. James C. VanderKam and William Adler; CRINT, Section 3, Jewish Traditions in Early Christian Literature 4; Assen: Van Gorcum; Minneapolis: Fortress, 1996), 33–101.

Speculation apparently extended to the rebellious angels, who, much like their beneficent counterparts, were named and associated with particular—in their case, forbidden— crafts (cf. *1 Enoch* 7 and 69); 4Q510 frg. 1.5–6, in which the sage seeks protection from ravaging angels, bastard spirits, liliths and demons, suggests the range of demons that were feared in antiquity (cf. also 4Q511 frg. 10.1–2).[61]

Otherworldly beings as manifestations of evil proliferate as well in literature of this period. These include Melchiresha (4Q280 frg. 1.2; 4Q286 frg. 7), Mastema (*Jub*. 10:8; CD 16:5; 1QM 13:12), Belial (1QS 1:16–2:8; 1QH 10:18, 24; 11:29, 30, 33; 12:11, 14; 13:28, 41; 14:24; 15:6; 4Q390 1:11; *T. Levi* 18:4; cf. also 2 Cor 6:14–15), satans (cf. *1 En.* 40:7; 54:6; 69:6), ὁ Σατανᾶς (= Satan; cf. Mark 3:23; Luke 13:16; John 13:27), ὁ διάβολος (= the devil; cf. Matt 4:5; Luke 4:3; John 6:70; Rev. 12:9), or opponents of the angels (like the army of Belial [1QM 1:13]; see also Matt 25:41). In contrast to these Second Temple period and late antique texts, *Hazon Gabriel* seems rather restrained in its angelology and mute with regard to demonology. What does this datum communicate? Though belief in demons was widespread in Second Temple and late antique Judaism, this apocalyptic text has more in common with proto-apocalyptic texts like Zechariah 3, where *satan* is but an accuser within a heavenly court.[62]

Does the angelology of *Hazon Gabriel* reveal anything of the text's provenance? Though perhaps not as telling with regard to situating the composition in space and time, the angelology of the inscription is instructive for situating the composition relative to other literature. Some readings of the text—for example, if one accepts the proposed reading of "three angels and Michael" for line 28 or "seven angels" for line 31—and the context of lines 29–32 as that of an interpreting angel providing revelations are reminiscent of what one finds in early Enochic literature. Still, many distinctive terms used for angels (e.g., "watchers") and some of the roles assigned to particular angels in the Enoch literature are not present in *Hazon Gabriel*. Further, the angelology of the inscription is not as elaborate or extensive as what one finds in many of the Qumran scrolls. The rich vocabulary

---

61. Alexander ("Demonology of the Dead Sea Scrolls," 332) also notes that the scrolls imply a complex demonic world with different orders and classes of demons. On the role of demonology in the community that preserved early Enoch writings, see Pierluigi Piovanelli, "'Sitting by the Waters of Dan,' or The 'Tricky Business' of Tracing the Social Profile of the Communities That Produced the Earliest Enochic Texts," in *The Early Enoch Literature* (ed. Gabriele Boccaccini and John J. Collins; JSJSup 121; Leiden: Brill, 2007), 257–81, esp. 277–78. The developing demonologies anticipate later apotropaic traditions that sought to ward off particular, named demons. See Joseph Naveh and Shaul Shaked, *Amulets and Magic Bowls: Aramaic Incantations of Late Antiquity* (Leiden: E. J. Brill, 1985), 159–214; and Schäfer, "Jewish Magic in Late Antiquity and the Middle Ages," *JSS* 41 (1990): 75–91. 4Q560 may have served the same purposes.

62. Alexander, "Demonology of the Dead Sea Scrolls," 351. Later Judaism also had a developed demonology, which, suggests Alexander, seems more complex and shares conceptual affinity with Greek magical papyri (p. 352).

used for heavenly beings in texts such as the *Songs of the Sabbath Sacrifice* is lacking in the inscription, as is an interest in demons. Moreover, there is little evidence from angelology for placing *Hazon Gabriel* in the immediate foreground of *hekhalot* and *merkabah* literature, which feature ascents, developed angelologies, celestial worship (*unio liturgica*, the liturgical union or "communion of humans and angels") and transformative experiences for the individual.[63] The angelology of *Hazon Gabriel* recalls especially Zechariah and the latter chapters of Daniel.

The recognition of similarities and differences in the angelology of *Hazon Gabriel* vis-à-vis other Second Temple and late antique angelologies does not necessarily offer dividends for speculation on provenance. Having no information on how the text was used or what texts or traditions were utilized alongside it is quite limiting.[64] It is possible that *Hazon Gabriel* could have been used at some time by a community at Qumran, though defining what we mean by "community" may be no small feat. Scholars now prefer to speak of the "diverse communities behind the Qumran Scrolls";[65] moreover, communities can evolve over time. Distinctive vocabulary might indicate "sectarian" tendencies, but the absence of such language does not necessarily imply that a composition was not utilized by a sect.[66] Even so, the angelology of *Hazon Gabriel* does not provide compelling reasons for associating this composition with many of the distinctive writings among the Qumran scrolls such as the *Serekh Ha-Yahad*.[67] Possible reference to

---

63. Schäfer's recent monograph (*The Origins of Jewish Mysticism* [Tübingen: Mohr Siebeck, 2009], esp. 341) is an important corrective to facile associations between early Jewish literature and *hekhalot* and *merkabah* mysticism. For example, Schäfer rejects attempts of many scholars to find points of connection between the *Songs of the Sabbath Sacrifice* and *hekhalot* or *merkabah* literature (pp. 144–45, 152–53). "Whereas the possibility cannot be ruled out that some of the ideas and motifs expressed in the songs are taken up in the Hekhalot literature, it is pointless to try and establish a literary and historical connection between the songs and Hekhalot literature" (p. 153).

64. I appreciate greatly the hypotheses offered by Hamidović, "La *Vision de Gabriel*," esp. 151–52, 161–63, that help to account for a context or setting for this composition; I look forward to further discussion of these proposals.

65. Alison Schofield, "Rereading S: A New Model of Textual Development in Light of the Cave 4 *Serekh* Copies," *DSD* 15 (2008): 96–120, esp. 120; see also eadem *From Qumran to the Yahad: A New Paradigm for the Textual Development for the Community Rule* (STDJ 77; Leiden: Brill, 2009). See also John J. Collins, *Beyond the Qumran Community: The Sectarian Movement of the Dead Sea Scrolls* (Grand Rapids: Eerdmans, 2010); and idem, "The Yahad and 'The Qumran Community,'" in *Biblical Traditions in Transmission: Essays in Honour of Michael A. Knibb* (ed. Charlotte Hempel and Judith Lieu; JSJSup 111; Leiden: Brill, 2006), 81–96.

66. Thus, Carol A. Newsom, "'Sectually Explicit' Literature from Qumran," in *The Hebrew Bible and Its Interpreters* (ed. William H. Propp, Baruch Halpern, and David Noel Freedman; Biblical and Judaic Studies 1; Winona Lake, Ind.: Eisenbrauns, 1990), 167–87, esp. 175–79.

67. Devorah Dimant, "The Qumran Manuscripts: Contents and Significance," in *Time to Prepare the Way in the Wilderness: Papers on the Qumran Scrolls by Fellows of the Institute*

groups of four or seven angels and the role of angels in revelations might tie the work to early Enoch literature. On the other hand, while the early literature associated with Enoch (i.e., the Book of the Watchers, the Animal Apocalypse) tends to be "this-worldly" in its eschatology, the seer still engages in an ascent and visits the heavenly temple, in addition to otherworldly sites, features lacking in the extant text of *Hazon Gabriel*. The vocabulary used for heavenly beings and the eschatological perspective of *Hazon Gabriel* are most like Zechariah and Daniel. Noting these similarities, however, does not shed more light on the provenance or use of this composition, the way it was read or by whom.

---

for Advanced Studies of the Hebrew University, Jerusalem, 1989–1990 (ed. Devorah Dimant and Lawrence H. Schiffman; STDJ 16; Leiden: Brill, 1995), 23–58, esp. 27–28; and also eadem, "Sectarian and Non-Sectarian Texts from Qumran: The Pertinence and Usage of a Taxonomy," *RevQ* 24 (2009): 7–18. But see also Charlotte Hempel, "Kriterien zur Bestimmung 'essenischer Verfasserschaft' von Qumrantexten," in *Qumran kontrovers: Beiträge zu den Textfunden vom Toten Meer* (ed. Jörg Frey and Hartmut Stegemann; Einblicke 6; Paderborn: Bonifatius, 2003), 71–85.

TEN

THE USE OF DANIEL IN THE *GABRIEL REVELATION*

Daewoong Kim

It has been widely recognized that the book of Daniel was used in the diverse Jewish literature of the Second Temple period. The popular use of Daniel in ancient Judaism finds additional support in a newly discovered inscription known as the *Gabriel Revelation*. Scholars generally agree that Daniel was formative in the shaping of the text of the inscription;[1] however, the Danielic elements remain unexplained. Despite its fragmentary state, the current form of the text does not deter us from discovering, as has already been demonstrated in previous studies, the numerous intertextual features between the *Gabriel Revelation* and the Jewish Scriptures. To understand the ways in which Daniel influenced the inscription, I will focus on the role of Gabriel, who announces the divine message and connects Daniel with other biblical traditions. I am concerned particularly with probing allusive words that the author of the *Gabriel Revelation* chooses in order to reactivate earlier scriptural texts.[2] Through my analysis of recognizable

---

1. See Ada Yardeni and Binyamin Elizur, "A Prophetic Text on Stone from the First Century BCE: First Publication" (in Hebrew), *Cathedra* 123 (2007): 155–66; Elisha Qimron and Alexey (Eliyahu) Yuditsky, "Notes on the Inscription 'The Vision of Gabriel'" (in Hebrew), *Cathedra* 133 (2009): 138–39; Israel Knohl, *Messiahs and Resurrection in 'The Gabriel Revelation'* (Kogol Library of Judaic Studies; London/New York: Continuum, 2009), 12–38; and Matthias Henze, "The *Gabriel Revelation* Reconsidered: A Response to Israel Knohl," paper presented at the SBL Annual Meeting in 2009 in New Orleans, Louisiana.

2. For the allusion as a device for the simultaneous activation of two individual texts, see Ziva Ben-Porat, "The Poetics of Literary Allusion," *PTL* 1, no. 1 (1976): 105–28; Carmela Perri, "On Alluding," *Poetics* 7, no. 3 (1978): 289–307; and William Irwin, "What Is an Allusion?" *JAAC* 59, no. 3 (2001): 287–97. For the biblical application of the theory of allusion, see Adele Berlin, "Qumran Laments and the Study of Lament Literature," in *Liturgical Perspectives: Prayer and Poetry in Light of the Dead Sea Scrolls. Proceedings of the Fifth International Symposium of the Orion Center for the Study of the Dead Sea Scrolls and Associated Literature, 19–23 January 2000* (ed. Esther G. Chazon; STDJ 48; Leiden: Brill, 2003), 6–17; Esther G. Chazon, "The Use of the Bible as a Key to Meaning in Psalms from Qumran," in *Emanuel: Studies in the Hebrew Bible, Septuagint, and Dead Sea Scrolls in Honor of Emanuel Tov* (ed. Shalom M. Paul et al.; VTSup 94; Leiden: Brill, 2003), 85–96; and Benjamin D. Sommer, *A Prophet Reads Scripture: Allusion in Isaiah 40–66* (Stanford: Stanford University Press, 1998).

meaningful allusions, I will argue that Gabriel as the main speaker provides the literary framework for the resonances with the earlier biblical sources.[3] I will also argue that the tradition of the coming of God is pivotal to the apocalyptic perspective of the Jewish group behind the *Gabriel Revelation*.

This paper is structured in three sections. I will begin by discussing the appearance of three Danielic figures in the inscription, with a special emphasis on the importance of the literary role played by Gabriel in the inscription. Two interpretive principles will be considered while exploring the meaning of the inscription. In the next two sections, I will concentrate my exegetical efforts mainly on identifying and deciphering allusions to the tradition of the coming of God, which is well integrated with the motif of the presence of God.

I. The Role of Gabriel in the *Gabriel Revelation*

The inscription contains three heavenly figures that are known only in Daniel in the Hebrew Bible. All the figures testify to the use of Daniel in the *Gabriel Revelation*. The first figure is the angel Gabriel. In the inscription, Gabriel speaks to a human addressee, playing the role of divine messenger in the dialogue that frames the inscription. The presence of the angel in the inscription is unmistakable. The name of Gabriel is mentioned no fewer than three times (Yardeni and Elizur, lines 77, 80, and 83). The connection between Gabriel in the inscription and the book of Daniel becomes clearer when it is observed that the angel speaks in ways evocative of an anonymous angelic speaker in Daniel. In line 21, Gabriel delivers a divine speech to the addressee, saying, "I shall tell you" (אגיד לכה). This language of Gabriel may well be traced back to Dan 10:21 and 11:2, where the anonymous angel makes a divine revelation to Daniel, stating, "I shall tell you" (לך אגיד).[4] Like the angels in Daniel, Gabriel in the *Gabriel Revelation* is shown to have a conversation with the human addressee. Although we do not know where and how the conversation begins, it seems reasonable to presume that Gabriel, as a messenger from God, is the only speaker to the human addressee.[5] I offer three pieces of evidence. First, as suggested in the addressee's question about the identity of the respondent, "Who are you?" (מי אתה), the addressee is speaking with only one respondent (line 77, Qimron and Yuditsky).[6] We hear of Gabriel's identity only in line 77, much later in the inscription. This seems to insinuate that Gabriel is already the unnamed respondent in the earlier lines of the text and divulges his identity only toward the end of the dialogue. Second, another archangel, Michael, who is mentioned in line 28, would hardly be regarded as another

---

3. Perri ("On Alluding," 301) suggests four kinds of effects in which the reader successfully understands allusion: recognizing, remembering, realizing, connecting.

4. Similarly, in Dan 8:19 Gabriel interprets the vision of Daniel, saying, "I will let you know" (מוֹדִיעֲךָ).

5. Yardeni and Elizur, "Prophetic Text," 156.

6. Yardeni and Elizur ("Prophetic Text," 158) suggests מי אנכי.

messenger in the inscription. Michael himself does not speak but is mentioned as part of the message of Gabriel. This implies that Michael is absent in the scene where Gabriel is talking to the addressee. True, in some early Jewish writings Michael appears as a speaker to human addressees.[7] By contrast, the *Gabriel Revelation* strictly follows the tradition of Daniel, where Michael does not speak but is always made known to a visionary by another angel (Dan 10:13, 21; 12:1). This, too, reflects the profound impact of Daniel on the inscription. Third and finally, the deliberate manner in which the speaker adopts a prophetic formula, "thus said the Lord/God,"[8] reinforces the likelihood that the *Gabriel Revelation* has a singular speaker. The series of the prophetic formulas strewn over the inscription appears to grant a literary coherence to the text. Put another way, the author effectively endows the whole inscription with the mood of biblical prophecy, as Gabriel constantly introduces divine speech by means of the formula.

Let me explain more about the conscious adoption of the prophetic formula by Gabriel. Although the inscription is often fragmentary, a closer reading finds that in almost every tenth line the author employs either the prophetic formula (e.g., lines 11, 19–20, 29–30, 58–59, and 69) or a variation of it (e.g., Yardeni and Elizur, lines 39–40).[9] Unfortunately, the text around line 50 is illegible, so we are unable to find the formula there. Fortunately, however, line 69 repeats the formula again, which demonstrates the rhythmic sequence of Gabriel's use of the formula. This observation leads us to expect that line 50 (or thereabout) should also contain either the formula or, as is the case in lines 39–40, a phrase modeled on the formula. It would seem, therefore, that the whole text of the *Gabriel Revelation* is formulated as a dialogue between a human visionary and the angel Gabriel, whose manner of speaking closely resembles that of the prophets.

In addition to Gabriel, whom I have identified as the only speaker of the inscription, the second and third heavenly figures corroborate the use of Daniel in the inscription. The angel Michael, who is mentioned in an anonymous angel's words to Daniel (Dan 10:13, 21), is introduced in the inscription by the angel Gabriel (line 28). Likewise, the mysterious character the "prince of princes" in Gabriel's interpretation of Daniel's vision in Dan 8:25, is referred to by Gabriel in line 81, though the immediate context is not known.

---

7. E.g., Seth (*Apoc. Mos.* 13:2), Enoch (*1 En.* 24:6), Abraham (*T. Abr.* A 7:11), Ezra (*Apoc. Ez.* 1:3; 4:2) and Baruch (*3 Bar.* 14:2).

8. The prophetic formula appears no fewer than eight times in the *Gabriel Revelation*. According to Yardeni and Elizur: כן אמר אלהים צבאות (line 11), כן] אמר יהוה אלהי ישראל] (line 13), כי אמר יהוה [ות]צבא אלהי ישראל (lines 29–30), כן אמר יהוה אלהים צבאות אלהי ישראל (lines 57–58), and כי אמר יהוה צבאות אלהי ישראל (lines 58–59). And according to Qimron and Yuditsky: כו אמר יהוה אלהים צבאות אלהי ישראל (lines 17–18), כו אמר [י]הוה צבאות אלהי ישראל (lines 19–20), and כה אמר יהוה צבאות אלהי ישראל (line 69).

9. Gary A. Rendsburg ("Linguistic and Stylistic Notes to the Hazon Gabriel Inscription," *DSD* 16 [2009]: 114–16) found eleven cases of variation, only some of which include the prophetic formula "thus says YHWH."

The use of these three Danielic figures in the inscription provides a valuable clue about the intended meaning of the inscription. The author was familiar with Daniel to such an extent that he could recast the biblical characters for his own composition. More importantly, the author could signal that the meaning of the inscription is closely related to the message of the biblical apocalypse. For example, the function of Gabriel as the primary speaker would have meant that the author expected the intended audience to grasp the point of the inscription on the basis of what Gabriel tells Daniel in the apocalyptic sections of Daniel.[10] For modern interpreters, accordingly, Gabriel's explanations of Daniel's visionary experiences may well be one of the key backdrops against which the meaning of the inscription emerges in greater detail. In the same vein, the author's appropriation of the other two Danielic figures in the *Gabriel Revelation* indicates that the author tried to communicate his thought to the audience through their shared knowledge of the book of Daniel.

What specific point did the author of the *Gabriel Revelation* attempt to make by remolding the three Danielic figures? In dealing with this question and exploring the other important textual elements of the inscription, I would like to suggest two principles. The first principle resides in the central role that the author assigns to Gabriel. We need to be mindful of how Gabriel delivers the divine message to the addressee during the military threat of the invading nations. Indeed, it is crucial that Gabriel takes a prominent role during the military crisis, which in the *Gabriel Revelation* is portrayed as the historical situation of Jerusalem. Such a characterization of Gabriel may be in line with that of the targumic tradition, which often views Gabriel as God's agent fighting for God's people against their foreign enemy. At the time of Hezekiah's reign, for example, the Assyrian king Sennacherib intends to make war on Jerusalem. During the night of Passover, God sends "the angel Gabriel" to the invading Assyrian armies, and the angel destroys them with a consuming fire (*Tg. 2 Chr* 32:21).[11] Gabriel, the guardian angel of Jerusalem, also stands against Babylon and Persia. Even after the destruction of Jerusalem, it is Gabriel, "prince of Zion," who declares in a poignant tone a blessing on the one that avenges Zion on her cruel murderer, Babylon (*Tg. Ps.* 137:8).[12] Gabriel is said to help in an invisible way Queen Esther thwart the scheme of the wicked Persian minister. Haman is pushed by Gabriel to lean over the bed of Queen Esther only to stir King Xerxes's burning rage against

---

10. God is the most eminent character in the *Gabriel Revelation*, to be sure. Nevertheless, the character of God in the inscription seems to be carefully designed and speaks only through Gabriel, which means that Gabriel serves as the primary speaker.

11. Roger Le Déaut and Jacques Robert, *Targum des Chroniques (Cod. Vat. Urb. Ebr. 1), Tome II, Texte et Glossaire* (AnBib 51; Rome: Biblical Institute Press, 1971), 155.

12. Luis Díez Merino, *Targum de Salmos: Edición príncipe del Ms. Villa-Amil n. 5 de Alfonso de Zamora* (Bibliotheca Hispana Biblica 6; Madrid: Consejo Superior de Investigaciones Científicas, Instituto "Francisco Suárez," 1982), 106, 316.

him (*Tg. Esth. I.* 7:8).[13] In short, Gabriel's role as the main speaker in the inscription would reflect the author's intention to inspire his community to expect the divine intervention by which the long-trusted angelic guardian of the Israelites would lead Jerusalem to survive the current military crisis. With this point in mind, the *Gabriel Revelation* is to be read in terms of the anticipation of the faithful remnant for the restoration of Jerusalem. The Jewish community behind the *Gabriel Revelation* may well have been interested in political independence from the domination of the Roman Empire.

The second principle for understanding the message of the *Gabriel Revelation* resides in the way Daniel is combined with other biblical traditions such as the Pentateuch and the Prophets. Gabriel not only is an iconic character who constantly leads the audience to remember what the biblical Gabriel taught Daniel. More interestingly, Gabriel's language, which alludes to earlier biblical passages, would have invited the audience to see how the biblical angel blends Daniel with other biblical traditions to create a new meaning. A good example for the mixture of Daniel with an earlier scriptural tradition is found in line 16, where we are given a hint regarding the identity of the addressee. Observe that the angel in Daniel employs a phrase from Ezekiel. Despite the first ten unintelligible lines of the text, we are able to get some knowledge of the initial literary setting of the inscription. In the divine speech Gabriel delivers, God informs the human addressee of the upcoming military campaign against Jerusalem (lines 13–14). Just two lines later, God calls him "my servant David" and commands, "ask me!" (line 16).[14] In response, the addressee demands God's answer to a question he had previously asked. Thus he speaks to Gabriel, "Answer me!" (lines 16–17). The next statement of the addressee, "I ask you for the sign" (lines 17), further implies that the answer the addressee wants from God is in some way related to the salvation of Jerusalem.

What does the addressee have in mind when he asks God for the sign? I suggest that a clue can be found in the epithetical phrase, "my servant David" (עבדי דוד). The phrase may well allude to the aspiration that God may reside in Israel (line 16). The word order of the phrase is worthy of our special attention.[15]

---

13. Bernard Grossfeld, *The First Targum to Esther: According to the MS Paris Hebrew 110 of the Bibliothèque nationale* (New York: Sepher-Hermon, 1983), 29, 65.

14. Following Knohl (*Messiahs and Resurrection*, 10), I take בקש to be a Piel imperative, not a Qal perfect, which is the reading of Yardeni and Elizur and Qimron and Yuditsky. However, as noticed by other scholars, Knohl's reconstruction of the object of the verb, "Ephraim," is highly problematic. I choose instead Qimron and Yuditsky's reading אֲמָרִים ("words"), which reflects the reading of Ronald Hendel, "The Messiah Son of Joseph: Simply 'Sign,'" *BAR* 35, no. 1 (2009): 8. This goes well with the next possible word, [הֲשִׁ]יבֵנִי, particularly considering the context of the vivid dialogue. Cf. תָּשִׁיב אֲמָרֶיהָ (Judg 5:29), אֱמֶת אֲמָרִים לְהָשִׁיב (Prov 22:21), וּבְאִמְרֵיכֶם לֹא אֲשִׁיבֶנּוּ (Job 32:14).

15. Yardeni and Elizur ("Prophetic Text," 159) distinguish two different phrases (עבדי

The biblical background of the phrase is Ezekiel 34 and 37, where God promises to set "my servant David" over the Israelites (Ezek 34:23, 24; 37:24). The deity announces that "the Lord their God is with them" (Ezek 34:23, 24, 30) and that God's "dwelling place is with them" (Ezek 37:27).[16] Once the prophecy is realized, Israel will no longer be plundered or insulted by the nations (Ezek 34:28, 29). The ordination of Ezekiel's shepherd-king David, therefore, leads to the fulfillment of the divine domination over Israel.

All these connotations of the phrase "my servant David" from the prophet Ezekiel are pertinent for the literary context of the military crisis of Jerusalem in the *Gabriel Revelation*. The audience could remember that David is the warrior par excellence with whom the divine presence ever resides. Prior to his contest with Goliath, for example, David is told that "the Lord will be with you,"[17] and right at the contest with his dreadful rival David says that "all the earth will know that there is a God in Israel" (1 Sam 17:37, 46). David's splendid victories, the result of God's special care for him, are confirmed as God states, "I have been with you wherever you went and have cut off all your enemies from before you" (2 Sam 7:9; 1 Chr 17:8). The addressee called "my servant David" was probably a leader of the group behind the *Gabriel Revelation*. That group hoped for the realization of Ezekiel's prophecy that God's servant David would appear to save Jerusalem.

II. The Danielic Divine Epithet "Prince of Princes" (line 81)

With the two principles in mind, I will consider the inscription in light of Daniel 8, where Daniel sees an apocalyptical vision of the ram and the goat. In Daniel 8, Gabriel leads Daniel to understand the vision, which is about a divine eschatological scenario that involves both the desecration of the Jerusalem cult by a deceitful king and its ultimate recovery through the victory of the "Prince of princes" (Dan 8:25). Addressing the relation between Daniel 8 and the inscription, Israel Knohl tries to identify the "Prince of princes" in line 81. Commenting on both Daniel's vision in Dan 8:11 ("it magnified itself, even up to the Prince of the host") and Gabriel's retelling in Dan 8:25 ("he shall even rise up against the Prince of princes"), Knohl concludes, "Thus, the 'prince of princes,' who would be defeated by the deceitful king 'of bold countenance,' is

---

דוד and עבד(י)ד) but do not discuss the connection of the first phrase with Ezekiel 34 and 37.

16. In addition to the term "my servant David," another term, "covenant," occurs both in Ezekiel and in the *Gabriel Revelation*. This further strengthens the possibility of a connection between the texts (Ezek 34:25; 37:26; line 18). Moshe Bar-Asher ("On the Language of 'The Vision of Gabriel,'" *RevQ* 23 [2008]: 506–15) rightly points out two distinctive linguistic features that link the inscription with Ezekiel: מושבו and קיטוט (line 24).

17. Josephus omits Saul's statement of divine presence with David, but instead puts it into the mouth of David: "εἶπε Δαβίδης ἐπαγγέλλομαι τῷ θεῷ θαρρῶν ὄντι μετ' ἐμοῦ" (Josephus, *Ant.* 6.181).

the 'prince of the host' seen by Daniel in his vision."[18] The "bad plant" in line 21, according to Knohl, is the Danielic rebellious king, whom the author of the *Gabriel Revelation* views as the one who will "destroy 'the people of the saints,' attack, and even kill their leader, the 'prince of princes'."[19] In the same vein, Knohl argues that in the inscription "the Prince of princes" refers to a human leader of Israel who is killed by his enemy and resurrected by Gabriel. Knohl also maintains that the notion of the death of the "Prince of princes" originates in Dan 8:25.[20]

Knohl's argument about the "Prince of princes" finds no purchase on the text of Daniel 8. In some sense, the view that the "bad plant" stands for the Danielic "king of bold countenance" is not entirely improbable (lines 21–22). In my view, however, the "bad plant" represents not an individual but rather a group of people. The collective nature of the Jewish apocalyptic expression "plant" is well attested, for example, in the *Apocalypse of Weeks,* where the Enochic group metaphorically calls itself the "plant of righteousness" (*1 En.* 93:1, 5, 10; cf. *1 En.* 10:16; *Jub.* 1:16; 36:6).[21] Moreover, the phrase in question is meant to distinguish the group behind the *Gabriel Revelation* from what the text calls the "bad plant." A useful analogy can be found in *Sib. Or.* 3:401–6 (163–145 B.C.E.).[22] The author adopts a faunal image to brand Phrygia an unfortunate nation, that is, "a defiled race, a perennial branch" (v. 403). Memorable here is that, like the *Gabriel Revelation,* the *Sibylline Oracles* are familiar with the tradition of Daniel. Thus, *Sib. Or.* 3:397–400 draws on the imagery of horns from Dan 7:7-8. Just as the pro-Hellenistic group reflected in *Sib. Or.* 3:401–6 adopts the term "perennial branch" to distinguish itself from Phrygia, a nation hostile to the Seleucid dynasty, so the Jewish group behind the inscription employs the epithetical phrase "bad plant" to differentiate itself from an antagonistic group, which in the literary context of the inscription refers most likely to the invading gentiles, "all the nations against Jerusalem" (lines 13–14). Like the "perennial branch," the "bad plant" serves as a metaphorical locution for a group that is faced with the forthcoming apocalyptic disaster accompanied by "a sign" (v. 401).[23]

---

18. Israel Knohl, "'By Three Days, Live': Messiahs, Resurrection, and Ascent to Heaven in *Hazon Gabriel*," *JR* 88 (2008): 156.

19. Ibid., 157.

20. Knohl, *Messiahs and Resurrection,* 37.

21. On the use of the term "plant" in Second Temple Judaism, see Loren T. Stuckenbruck, "The Plant Metaphor in Its Inner-Enochic and Early Jewish Context," in *Enochic and Qumranic Origins: New Light on a Forgotten Connection* (ed. Gabriele Boccaccini et al.; Grand Rapids: Eerdmans, 2005), 210–12; idem, *1 Enoch 91–108* (CEJL; Berlin: de Gruyter, 2007), 76–79.

22. On the matter of date, see John J. Collins, "Sibylline Oracles," *OTP* 1:354–55; recently, Rieuwerd Buitenwerf (*Book III of the Sibylline Oracles and Its Social Setting: With an Introduction, Translation, and Commentary* [SVTP 17; Leiden: Brill, 2003], 124–34) dates the *Sibylline Oracles* around 80–40 B.C.E.

23. The Alexandrian Jewish depiction of the perdition of the Phrygian race (*Sib. Or.*

If the "bad plant" designates a doomed group of gentile armies that threaten Jerusalem, it would be reasonable to suggest that in the inscription Gabriel characterizes the "Prince of princes" as bringing the group to an end. In Daniel 8, the "Prince of princes" is the divine warrior who is central to the eschatological restoration of Jerusalem that previously was devastated by the *gentile* king (Dan 8:25). Given that the "Prince of princes" in Gabriel's interpretation in Daniel 8 is neither killed nor resurrected, how could the author of the *Gabriel Revelation* characterize the "Prince of princes" in line 81 as slain and revived, as Knohl claims? There is no textual evidence to maintain that the author disregards the fact that the "Prince of princes" in Daniel 8 is invincible.

The author of the inscription, who used Daniel 8 to encourage his community, presumably continued to use the Danielic figure in a prophetic role rather than distorting it. Considering how Gabriel describes the Prince in Daniel 8, I posit that the author appropriated the Danielic divine epithet to convince the audience that it is the "Prince of princes" alone who defeats the "bad plant," a symbol of "all the nations" that storm against Jerusalem (lines 13–14). It further means that, contrary to Knohl's claim, what is envisioned in the *Gabriel Revelation* is not a clash between the human Messiah (the "Prince of princes") and an Antichrist figure (the "bad plant").[24] Rather, the epithet of God, the "Prince of princes," serves to describe a clash between God (the "Prince of princes") and the invading gentiles (the "bad plant") only to reaffirm the point of Gabriel's speech in Daniel 8 that God will ultimately defeat the archenemy of God's people.

As observed above, Knohl's argument about the "Prince of princes" in line 81 stems from his assumption that the author of the *Gabriel Revelation* understood the Prince to be a *human* messianic leader. Thus, he holds that "the ideology of Catastrophic Messianism . . . is reflected in *The Gabriel Revelation* by the use of the scriptures of Daniel."[25] Indeed, Knohl's interpretation of the "Prince of princes" in Dan 8:25 is pivotal to his overall interpretation of the inscription. But how can one assert that the author of the inscription viewed the "Prince of princes" as a human being "based on Gabriel's address to Daniel"?[26] Knohl's hypothesis concerning the "Prince of princes" as the slain yet resurrected human Messiah is irrelevant to Daniel. Daniel identifies the "Prince of princes" as God,

---

3:401–5) is in many respects reminiscent of the Jewish depiction of the "bad plant" in the *Gabriel Revelation* (lines 21–22). "A sign" appears for the doomed race, and the race "disappears" in a single night by the hand of the "earth-shaker." It could be that the group responsible for the inscription uses a different, epithetical term for self-identification, as the group reflected in the apocalyptic section of Daniel takes the term *maśkîlîm*. The analogy between "plant" and "race" is found also in Philo, *Det.* 1.85, where human beings are described as "the only heavenly plant" that the creator placed on the earth.

24. Knohl, *Messiahs and Resurrection*, 12–13, 52–84.
25. Ibid., 38, 45.
26. Ibid., 95.

not only in Gabriel's talk in ch. 8 but *throughout the whole apocalyptic section* in Daniel, where the phrase refers exclusively to God, the heavenly King who surpasses the wicked champion of all earthly kings.

To make my case, I wish to investigate more rigorously the matter of the identity of the "Prince of princes" in the book of Daniel. The angel Gabriel in the inscription is reminiscent of the Danielic Gabriel in that both report the upcoming war that involves Jerusalem. In his visionary experience about a horn, Daniel highlights its marvelous enlargement. After the horn came forth, it "grew" (תִּגְדַּל) exceedingly toward the south and all the way toward the glorious land, Jerusalem (Dan 8:9). It continues to "grow up" to the host of heaven, to the extent that it "grew up" against the Prince of the host (Dan 8:10, 11). The horn's arrogant self-magnification is intensified by its desecration of the Jerusalem cult. The horn removed the daily sacrifice from the "Prince of the host" and overthrew his sanctuary (Dan 8:11). As the desecration occurred in the course of "transgression" (פֶּשַׁע), the horn "prospered" (הִצְלִיחָה) (Dan 8:12).[27]

Knohl rightly suggests that the "Prince of the host" stands for God,[28] but, curiously enough, he does not admit that the "Prince of the host" in Daniel's vision is the "Prince of princes" in Gabriel's interpretation of the vision (Dan 8:11, 25). As is clear from the expression "his sanctuary," the "Prince of the host" against whom the horn acts disdainfully stands for God. This violent conflict between the horn and God is represented in Gabriel's explanation of Daniel's vision. Gabriel identifies the horn as a "king of bold countenance" (Dan 8:23). The three words used of the horn are repeated to depict the king and thus establish the link between both characters. Gabriel says that the king appears at the time of the "transgressions,"[29] "prospers," "magnifies" (יַגְדִּיל) himself in his heart, and, at last, stands against the "Prince of princes," the phrase also found in the *Gabriel Revelation* (Dan 8:23, 24, 25; line 81). It is here, in Dan 8:25, where Gabriel identifies the "Prince of the host" as the "Prince of princes." All of the terminological connections between Daniel's vision and Gabriel's interpretation are deliberately chosen and carefully measured, so much so that Gabriel reidentifies God, who was formerly called the "Prince of the host," as the "Prince of princes."[30] Note also the ideological parallel between the Daniel's depiction that the horn grows up toward the "Prince of the host" and Gabriel's depiction that the king stands against the "Prince of princes" (Dan 8:11, 25).

The "Prince of princes" is clearly identified in Dan 11:21–45, where Gabriel's interpretation of the horn in Dan 8:23–25 is reworked.[31] Preserving

---

27. Regarding the translation of this verse, see John J. Collins, *Daniel: A Commentary on the Book of Daniel* (Hermeneia; Minneapolis: Fortress, 1993), 335.
28. Knohl, *Messiahs and Resurrection*, 28.
29. The reading is reflected in the LXX, τῶν ἁμαρτιῶν αὐτῶν. See Collins, *Daniel*, 327.
30. H. Louis Ginsberg, *Studies in Daniel* (Texts and Studies of the Jewish Theological Seminary of America 14; New York: Jewish Theological Seminary of America, 1948), 53.
31. Matthias Henze ("The Use of Scripture in the Book of Daniel," in *A Companion to*

Gabriel's previous point that the horn desecrates the Jerusalem cult, an anonymous angel elaborates on the clash between the horn and God. On the one hand, the king, identified as "the northern king," is reported to "magnify" himself above all (Dan 11:36–37), in a way reminiscent of Gabriel's wording. The king's opposition to the "Prince of princes," on the other hand, comes to be more particularized as the king's act of speaking horrendous things against "the God of gods" (Dan 11:36–37). The reiteration of the clash between the king and God, therefore, serves to identify the "Prince of princes" as the "God of gods."[32] In sum, the "Prince of princes" in Daniel consistently and powerfully refers to God. Knohl's claim that the author of the *Gabriel Revelation* applies the epithet of God in Dan 8:25 to a human messianic leader of the Israelites is purely conjectural.

III. THE ALLUSION TO THE TRADITION OF THE COMING OF GOD

(1) לשלשת ימין, "ON THE THIRD DAY" (LINE 11)

Rather than dwell more on the way in which the author of the *Gabriel Revelation* understands the Danielic "Prince of princes," I turn to the matter of the end-time as it is based on Gabriel's interpretation of the vision of Daniel. As we have seen, Gabriel's interpretation reaches a climax with the depiction of the ultimate fate of the archenemy of the "Prince of princes" in Dan 8:25, where the "king of bold countenance" is said to be "destroyed" (יִשָּׁבֵר). The Danielic scene of the destruction of the rebellious king foreshadows the scene of "the evil" that is "destroyed"

Biblical Interpretation in Early Judaism [ed. Matthias Henze; Grand Rapids: Eerdmans, Forthcoming]) applies the interpretive technique of *Fortschreibung* to the book of Daniel. See Walther Zimmerli, "Das Phänomen der 'Fortschreibung' im Buche Echeziel," in *Prophecy: Essays Presented to Georg Fohrer on His Sixty-fifth Birthday, 6 September 1980* (ed. J. A. Emerton; Berlin: de Gruyter, 1980), 174–91; more recently, William S. Morrow, "Fortschreibung in Mesopotmian Treaties and in the Book of Deuteronomy," in *Recht und Ethik im Alten Testament: Beiträge des Symposiums „Das Alte Testament und die Kultur der Moderne" anlässlich des 100. Geburtstags Gerhard von Rads (1901–1971), Heidelberg, 18.–21. Oktober 2001* (ed. Eckart Otto et al.; Münster: LIT, 2004), 111–23.

32. The "Prince of princes" is a calque of Akkadian *šar šarrāni* that refers to "King of kings," which is used, in turn, of God in the Old and New Testament (H. Niehr, "שר," *TDOT*, 214; Marie-Joseph Seux, *Épithètes royales akkadiennes et sumériennes* [Paris: Letouzey et Ané, 1967], 318–19); 1QH[a] 18:8 שר אלים ומלך נכבדים ואדון לכול רוח ומושל בכל מעשה, "You are the Prince of gods and the King of the glorious ones, Lord of every spirit, Ruler of every creature"; see also *The Syriac Apocalypse of Daniel* 28, where the description of the coming of God combines the divine titles from Daniel 8 and the divine fiery image. The text refers to the "God of gods, Lord of lords, and King of kings" and clearly alludes to the Danielic Prince of princes. Matthias Henze (*The Syriac Apocalypse of Daniel: Introduction, Text, and Commentary* [STAC 11; Tübingen: Mohr Siebeck, 2001], 100–101) lists numerous (non-)biblical parallels to the Danielic expression.

(נשבר) by justice (line 20). The *Gabriel Revelation* focuses on the time when the king is destroyed. This becomes palpable when we compare two temporal expressions, "many days" and "three days." Gabriel says that Daniel's vision "refers to many days" (לְיָמִים רַבִּים; Dan 8:26). This means that the termination of the rebellious king, too, will happen only in the distant future. In the *Gabriel Revelation*, by contrast, the extinction of the evil is said to happen in quite a short term, that is, "by three days" (לשלשת ימין; line 19).[33] Does this mean that the author feels that the annihilation of evil has become imminent? The answer seems to be positive. The author revises in a bold way the prophesied long period of the tribulation of Jerusalem by shortening the "many days" to "three days." In other words, remembering what Gabriel previously foretold about the devastation of Jerusalem, the author tries to persuade the audience that the present military crisis of Jerusalem was part of the divine plan already foretold by Gabriel which is now about to be finished.

The profound interest of the author of the *Gabriel Revelation* in the divinely appointed time may well flow not only from Daniel 8 but also from Daniel 9. There Gabriel comments on the end-time, when the things Daniel sees in the vision in ch. 8 will happen. In Daniel 8 Gabriel begins his interpretation of the vision by commanding Daniel to "understand that the vision concerns the time of the end" (8:17). Gabriel repeats the point, just two verses later, saying, "The vision concerns the appointed time of the end" (8:19). Later Gabriel concludes his words with the same note that the vision "pertains to many days."

Gabriel's emphasis on the element of time in understanding the vision of Daniel continues in Daniel 9. The encounter with Gabriel appears to make Daniel have greater interest in the matter of time. Daniel thus says that he perceives the truth about the duration of the period of the devastation of Jerusalem (9:2). But his view of the time is wrong. For Gabriel comes swiftly back to Daniel in order to rectify Daniel's perception. The angel enlightens Daniel about the divinely planned restoration of Jerusalem. We see here that Gabriel recapitulates the point he made previously in Daniel 8. As in ch. 8, Gabriel urges Daniel to understand that the vision is concerned with the time of the end, and so in ch. 9 Gabriel admonishes Daniel the same way, saying, "Understand the vision!" (8:17; 9:23).

The author of the *Gabriel Revelation* also has a strong interest in the divinely appointed end-time. So he announces that the "many days" now become shorter and will last only "three days," during which Jerusalem will see the destruction of her enemies and the subsequent homecoming of the children of Jerusalem. Therefore, unlike God in Daniel 9, who dispatches Gabriel to Daniel and clarifies the fact that the appointed time will be much longer than Daniel understands, in the inscription God sends the angel to the addressee and says that the deity

---

33. Compare "לשלשת ימין" (line 19) with the "לִשְׁלֹשֶׁת הַיָּמִים" (Ezra 10:8), which is best translated as "within three days."

will "listen to the [cr]y of Jerusalem." God will return the Israelites back to the "place," that is, Jerusalem (Qimron and Yuditsky, lines 27, 71–72).

Most important, a closer reading of the *Gabriel Revelation* demonstrates that the temporal expression לשלשת ימין (line 19) is significant not so much because the elimination of Jerusalem's enemy is thought to happen soon but because of the author's expectation that the advent of God is imminent. The author's perspective on the way in which the end of the enemy of Jerusalem is expected should be examined in terms of the relevant biblical texts that the phrase in question evokes. The biblical texts that contain the biblical tradition of the coming of God should therefore be interpreted properly. The coming of God is a renowned Old Testament tradition that has widely influenced the New Testament and other early Jewish and Christian literatures. Our author, too, uses the phrase as a vehicle to express the coming of God to God's people.[34] Translating the phrase לשלשת ימין as "by three days,"[35] Knohl holds that it refers to the time Gabriel resurrects the "Prince of princes," a slain leader of Israel (line 81). Knohl's hypothesis is tantamount to claiming that the author of the *Gabriel Revelation* dismisses Gabriel's prophecy of the most decisive moment of the end-time, that is, the destruction of the king by the "Prince of princes."

To do justice to the phrase לשלשת ימין, one needs not only to trace it back to the relevant biblical texts from which the tradition of the coming of God derived but also to observe how the theme is blended with the Danielic apocalyptic background of ch. 8. The first step is to translate the temporal phrase as "on the third day." For the ordinal meaning of the phrase, it is essential to acknowledge the continuity of the tradition of the coming of God. The tradition derives from Exodus, is transmitted to Hosea, and then to the *Gabriel Revelation*. The corresponding form in the Hebrew Bible occurs only twice (Exod 19:15 and Amos 4:4).[36] This strengthens the probability that the phrase depends on one of the two biblical occurrences.[37] I propose that the origin of the phrase "on the third day" (לשלשת ימין) can be found in Exod 19:15, where Moses commands the Israelites to prepare themselves "for the third day" (לִשְׁלֹשֶׁת יָמִים),[38] the very moment

---

34. For the tradition of the coming of God, see Edward Adams, "The 'Coming of God' Tradition and Its Influence on New Testament Parousia Texts," in *Biblical Traditions in Transmission: Essays in Honour of Michael A. Knibb* (ed. Charlotte Hempel and Judith M. Lieu; JSJSup 111; Leiden: Brill, 2006), 1–19; Richard Bauckham, "Eschatology in the Coming of God," in *God Will Be All in All: The Eschatology of Jürgen Moltmann* (ed. Richard Bauckham; Edinburgh: T&T Clark, 1999), 1–34.

35. Israel Knohl, "The Messiah Son of Joseph: 'Gabriel's Revelation' and the Birth of a New Messianic Model," *BAR* 34, no. 5 (2008): 62;, and idem, *Messiahs and Resurrection*, 11.

36. I regard the phrase לִשְׁלֹשֶׁת יָמִים in Amos 4:4 to be irrelevant for the inscription.

37. The repetition of words and expressions, which is rare in the Bible, makes it easier to discover an allusion. See Chazon, "Use of the Bible," 95.

38. For the ordinal nuance of this phrase, see GKC, p. 437, §134, note 4. In *m. Šabb.* 9:4, R. Aqiba also takes the phrase as ordinal. For an English translation of the Mishnaic text, see Michael L. Rodkinson, *New Edition of the Babylonian Talmud* (20 vols. in 10; Boston: Boston

God is announced to descend from heaven to Mount Sinai to make a covenant with Israel. It is critical to see that Moses' command in Exod 19:15 is based on God's command in Exod 19:11, which reads: "[L]et them prepare 'for the third day' (לַיּוֹם הַשְּׁלִישִׁי), for 'on the third day' (בַּיּוֹם הַשְּׁלִישִׁי) the Lord comes down on Mount Sinai in the sight of all the people." Notice here that the Mosaic expression לִשְׁלֹשֶׁת יָמִים replaces God's expression לַיּוֹם הַשְּׁלִישִׁי without changing the *ordinal* meaning of God's expression.

The author of the inscription is also aware of the ordinal meaning of the Mosaic expression and reuses the expression in line 19. Proclaiming that the deity has a new "covenant,"[39] the author announces God's coming, saying "on the third day you shall know" (lines 18–19). As a result, the Sinaitic temporal expression from the Exodus theophany is reused in a new apocalyptic context. The author of the inscription invites the audience to recognize that the current situation of Jerusalem is part of the realization of Gabriel's prophecy. Moreover, he implies that it is at the coming of God that this turbulent period of the appointed time, during which Jerusalem is dominated by Rome, will be completed. The author eschatologizes the Sinaitic theophany by transferring it into the apocalyptic context of what Gabriel foretells about the destruction of God's enemy (Dan 8:25).[40]

Moreover, the author's solution to the crisis of his community appears to be motivated by the prophecy of Hosea. Thus, the author's appropriation of the Sinai tradition through the Mosaic expression "on the third day" finds a remarkable precedence in the prophecy of Hosea. The idea of "the numerical progression from two days to on the third day"[41] in Exodus 19 became so important that it was reworked in Hos 6:2–3. There the Exodus idea of the coming of God on the third day recurs as a desire for the restoration of the broken relation between God and Israelites. "He will revive us after two days. . . . On the third day (בַּיּוֹם הַשְּׁלִישִׁי) he will raise us up that we may live before him. . . . He will *come to us* like the rain, like the spring rains that water the earth." As the prophet Hosea adapts the Exodus idea of the coming of the divine to Hosea's own time, so the author of the inscription, putting the Mosaic phrase "on the third day" into the

---

New Talmud Pub. Co., 1903), 1:157. Similarly, *Tg. Onq.* reads לתלתת יומין, which Israel Drazin and Stanley M. Wagner (*Onkelos on the Torah: Understanding the Bible Text.* שמות *Exodus* [Jerusalem: Gefen, 2006], 121) translate as "for the third day." The majority of modern English versions (KJV, NASB, NRSV, NIV, ESV, TNK) render the phrase as ordinal ("for the third day").

39. The reading of Qimron and Yuditsky.

40. Similarly, *Sifre Deuteronomy* puts the Sinai theophany in an eschatological context. Portraying God as coming from Sinai, *Sifre* announces that at the time of the final shake-up of the whole world Israel will succeed Seir, a designation for the Roman Empire. See Steven D. Fraade, *From Tradition to Commentary: Torah and Its Interpretation in the Midrash Sifre to Deuteronomy* (SUNY Series in Judaica; Albany: State University of New York Press, 1991), 25–68, here 38.

41. Edwin M. Good, "Hosea 5:8–6:6: An Alternative to Alt," *JBL* 85 (1966): 280.

mouth of Gabriel, further continues to adapt the theophany on Mount Sinai to his own time.

In his explanation of the expression לשלשת ימין in light of Hos 6:1–2, Knohl claims that the inscription reflects the idea of "metaphorical resurrection."[42] However, one should not overlook the fact that the expression, as suggested by the parallel between לשלשת ימין (line 19) and לִשְׁלֹשֶׁת יָמִים (Exod 19:15), retains its deeper root in the Exodus text that is involved not with any idea of resurrection but rather with the powerful coming of God. Furthermore, considering the fact that the implication of the Exodus expression "on the third day" (line 19) has nothing to do with the idea of resurrection, it remains groundless to make an attempt, as Knohl does, to explain the resurrection of Jesus on the third day in terms of the *Gabriel Revelation*.[43]

In addition, the biblical tradition of the coming of God, to which the expression alludes, is perfectly in line with Gabriel's interpretation of Daniel's vision in Daniel 7, which contains the same tradition. Although the name of the angel is first mentioned in Dan 8:16, where Gabriel helps Daniel understand his visionary experience, it becomes clear that Daniel has already met Gabriel in Daniel 7. Thus, in 9:21, Daniel identifies Gabriel as the one "whom I have seen in the vision at the beginning." Gabriel is unveiled to be the "one of the attendants" whom Daniel had approached to ask the meaning of the vision in 7:16.[44] This means that the author of the *Gabriel Revelation*, too, may well have considered Gabriel's interpretation of Daniel's vision in Daniel 7. This point finds further support when we observe that the tradition of the coming of God is attested in Daniel 7. There God is presented as the eschatological savior who saves the saints from their great persecution. In the vision of Daniel, God is depicted as an enthroned deity who is called the "Ancient of Days" (7:9). Speaking of a terrifying horn that wages a war against the saints, Daniel states that the war is finally ended at the time the "Ancient of Days comes" (7:22). That in Daniel 7 Gabriel, as the angelic speaker, forecasts the coming of the Ancient of Days, therefore, might have been formative in the author's shaping of the theme of the coming of God in the inscription.

(ii) האות "The Sign" (lines 17, 80).

Our hypothesis that the author uses the phrase "on the third day" (line 19) to connote the coming of God finds further support in the use of the biblical motif of the divine "sign" (line 17). The motif alludes to God's dwelling among God's people. The author uses both phrases to imply that the hoped-for redemption of Jerusalem will be wrought through God's coming and dwelling with the people of God. Just as Gabriel alludes to the coming of God by using the expression "on

---

42. Knohl, *Messiahs and Resurrection*, 39.
43. Ibid., 87.
44. Collins, *Daniel*, 311, 351.

the third day," so the "sign" is evocative of the tradition of the presence of God. Through the use of both allusions, Gabriel informs the audience of the way in which Daniel's prediction concerning the restoration of Jerusalem's cult in the end-time is being realized.

Indeed, the author's use of the "sign" is remarkable. The term "sign" occurs in lines 80 and 82,[45] but its implication as a motif has received little attention.[46] In the *Gabriel Revelation,* the "sign" occurs in the dialogue between Gabriel and the addressee, who is called "my servant David" and "my Son" (lines 16, 18). Gabriel encourages the addressee to ask God for the sign, which the addressee does (line 17). Knohl associates the sign with "Ephraim," which is a contested reading.[47] There is no biblical precedence for Ephraim described as placing the sign. In the Hebrew Bible it is always God who is asked by a human being to give a sign. To deal properly with the term "sign," therefore, special attention should be paid not so much to the hypothetical reading of "Ephraim" but to the dialogical situation in which the biblical motif of the divine sign is attested. The situation in the Bible in which a human addressee is prompted by a messenger of God to ask God for a sign provides the key to the meaning of the "sign" in the *Gabriel Revelation.*

The parallel situation helps us comprehend how the biblical motif of a divine sign is used in the *Gabriel Revelation.* Three texts in the Old Testament hint at the nature of the sign in the inscription. In all three biblical texts, the sign functions as a guarantee of the divine presence with a political leader of the Israelites. King Hezekiah, for example, is told of his upcoming death by the prophet Isaiah. The dialogue between Hezekiah and Isaiah is significant. King Hezekiah asks God for a "sign" of his recovery, and the prophet Isaiah conveys the divine reply (2 Kgs 20:8-9; cf. Isa 38:7, 22). Despite the similar conversation, however, the situation of Hezekiah and that of the addressee in the *Gabriel Revelation* are not the same. The sign of Hezekiah lacks an element of military crisis, which prompts the addressee to ask God for the sign. Moreover, the sign involving Hezekiah's miraculous healing by God is deeply personal and has no implications for the divine presence with God's people.

An equally intriguing and even more relevant situation is found in the story of Gideon. The judge Gideon hears that the Lord is with him and that he will save Israel (Judg 6:12, 14, 16). However, distrusting the divine presence with Israel under foreign domination, Gideon asks God to show him a "sign," in which Gideon can recognize the Lord's presence with him (Judg 6:17). Again, this parallel does not constitute an exact analogy. In the episode of the biblical judge,

---

45. Following Qimron and Yuditsky.
46. Yardeni and Elizur find a similar expression, "three signs," in a mid-tenth-century Persian composition, which was written much later than the inscription (Qimron and Yuditsky, 141). Further, Knohl comments briefly on the meaning of the term "sign," stating, "The nature of the sign remains unclear" (*Messiahs and Resurrection,* 10).
47. Knohl, *Messiahs and Resurrection,* 33.

Jerusalem, which is the setting of the inscription, does not occur. Likewise, the idea of the divine protection of Jerusalem is completely missing in Gideon's case.

The closest analogy to the *Gabriel Revelation* is the motif of "sign" in Isa 7:1–17, the conversation between Isaiah and Ahaz. Parallels are linguistic and ideological as well. Like the angel Gabriel, the prophet Isaiah delivers to King Ahaz the divine message that invading nations will wage against Jerusalem (cf. על ירושלם, line 14 [Qimron and Yuditsky] and יְרוּשָׁלַם מִלְחָמָה עָלֶיהָ, Isa 7:1). Both Gabriel and Isaiah reassure their human addressee, saying, "do not fear!" (Qimron and Yuditsky, line 23; Isa 7:4). Most notably, the two conversations make use of the motif of the divine sign as integral to the survival of Jerusalem. The essence of the divine sign, which Isaiah ultimately prophesies independently of the king's reluctance, is related to the birth of the son called "Immanuel," which means "God is with us" (Isa 7:14). The meaning of the sign given to Ahaz depends on the meaning of the name of the son, that is, God's abiding presence. Thus, Isaiah declares that the military threat to Jerusalem will be averted while Immanuel is still young. The divine protection of Jerusalem comes through the divine presence in the holy city, as the name of Immanuel implies (Isa 7:16). In addition, Gabriel urges the addressee to request a sign from God, and he predicts that "the evil shall be destroyed before justice" (lines 20–21), a prophecy that the crisis of Jerusalem will be resolved through God's salvific power. We find a close analogy in the Qumran text 1Q27 1 i 5, where the speaker, who gives "the sign" (האות) to the addressee, proclaims, "[E]vil will disappear before justice" (גלה הרשע מפני הצדק).[48]

My point here is that the inscription alludes in a clear way to the Isaianic idea that God's defense of Jerusalem against the enemy nations is possible only after God's indwelling is realized in God's people. The author of the inscription adopts the Isaianic theme elegantly. Not only does he reactualize the Isaianic theme by repeating the situation in which the motif of the sign operates; he also adds a revisionary touch to the text from Isaiah 7. Knohl insists that what the inscription "adds to the original prophecy" of Gabriel in Daniel 8 is that the "Prince of princes" is killed by a king of bold countenance and resurrected by Gabriel.[49] However, the author's modification of a biblical text should be found in Isaiah 7 rather than in Daniel 8. The author's revisionary use of the prophetic text in Isaiah 7 presupposes the scene in which Isaiah prompted Ahaz to request a divine sign but Ahaz declined it (Isa 7:10–12).

Moreover, the allusive nature of the term "sign," which ties the *Gabriel Revelation* to the story of Ahaz in Isaiah 7, accentuates the unstated details of the story that revolve around the term "sign" in Isaiah 7.[50] Thus, considering the negative

---

48. Florentino García Martínez and Eibert J. C. Tigchelaar, *The Dead Sea Scrolls Study Edition* (2 vols.; Leiden: Brill, 1997, 1998), 1:66–67.

49. Knohl, *Messiahs and Resurrection*, 28.

50. On this nature of allusion, see Richard B. Hays, *Echoes of Scripture in the Letters of Paul* (New Haven: Yale University Press, 1989), 20–21. Hays uses the theory of John J. Hol-

model of Ahaz, the author deliberately creates an obedient recipient of the sign. In doing so, the author succeeds in creating the expectation of a reenactment of what Isaiah had earlier prophesied to Ahaz regarding the divine dwelling in Jerusalem. The author was convinced that once the divine presence was established in Jerusalem, the city's enemies would be thoroughly swept away.[51]

Special attention needs to be paid to the fact that in the *Gabriel Revelation* the Isaianic sign takes on distinctive eschatological overtones. Gabriel's prediction of the triumph of justice over evil is of a significant apocalyptic bent. Thus, the prediction is followed by a prophecy of an eschatological woe in lines 24–25, where God proclaims to "shake heaven and earth." The woe is reminiscent of that in Isa 13:13, where God is described as shaking the heavens and the earth as the deity judges Babylon, the principal enemy nation that ultimately destroys Jerusalem.[52]

My interpretation of the "sign" as an allusion to God's protective presence in Israel turns out to be on the right track for this understanding of the apocalyptic depiction of theophany in lines 24–25: "In a little while I will shake the heavens and the earth" (עוד מעט קיטוט היא ואני מרעיש את השמים ואת הארץ). This portrayal is based on Hag 2:6, "Once again, in a little while, I will shake the heavens and the earth" (עוֹד אַחַת מְעַט הִיא וַאֲנִי מַרְעִישׁ אֶת־הַשָּׁמַיִם וְאֶת־הָאָרֶץ). Here the author of the inscription puts the visionary language of Haggai into the mouth of the angel Gabriel. This literary phenomenon of linking the Danielic interpreting angel to the Haggaic apocalypticism could be compared to the rabbis' associating the angel's remark in Dan 7:25 with the prophet's vision in Hag 2:6 (*m. Sanh.* 11:1).[53]

What really matters, however, is not simply the almost verbatim reuse of Haggai's prophecy.[54] Rather, I am interested more in the original context. The literary context of the biblical prophecy emphasizes the divine presence, which is captured and used by the author of the *Gabriel Revelation* as its prominent theme. Through the mouth of the prophet Haggai, God announces to postexilic Israel, "I am with you . . . my Spirit remains among you" (Hag 2:4, 5; cf. 1:13). Haggai's context would have been useful for expressing the theological outlook of the *Gabriel Revelation*. The early postexilic community had known that "the

---

lander, *The Figure of Echo: A Mode of Allusion in Milton and After* (Quantum Books; Berkeley: University of California Press, 1981), 113–49.

51. The origin of the author's expectation may well be found in Daniel 9, where Daniel prays to God for the restoration of Jerusalem. Asking in a passionate way for God's redemption of Jerusalem, Daniel requested "God's face to shine on the holy city" (Dan 9:17).

52. *Sibylline Oracles* 3:401–10 contains a prophecy of eschatological woes that are announced in terms of sign(s) and disasters such as the shaking of the earth. See Collins, "Sibylline Oracles," 371; and my n. 23 above.

53. See Jacob Neusner, *Zephaniah, Haggai, Zechariah, and Malachi in Talmud and Midrash: A Source Book* (Lanham, Md.: University Press of America, 2007), 69.

54. Yardeni and Elizur, "Prophetic Text," 162.

Lord of hosts" (יְהוָה צְבָאוֹת) would fill the rebuilt temple with the divine "glory" (כָּבוֹד), would shake "all the nations" (כָּל־הַגּוֹיִם), and would overthrow their "chariots" (מֶרְכָּבָה; Hag 2:7, 22). Likewise, the readers of the inscription could expect that "the glory of the Lord the God of hosts" and God of the "chariots" would be revealed in Jerusalem, while "all the nations" were on the attack (Qimron and Yuditsky, lines 13, 25–27).

As we have seen, the divine message of Gabriel includes two allusions. The word "sign" alludes to divine dwelling, and the phrase "on the third day" alludes to the divine coming. The association of these two expressions points to the same association in line 80: "On the third day, the sign!" (לשלשת ימין האות).[55] This elliptical expression amalgamates the two allusions, God's dwelling in and coming to God's people, and effectively intensifies the yearning for the restoration of Jerusalem through the divine intervention.

In the *Gabriel Revelation*, the divine coming and indwelling together connote the divine restoration of Jerusalem. The connection between the coming of God and the recovery of Jerusalem is well attested in Haggai 2, where the theophany is accompanied by the divine judgment of Israel's enemy. I now turn my attention to another allusion to the motif of coming of God (lines 25–27):

25. Readily the "glory of YHWH" (כבוד יהוה) the God of
26. Hosts, the God of Israel, the God of the chariots will listen to
27. the [cr]y of Jerusalem (ירושלם) and will console (ינחם) the cities of Judah (ערי יהודה).[56]

The scene in lines 25–27 contains many textual components that are evocative of God who is anticipated to comfort the exiled. According to the scene, the "glory of YHWH" comes upon both "Jerusalem" and "the cities of Judah" in order to "console" them. This idea has a conceptual affinity with Isa 40:1–10. There God's commandment to "console" (נַחֲמוּ) God's people (v. 1) is repeated, and the "glory of YHWH" (כְּבוֹד יְהוָה) is proclaimed to be revealed to them (v. 5). Moreover, "Jerusalem" (יְרוּשָׁלַםִ) and "the cities of Judah" (עָרֵי יְהוּדָה) are invited to welcome their God (v. 9). Eventually, Isaiah's encouraging message culminates in the prophecy that "the Lord God will come with power" (v. 10). The image of the coming of God fits well with the description of God as driving "chariots" (המרכבות), forging another connection with another Isaianic text. In Isa 66:15, the Lord is announced to "come in fire and 'his chariots' (מַרְכְּבֹתָיו) like the whirlwind to pay back his anger in fury and his rebuke in flames of fire."[57] The link

---

55. I translate the Hebrew in line 80 as "the sign" (האות); cf. Hendel, "Simply Sign," 8; Qimron and Yuditsky ("Notes," 140–41) compare the phrase to other sentences that comprise three parts, such as האות אני מבקש (line 17) and לשלושת ימין תדע (line 17), and suggest לְמָחָר יִהְיֶה הָאֹת הַזֶּה to be a biblical parallel (Exod 8:19; Eng. 8:23).
56. See the English translation of Qimron and Yuditsky in this volume.
57. Henze, "The *Gabriel Revelation* Reconsidered," 5.

between line 26 and Isa 66:15 becomes even clearer when we see the contextual similarity between the texts. The comfort of Jerusalem is mentioned three times in the context of Isa 66:15 (66:10, 11, 13), which is consonant with lines 25 and 27.

In lines 25–27, therefore, Gabriel blends in an elegant way Isa 40:1–10 with Isa 66:10–15 to allude to the coming of God, which triggers the divine anger about Israel's enemies. This fiery image of God's coming in chariots accords well with the previous allusion to Haggai in lines 24–25, where God declares that the heavens and the earth will be shaken.[58] The allusion to those Isaianic texts embraces the apocalyptic vision of Jerusalem's salvation under the military pressure of the Roman Empire.

Concluding Remarks

I have demonstrated that Daniel is remembered and appropriated in many ways in the *Gabriel Revelation*. The author of the inscription strategically employs the angel Gabriel as the speaker of the divine message. While reactualizing the major points of biblical Gabriel, the angelic speaker interprets the earlier scriptural texts by making them part of the apocalyptic milieu of the inscription. In doing so, the author of the *Gabriel Revelation* highlights the eschatological nature of the historical crisis Jerusalem presently suffers.

In particular, I have examined the theological perspective of the inscription through an analysis of a series of remarkable allusions, in which the author inspires the audience in an elegant way to expect the imminent fulfillment of the prophetic visions about the redemption of Jerusalem in the end-time. This interpretation of the *Gabriel Revelation* is greatly enriched once we appreciate the many ways in which its author alludes to the coming of God and the presence of God.

---

58. Cf. Hab 3:8, 12, where Habakkuk's vision of God integrates the fiery image of God's coming with the terrifying cosmic catastrophe. With flames coming from his feet, God drives chariots of salvation, shakes the earth, makes the nations tremble, and threshes the nations.

ELEVEN

"Jerusalem" in the *Gabriel Revelation* and the Revelation of John

David B. Capes

When the scribe incised the guidelines into the soft limestone and began copying the text we know today as the *Gabriel Revelation,* or *Hazon Gabriel* (HazGab), Jerusalem had been the center of Jewish life, hope, and imagination for centuries. More than half a millennium had passed since Ezekiel described the holy city as the center of the world (Ezek 5:5; cf. 38:12), a theme picked up and elaborated by other writers (*1 En.* 26:1; *Jub.* 8:11, 19).[1] When David captured the Jebusite settlement (2 Sam 5:6-10) and moved the ark of the covenant there, he set in motion a process whereby his capital came to be regarded as the nexus of earthly and heavenly power, the locus of God's final, definitive actions to redeem God's people. Even when it was attacked, destroyed or controlled by foreigners, Jewish imagination did not relinquish the hopes fixed on this city. As Carey Newman writes, "ideal figurations of this holy city, this Zion, became stock symbols for Jewish worship and eschatology."[2]

Around the turn of the millennium—when the *Gabriel Revelation* was inscribed—these ideal figurations were expressed in a variety of ways in Jewish and Christian literature. First, some Jews envisaged a day when the earthly Jerusalem would be restored and purified. *Second Baruch,* for example, describes a time when the Mighty One will shake the entire creation and the building of Zion will be razed in order to be rebuilt, "renewed in glory" and "perfected into eternity" (*2 Bar.* 32:2-4; cf. Tob 13:9-18; *T. Dan* 5:12).[3] Second, other Jews and Christians situated the perfect Jerusalem in heaven and considered it the place to which God's covenant people will ascend. In contrasting the two covenants, Heb 12:22 portrays true believers as arriving at Mount Zion, the city of God, the new Jerusalem in the company of angels, God, and Jesus, the mediator of a new

---

1. Pliny the Elder (*Natural History* 5.14) remarked that Jerusalem was one of the most well known and significant cities in the east.
2. Carey Newman, "Jerusalem," *Dictionary of the Later New Testament and Its Developments* (ed. Ralph Martin and Peter Davids; Downers Grove, Ill.: InterVarsity, 1997), 561.
3. A. F. J. Klijn, "2 (Syriac Apocalypse of) Baruch," *OTP* 1:615-52.

covenant (cf. *2 Bar.* 4:1-7; *4 Ezra* 8:52; *4 Bar.* 5:35). Third, yet others looked for a new, perfect Jerusalem to descend from heaven to earth sometime in the future (Rev 3:12; chs. 21-22; *4 Ezra* 7:26; 10:25-54; 13:36).[4]

In the community of the Dead Sea Scrolls, the covenanters held "three distinct but related notions" of Jerusalem.[5] On the one hand, the community of the faithful—when properly disciplined—is described metaphorically as "a holy house" where "the offering of the lips" is sufficient and no burnt offerings or sacrifices are required (1QS 9:3-6; cf. 4Q164 1-7; 11QMelch 2:23-34).[6] This conviction coexisted without contradiction with two other, related notions: the covenanters believed (a) that God wanted them to establish a temple and maintain its purity and sacrifices "until the day of creation," and (b) that God would one day build the final temple, an eternal temple (11QTemple 29:6-10; cf. 4QFlor [4Q174] 1:1-2). The majority of references to Jerusalem in the scrolls depict the holy city in these idealistic terms; however, the real situation on the ground at the time when the scrolls were written shows deep divisions over issues of purity and scriptural interpretation.[7] The Habakkuk pesher (1QpHab 12:7-9) complains that Jerusalem had been corrupted and the temple defiled by the wicked priest. Other scrolls protest that God's people will suffer because Jerusalem is ruled by arrogant men who reject the law (4QpIsa^b 2:1-9) and look for easy interpretations (4QpIsa^c 23 ii 10-12; 4QpNah 3-4 iii 6-7). These tensions provoked a variety of reactions but, perhaps more than anything, a longing for a new Jerusalem.

The *Gabriel Revelation* provides further evidence that Jerusalem is the one place on earth that captured the Jewish imagination. The holy city figures prominently in this brief, fragmentary prophecy that originated likely before or at the beginning of the first century C.E.[8] This essay explores the role of Jerusalem in this prophecy and in the Revelation of John. It suggests that these prophecies portray what appear to be different versions of an accepted apocalyptic scenario regarding Jerusalem and its future. While these texts have much in common, there are some important differences, as we will see. In addition, Revelation's account of Jerusalem in ch. 11 may provide some help in interpreting particular aspects of the *Gabriel Revelation*.

---

4. Philip King, "Jerusalem," *ABD* 3:747-66.

5. Adela Yarbro Collins, "The Dream of a New Jerusalem at Qumran," in *The Bible and the Dead Sea Scrolls: The Second Princeton Symposium on Judaism and Christian Origins* (ed. James H. Charlesworth; 3 vols.; Waco, Tex.: Baylor University Press, 2006), 3:238.

6. Florentino García Martínez and Eibert J. C. Tigchelaar, eds., *The Dead Sea Scrolls Study Edition*, vol. 1 (Leiden: Brill, 1997).

7. Jerome Murphy-O'Connor, "Jerusalem," in *Encyclopedia of the Dead Sea Scrolls* (ed. Lawrence H. Schiffman and James C. VanderKam; 2 vols.; Oxford: Oxford University Press, 2000), 1:402-4.

8. Ada Yardeni and Binyamin Elizur, "A Prophetic Text on Stone from the First Century BCE: First Publication" (in Hebrew), *Cathedra* 123 (2007): 155-66.

Jerusalem in the Gabriel Revelation

According to Ada Yardeni, Binyamin Elitzur, and Israel Knohl, the word "Jerusalem" occurs seven times among the legible lines of the *Gabriel Revelation* (lines 12, 14, 27, 33, 36, 39, 57).[9] Elisha Qimron and Alexey Yuditsky restore the text to suggest three other occurrences of the word (lines 32, 60, 66).[10] Thus, the extant part of the inscription contains seven to ten references to the holy city. References to David ("my servant David" in line 16, and "David, the servant of YHWH" in line 72) may indicate that the people who read and were influenced by the *Gabriel Revelation* supported the Davidic dynasty, which may in turn reinforce Jerusalem's importance in this prophecy.[11]

Knohl argues that the *Gabriel Revelation* focuses on two themes. Our concern here initially is with the first:

> The first half [of the inscription] describes an eschatological war, in which the nations of the world besiege Jerusalem, expelling its residents from the city. God, in response, sends "My servant David" to ask Ephraim—the Messiah son of Joseph—to place a "sign," presumably heralding the coming redemption. The text goes on to describe the vanquishing of the Antichrist and its forces of evil. God Himself appears together with His angels to defeat the enemies.[12]

Knohl attempts to situate the text in the aftermath of Rome's crushing defeat of Jerusalem and Judea prior to the turn of the millennium. In the political vacuum left by Herod's death, insurgents revolted against Rome's domination and were soundly defeated when thousands were killed, cities and villages were destroyed, and the temple burned.[13] According to Knohl, those who composed the *Gabriel Revelation* desired to raise the spirits of God's faithful and offer them hope that redemption was indeed at hand. Despite what they had seen and experienced, God was still in control and would soon judge his enemies.

In the first column of the revelation, God appears to address a human being directly, but the extant text does not identify the seer. In what can be read, a dialogue takes place in which God does most of the talking.[14] The "God of Hosts" begins to tell of Jerusalem and its greatness[es] (בגדלות, line 12). Knohl remarks

---

9. Yardeni and Elizur, "Prophetic Text"; Israel Knohl, *Messiahs and Resurrection in 'The Gabriel Revelation'* (Kogod Library of Judaic Studies; London/New York: Continuum, 2009), 1–7.

10. Elisha Qimron and Alexey (Eliyahu) Yuditsky, "Notes on the Inscription 'The Vision of Gabriel'" (in Hebrew), *Cathedra* 133 (2009): 133–44.

11. Knohl (*Messiahs and Resurrection*) restores "Son of David" in line 8. "Son of David" is taken as a messianic title in *Ps. Sol.* 17:21 and Matt 9:27.

12. Knohl, *Messiahs and Resurrection*, xii.

13. Josephus, *J.W.* 2.1.1–2.5.3 §§1–79; *Ant.* 17.10.8–10 §§285–297.

14. Based on the poor preservation of the text, this seems to be the case.

that this line provides an introduction to "the miraculous salvation of Jerusalem."[15] One day "all the nations" (כול הגאים, line 13) will surround and besiege Jerusalem in a great eschatological battle. Though he calls it doubtful, Knohl reconstructs the text at the end of that line "and from it are exi[led]," partly on the strength of the intertextual play between the *Gabriel Revelation* and Zech 14:2. Clearer references to exile in lines 37–39 may well confirm his suspicions. On a strictly human level, the situation seems dire, but as the prophecy unfolds it becomes clear that deliverance is not far away. A sign of redemption is set (lines 16–17), and the Lord of Hosts, the God of Israel, announces that evil will be broken before righteousness (lines 19–21). Qimron and Yuditsky suggest that lines 17–19 be read: "Thus said [Y]HWH of Hosts, the God of Israel: My son, I have a new testament for Israel, by three days you shall know." This restoration seems consistent with the rest of the prophecy and provides a more satisfying reading than either Knohl's or Yardeni's and Elizur's. If correct, it clearly reflects the "new covenant" language of Jeremiah (31:31). Six centuries earlier Jeremiah had announced the terrible news of God's coming judgment against Israel and Jerusalem. The holy city, once thought to be invincible, was destined for destruction, according to the prophet. Yet even as God threatened to punish Israel for her sins, he promised to restore the fortunes of Judah and make Jerusalem again a place of joy (Jer 33:6–9). Jeremiah's prophecy of destruction and "new covenant" may well be imprinted on this turn-of-the-millennium prophecy. However, God promises to shake the heavens and earth "in a little while" (lines 24–25; cf. Hag 2:6) and to reveal his glory (כבוד, line 25).

There seems little doubt that Zechariah 14 and Haggai 2 provide scriptural inspiration for the future of Jerusalem envisioned in this revelation. The closing chapter of Zechariah's prophecy presents a broad description of an eschatological battle in which "all the nations" gather against Jerusalem, overthrow the city, loot the houses, rape the women, and carry half of the citizens into exile (Zech 14:2). But when all seems lost, the Lord goes forth to fight against the nations. As in other theophanies, the divine appearance disrupts nature, shaking the earth and carving out a valley toward the east. As for those who survived and remained in Jerusalem after the initial attack, they will leave the city and escape the coming battle. The Lord arrives and "all the holy ones"—a reference to the angelic army—are with him (Zech 14:5). Plagues fall upon those who have waged war against Jerusalem; even the animals in their camps succumb to sickness and disease (Zech 14:12–15). In Zechariah's idyllic vision, living waters flow from Jerusalem to the east and west as the holy city sits high above the surrounding plains. The victory of God in this final war causes the world to recognize the one, true God. Zechariah writes: "The Lord will become king over all the earth; on that day the Lord will be one and his name one" (Zech 14:9). Thereafter Jerusalem, the holy city, will be safe and inhabited once again by God's people. Never again will

---

15. Knohl, *Messiahs and Resurrection*, 9.

she be threatened with destruction (Zech 14:10–11). In the years that follow, all the nations that once attacked her will stream up her slopes to worship the King, the Lord of Hosts, and to keep the feast of Sukkoth. Those who do not will face plagues and punishments (Zech 14:16–19)

Zechariah's eschatological vision appears to provide the basic outline for the future role of Jerusalem in the *Gabriel Revelation*: (a) all nations gather to battle against Jerusalem (lines 13–16); (b) key citizens are taken into exile; (c) the Lord and his angelic army arrive to fight for his people and their city (lines 24–31); and (d) Jerusalem is miraculously delivered. Zechariah's vision has to do with the earthly Jerusalem, judged, restored, and protected by God. Whereas God had allowed Jerusalem to fall to imperial forces in the past, in the future God would repulse any attack and defeat his enemies soundly.

Haggai's prophecy has well shaped the eschatological expectation regarding Jerusalem in the *Gabriel Revelation*. The sixth-century prophet Haggai uttered his message in the shadows of an inglorious Jerusalem. When Cyrus issued his decree allowing the exiles to return home, he encouraged them to rebuild the temple (Ezra 1:1–4); but nearly twenty years later, little progress had been made. So Haggai addressed Zerubbabel the governor and Joshua the high priest to take the lead in rebuilding God's house. Not only would this momentous act unite a fractured people and bring prosperity back to the land, but it might also issue in the messianic age (Hag 2:20–23). Haggai grounded the future work of rebuilding the temple in God's promise made in the distant past when Israel came out of Egypt: "My spirit abides among you; do not fear" (Hag 2:5; cf. Exod 13:21–22; 14:19–20). He continues (Hag 2:6–7):

> For thus says the Lord of hosts: Once again, in a little while, I will shake the heavens and the earth and the sea and the dry land, and I will shake all the nations, so that the treasure of all nations shall come, and I will fill this house with splendor [or glory = כָּבוֹד], says the Lord of hosts.

The phrase "once again" recalls how God came in power to Mount Sinai (Exod 19:16–25) and reflects a new exodus perspective.[16] In the oracle, God promises to shake the heavens, earth, sea, and dry land—the first realms of God's creative actions (Gen 1:1–13). The shaking of the heavens and earth is clearly theophanic: YHWH appears and the earth shakes. Indeed this future event ("in a little while") is both imminent and cosmic in scope. All of creation and those who inhabit it will be affected. Therefore, God will shake the nations and they will in turn bring their precious, natural resources to Jerusalem to rebuild and refurbish the temple (Isa 60:5; 61:6; 66:20). The material "glory" of the nations reflects the divine "glory" that will fill God's new house one day so that Solomon's temple

---

16. A connection made by the writer of Hebrews (12:25–27).

will not "out-glory" Zerubbabel's. The prophecy ends: "and in this place [the new temple] I will give peace [שלום], says the Lord of Hosts" (Hag 2:9).

Hazon Gabriel 24–25 echo Haggai's prophecy. The reference to God's "place" at the beginning of line 24 may well refer to the temple or Jerusalem.[17] If so, we may surmise that the oracle proceeds from Jerusalem. God promises, "In a little while, I will shake . . . the heavens and the earth." Here the shaking of the heavens and the earth is a prelude to the arrival of glory. The juxtaposition of the shaking of the heavens and earth and the arrival of glory depend on Haggai's prophecy concerning the future of Jerusalem and an eschatological age anchored by a glory-filled temple. As the prophecy unfolds, God's glory is associated with seven chariots at the gate of Jerusalem and gates of Judea.[18] Although the text is fragmentary, this appears to refer to angels descending on chariots to wage war against the enemies of Jerusalem.[19] The appearance of Michael (line 28) suggests that he leads the angelic hosts into battle.

Qimron and Yuditsky restore line 32 to read: " . . . [Je]rusalem [shall be] as in early times. . . ." They take the phrase "as in early times" to refer to the tree in line 31, symbolizing "rest and longevity" (cf. Isa 65:22; Amos 9:11). This suggestion seems plausible and clearly comports with the theme of Jerusalem's restoration. The Jerusalem to come will become as Jerusalem was in the days of old, when heroes like David, God's servant, lived. Line 33 follows with another reference to Jerusalem and her greatness (cf. line 12).

The references to exile (גלות) in lines 37–39, according to Yardeni and Elizur, suggest that the author and his community were forced out of Jerusalem and made to live in exile.[20] If so, then the *Gabriel Revelation* would be the kind of apocalyptic text that provided consolation to a defeated, humiliated, marginalized people. Exile from Jerusalem may well provide some of the historical backdrop, but we should note also that exile serves as an important, generative theme from Zechariah's vision of Jerusalem and her future. Since Zechariah's vision shaped this apocalypse, exile may be more of a potential threat to this community rather than its current reality.[21]

Fewer references to Jerusalem are found in what remains of the second column of the inscription. The clearest line is *HazGab* 57: סתום דם טבחי ירושלם כי אמר יהוה צבא]ות]. Although the text is clear, its meaning is not. Yardeni and Elizur suggest that the phrase דם טבחי ירושלם refers to the sacrifices made in

---

17. Qimron and Yuditsky and Yardeni and Elizur read "his place" (מקומו) at the beginning of line 24, while Knohl reads "his seat" (מושבו).
18. So Knohl and Yardeni and Elizur. Qimron and Yuditsky restore this as "the God of the chariots will listen to the [cr]y of Jerusalem and will console the cities of Judah. . . ."
19. Knohl, *Messiahs and Resurrection*, 17.
20. Yardeni and Elizur, "Prophetic Text," 6.
21. Alternatively—as with the Qumran sectarians and early Christians (e.g., Matthew 21–25; Gal 4:21–31)—exile from Jerusalem and the temple may be self-imposed based on a negative evaluation of the current temple and its leadership.

Jerusalem. Though they regard it as unclear, they suggest that *satum* (סתום) be read as a reference to a temporary interruption or interlude of the sacrifices at the Jerusalem temple.[22] Knohl, however, seems more confident that it refers to the bloody massacre of Jerusalem's slain citizens. He bases this on subsequent references to "the blood of those slain" (line 67) and to the resurrection (line 80).[23] Furthermore, he translates *satum* (סתום) over against Daniel's prophecy (ch. 8) and renders it: "Seal up the blood of the slaughtered of Jerusalem." In other words, the seer is urged to suppress the prophecy regarding those who will be massacred in Jerusalem when the gentiles lay siege to the city.

Qimron and Yuditsky restore lines 66–67 as follows: "[Je]rusalem saying: (only) on You we rely, [not on]/flesh (and) not on man. This is the chariot . . . ." Neither Yardeni and Elizur nor Knohl restores Jerusalem at the beginning of line 66. Instead, they read the word "peace." Qimron and Yuditsky restore the text based on the potential influence of Jer 17:5–8, a prophetic oracle that pronounces a curse on all who put their trust in mortals and fleshly strength and a blessing on those who trust in the Lord. If "Jerusalem" is correct in line 66, we may have a situation in which the faithful survivors or martyrs of the nations' attack on Jerusalem express their faith in the one who rescued them.

Given the fragmentary nature of the inscription, any reconstruction or interpretation of Jerusalem's place in the *Gabriel Revelation* is necessarily provisional. Until further evidence can be brought to bear on this text to fill in vacant lines, we may never know the exact nature of this prophecy. Still, enough remains to begin to sketch out a few contingent conclusions. Inspired by earlier apocalypses and prophecies (Zechariah, Daniel, Jeremiah, Haggai, and possibly others), the community of the *Gabriel Revelation* is told that a great eschatological war is coming that pits the nations of the world and their military might against Jerusalem and her faithful. When the nations arrive, they surround Jerusalem. In the attack, many of the faithful will be slaughtered, and Jerusalem's key citizens will be taken into exile. However, a sign of redemption will be given (in Jerusalem ?), and God promises that evil will be broken by righteousness and the "wicked branch" will be exposed (cf. 2 Thess 2:3–12).[24] Jeremiah's vision of a new covenant is in the process of being fulfilled in their midst. As the battle rages, the Lord arrives and the heavens and the earth quake in his presence. Divine glory eclipses the might and power of the nations as holy angels join the battle led by Michael, the archangel. In the end, heaven and earth come together in the miraculous deliverance of Jerusalem, and the city is restored to her former glory. "The place

---

22. Yardeni and Elizur, "Prophetic Text," 10.
23. Knohl, *Messiahs and Resurrection*, 21.
24. Knohl (*Messiahs and Resurrection*, 12) argues that the "wicked branch" is "a wicked messianic king, a precursor to what would subsequently be termed the Antichrist." "Branch" may well be used here with messianic import. Jeremiah envisioned a day when the Lord will raise up a "righteous branch" for David. He will reign with integrity and wisdom and his name will be "The Lord is our righteousness" (Jer 2:5; cf. Isa 11:1–3; Matt 2:23).

of David, the servant of the Lord" (line 72) is once again secure and will be for all time. The faithful remnant returns from exile and declares absolute faith in the one, true God. And the God who once promised to show steadfast love to the thousands who love him and keep his commandments (Exod 20:6) has proven once again to be faithful to his covenant (lines 68, 74).

The eschatological figuration of Jerusalem in the *Gabriel Revelation* is heavily dependent on images and prophecies found in the Hebrew Scriptures. It is clearly a this-worldly Jerusalem, even though heaven comes in power to redeem her. Absent here is any reference to a heavenly Jerusalem—as the home of true believers—or a new Jerusalem that comes down out of heaven to earth. Nor is there any reference to the current community as somehow embodying Jerusalem or its temple, as we see among the Dead Sea Scrolls or the New Testament (e.g., 1 Cor 3:16-17; 6:19-20).

Jerusalem in the Revelation of John

As one writer put it, "the plot of Revelation can be read as the tale of two cities—the new and heavenly Jerusalem and the corrupt and sinful Babylon."[25] Babylon the great, of course, is destined for destruction (Rev 14:8). The cryptic city is metaphorically portrayed as a woman donning royal garb and bearing blasphemous names (17:1-4). She is described as "Babylon the great, the mother of whores and the earth's abominations" (17:5).[26] When the angelic guide escorts John into the wilderness to see her, she is drunk with the blood of the saints and the martyrs of Jesus (17:6). Tragically, her influence has extended throughout the world, but her destiny—and the destiny of the world for that matter—is soon to change, as the vision reveals God's judgment falling swiftly (ch. 18). In a single day plagues will descend on her and she will be burned with fire (18:9). In a single hour her judgment comes (18:10). Though her allies mourn her destruction, heaven erupts in praise when God avenges the blood of his servants (19:1-4).

Within the prophetic narrative of Revelation, both the character and the destiny of Jerusalem, the holy city, are far different from those of Babylon. The first reference to Jerusalem occurs in the letter to the church in Philadelphia (Rev 3:12): "I will make the victor a pillar in the temple of my God and he shall never again have to leave it and I will write the name of my God upon him and the name of the city of my God, the new Jerusalem, which comes down out of heaven from my God, and my own new name." The promises made to the Philadelphia faithful by the risen Jesus[27] situate them as a permanent feature in God's final temple. Never again will they be separated from the beloved city and its temple;

---

25. Newman, "Jerusalem," 564.
26. All translations of Revelation are my own.
27. The predications at the beginning of this and other letters should be read christologically.

never again will exile be a real threat. Likewise, the names they bear indicate an abiding relationship with God and the revealer and lasting citizenship in the new Jerusalem. These promises are clearly eschatological and foreshadow the descent of the new Jerusalem from heaven to earth (chs. 21–22). They help the persecuted minority in Asia Minor anticipate the kind of future they will experience if they stay true to the faith.[28]

Before the glorious new Jerusalem arrives, however, the earthly Jerusalem—like Babylon—must endure a time of judgment. John is given a measuring rod like a staff and told to measure the temple, the altar, and those who worship there.[29] Yet he is warned not to measure the court outside the temple, because it is given over to the nations, who will trample the holy city underfoot for forty-two months (Rev 11:1–2). No reason is offered as to why Jerusalem must suffer this disaster, but it is clear from what follows that God will not abandon Jerusalem forever and will indeed restore her. Two witnesses appear and prophesy powerfully for 1,260 days (= forty-two months). When their work is finished, they are killed by the beast that ascends from the abyss. Their bodies lie unburied in "the great city which is called prophetically Sodom and Egypt, where their Lord was also crucified" (Rev 11:8). These prophetic descriptions of Jerusalem as "Sodom" and "Egypt" and "where their Lord was also crucified" do not provide a reason for the judgment. Still, the association with such infamous places suggests that Jerusalem itself has been co-opted and corrupted by powerful, foul forces. Yet judgment and death are not the final word; their bodies do not lie like dung in the streets. After three and one-half days of their enemies' celebrations, the breath of God enters them and they stand to their feet to the dread of all those who rejoiced over their demise. Their complete vindication is assured when a heavenly voice calls them to come up to heaven and the city is rocked by an earthquake (Rev 11:9–13).

A similar account regarding Jerusalem's fate is found in Revelation 20. At an appointed time, "the dragon, the serpent of old, who is the devil and the Satan" will be locked up in the abyss for one thousand years (vv. 1–3). When the thousand years have ended, the devil will be released from the pit and will go about deceiving the nations and gathering them for battle. The enemies of God and his people surround "the camp of the saints and the beloved city [Jerusalem]" (v. 9). But even before the battle begins, it seems, the fire of heaven falls and consumes them; then the devil is seized and thrown into the lake of fire and sulfur for an eternity of torment (vv. 7–10). This visionary episode of the nations' attack on Jerusalem recapitulates the earlier account and intensifies it. It reveals the true power behind the scenes on earth (the Satan) and the impulse that drives powerful nations to line up against Jerusalem. Likewise, it shows how quickly and definitively heaven responds to the threat. In this episode there are no martyrs,

---

28. Yarbro Collins, "Dream of a New Jerusalem," 252.
29. The word translated "measure" (μέτρησον) can also mean "count."

no exiles, and no long, drawn-out battles; instead there is heaven's swift, powerful response to the peril.

The prophet refers to the heavenly Jerusalem in an interlude of three visions (Rev 14:1–20) intended to provide comfort to the church as she faces persecution. The seer looks to see the Lamb standing on Mount Zion in the company of 144,000 who have his name and his Father's name written on their foreheads. John listens as they sing a new song—a song only the redeemed can learn (cf. Rev 5:8–10)—before the throne and heavenly creatures. The number 144,000 is a symbolic number representing the faithful of all generations. Although the word "Jerusalem" does not occur in these verses, the association of Mount Zion with Jerusalem is unmistakable. The fact that this scene takes place before the throne, the elders, and the four living creatures suggests that John refers to the heavenly Jerusalem, for the new Jerusalem has yet to come down from heaven to earth (Revelation 21–22; cf. Heb 12:22).

The longest and most sustained treatment of Jerusalem in Revelation comes in the final chapters. The new Jerusalem foreshadowed in 3:12 becomes a reality, following a great battle between the kings of the earth (16:12–16) and heavenly armies led by a rider on a white horse who bears the name "The Word of God" (19:11–21). The battle is swift and decisive. Satan and his minions are soundly defeated. The dead are raised to life, and death itself is consumed in the lake of fire (ch. 20). It is at this point in the storied prophecy that the holy city, the new Jerusalem, appears, coming down out of heaven from God. In contrast to the harlot Babylon, she is described as a beautiful bride ready to meet her husband. The new Jerusalem experiences the unmediated presence of God that chases away sorrow, tears, and death. In the language of the Zion tradition,[30] the new Jerusalem is situated on a great, high mountain (21:10), and the glory of God radiates from the citiy. Revelation de-emphasizes the temple in favor of the city itself. No temple is found there because the eschatological gathering of the faithful constitutes the temple (cf. 1 Cor 3:16–17). As Rev 3:12 foreshadowed, God's faithful become pillars in the new Jerusalem, and the heavenly city itself becomes the temple. This is perhaps why the city is described as a perfect cube fifteen hundred miles in length, width, and height (Rev 21:15–16). As Adela Yarbro Collins notes, the cube shape suggests that the city "plays the role of the holy of holies of the temple of Solomon" (cf. 1 Kgs 6:19–20).[31]

As John's story draws to a close, the angel shows him "the river of the water

---

30. For a description of the Zion tradition, see Jimmy J. M. Roberts, "The Davidic Origin of the Zion Tradition," *JBL* 92 (1973): 329–44.

31. Yarbro Collins, "Dream of a New Jerusalem," 253. The four walls of the new Jerusalem are measured to be about seventy-five meters high. They surround a city made of gold and yet clear as glass. The city walls are founded and ornamented with precious jewels. The description here of the new Jerusalem in Revelation is similar to that in the Qumran document known as the Description of the New Jerusalem (5Q15 [5QNew Jerusalem]). Isaiah's prophecy (54:11–12) may have inspired such apocalyptic imaginations.

of life" that proceeds from the throne of God and the Lamb (Rev 22:1) and the tree of life. John's language here clearly reflects biblical imagery associated with a newly restored temple and the holy city, the new Jerusalem, as a new Eden.[32] In Ezekiel's vision of the restored temple, a sacred river runs beneath the threshold of the temple's entrance, flowing east to the Arabah, growing deeper until it becomes a mighty river that freshens the salty waters of the Dead Sea. The waters teem with life, and all sorts of trees grow on the banks of this river providing fresh fruit monthly even as their leaves offer healing (Ezek 47:1–12; cf. Zech 14:8). The reference to "the tree of life" in John's description borrows from Ezekiel's vision but also alludes to "the tree of life" in the garden of Eden (Gen 2:8–9).

As we have seen, Jerusalem functions in the Revelation of John in three ways. First, the earthly Jerusalem is a "great city" destined for judgment. Gentiles will surround her and ultimately trample her for an appointed time determined by God. But, unlike Babylon—the other "great city" in Revelation—God does not abandon her and will restore her (Rev 11:1–13; 20:1–10). Second, Mount Zion and Jerusalem refer to the heavenly city where the Lamb and those who bear his and his Father's name worship before the throne. These have remained pure and true despite threats and persecution (Rev 14:1–5; cf. Heb 12:22). Finally, at the end of John's visionary account, when the old order is eclipsed by a new heaven and new earth, the new Jerusalem comes down from God out of heaven. The entire city is construed in idyllic terms as an immense temple where God is immediately present with his people and where evil has been destroyed and impurity banished. In John's apocalyptic imaginings, various lines of biblical prophecy find their fulfillment in the temple city, configured ultimately as a new Eden (Rev 21:1–22:5).

Conclusion

The *Gabriel Revelation* and the Revelation of John are excellent examples of Jewish apocalyptic literature. As with other literature in this genre, they are written against the backdrop of persecution, martyrdom, and exile. Both attempt to comfort their communities with the promise that God is soon to act to rescue his suffering people (*HazGab* 24; Rev 1:3; 22:20). Both depend heavily on earlier biblical prophecies and revelations.[33] Both describe Jerusalem as a great city whose destiny influences the future of the world (*HazGab* 12; Rev 11:8; 21:10, 12, 16). Both envisage a great eschatological battle in which the nations of the world march against Jerusalem (*HazGab* 13–14; Rev 11:1–2; 20:7–10). In both accounts martyrs are many; but heaven answers, the Lord arrives,[34] and his

---

32. Yarbro Collins, "Dream of a New Jerusalem," 253.

33. In a similar way, 1 Macc 7:16–18 describes the massacre of a group of scribes by Alcimus and Bacchides as fulfilling Ps 79:2–3.

34. In Revelation, the rider on the white horse bears the names "The Word of God," "King of kings," and "Lord of lords" (19:11–16). In the narrative vision, this can be none other than the risen Jesus.

arrival disrupts the natural course of events (*HazGab* 24-25; Rev 11:3-7, 11-13; 19:11-21). He comes with his holy angels (*HazGab* 26-29)—a vast angelic army (Rev 19:14)—to destroy evil and its representatives (*HazGab* 20-22; Revelation 13; 20:7-10) and to establish righteousness. Ultimately, Jerusalem is restored and is once again a great city (*HazGab* 32-33; Rev 21:1-22:5). Given the similarities found between these and other texts (e.g., Zechariah 14 and Daniel 11-12), we may well be dealing with various versions of an eschatological scheme regarding Jerusalem that was current among apocalyptic Jewish and early Christian communities.[35]

These two apocalypses differ in the nature of Jerusalem's future. In contrast to Jerusalem's destructions in the past, the *Gabriel Revelation* envisages an earthly Jerusalem, attacked and yet, this time, miraculously rescued by God. John's Revelation, on the other hand, finds ultimate hope not in an earthly Jerusalem but in a new creation and a new Jerusalem that comes down from heaven. In John's vision, God is immediately and eternally present with his faithful people (especially the resurrected martyrs) in the temple city.

John's Revelation may also assist in interpreting obscure aspects of the *Gabriel Revelation*. In particular, Knohl reads lines 80-81 as Gabriel commanding the son of Joseph, "the prince of the princes," to be raised from the dead on the third day after dying in battle. According to Knohl, the suffering of the "Messiah son of Joseph" is considered "a necessary stage in the redemptive process," for his death moves God to come down at the Mount of Olives to avenge his suffering people.[36] If Knohl's reading is correct, then the idea of a suffering-resurrected Messiah is earlier than Jesus and may have inspired the Nazarene carpenter to see his messianic vocation in terms of suffering and resurrection on the third day. But not all agree.

The book of Daniel and John's Revelation offer a more appropriate context for how the *Gabriel Revelation* should be read at this point. Daniel envisions a day when a wicked king will set his heart against the covenant and its people (Dan 11:28). When his forces move south and are initially repulsed by the Kittim, the unnamed king (Antiochus IV) turns angrily against Jerusalem, profanes the temple, abolishes the sacrifices, and sets up the abominating sacrilege (11:31). He is able to seduce some to his wicked ways, but those loyal to God and his covenant resist. "The wise," as they are called, fall by the sword and flame; some are taken into captivity (11:33-35). But this suffering is portrayed as a refining, purifying event until the end. At the appointed time, Michael, the great prince and protector of the people, arises and great tribulation proceeds (12:1). But Daniel is assured that his people—those whose names are found written in the book—will be delivered. The text concludes (12:2-3):

---

35. Compare the role of Jerusalem in the eschatological discourse in the Synoptic Gospels (Matt 24:1-36; Mark 13:1-37; Luke 21:5-36).

36. Knohl, *Messiahs and Resurrection*, xii-xiii.

Many of those who sleep in the dust of the earth shall awake, some to everlasting life, and some to shame and everlasting contempt. Those who are wise shall shine like the brightness of the sky, and those who lead many to righteousness, like the stars forever and ever.

This is the first clear reference to resurrection in the Hebrew Bible (cf. Isa 26:19; Ezekiel 37).[37] For our purposes, it is important to note that the Danielic text does not refer to the resurrection of a single individual but to that of a group who have remained faithful unto death. George W. E. Nickelsburg notes correctly that the period when Daniel was written was formative for Jewish views of the afterlife. The persecutions of Antiochus IV and the death of many *ḥāsîdîm* created a theological problem: How can those obedient to Torah die such horrid deaths? The answer is resurrection.[38] Daniel underscores that the righteous martyrs will one day live, and the wicked—often those who afflicted them—will be resurrected for eternal shame and punishment. Thus, God's justice is satisfied.[39]

As we have seen, the Revelation of John presents a scenario similar to what we find in Daniel (Revelation 11). For a time Jerusalem and its temple are trampled by the nations. Resistance to the onslaught comes from the two witnesses—representatives of God's loyal people—who bear witness to the one, true God and to whom God grants authority reminiscent of Moses and Elijah. Eventually, they too are captured and killed, and their bodies lie unburied for three and one-half days in Jerusalem. But even as wickedness seems to triumph, God answers this injustice by resurrecting his two witnesses and assuming them up into heaven in full view of their terrified enemies. A great earthquake ensues, thousands are killed, and the survivors turn to give glory to the true God (Rev 11:1–13). In both Daniel and Revelation, God's faithfulness to his people and their vindication is demonstrated when they are raised from the dead. Resurrection here is clearly not individual but corporate.[40]

---

37. When 4 Maccabees was written, Ezekiel 37 was read as a promise of bodily resurrection for those who do the will of God (4 Macc 18:16–19).

38. George W. E. Nickelsburg, *Resurrection, Immortality, and Eternal Life in Intertestamental Judaism and Early Christianity* (expanded ed.; HTS 56; Cambridge: Harvard Divinity School, 2006), 33–53.

39. These convictions are worked out narratively in the celebrated account of the seven brothers and their mother (2 Maccabees 7). The devout family is captured by Antiochus IV, forced to eat pork, and afflicted with torture. Despite threats of dismemberment and death, all the brothers pledge fidelity to God and his law. One by one they are killed, as their pious mother looks on, each expressing confidence that the true king of the world will raise them to eternal life (see 4 Macc 17:5).

40. There is little in the vision recorded in Revelation 11 that is distinctively "Christian." Unlike, for example, Paul, who links the resurrection of believers directly to the resurrection of Jesus (e.g., 1 Thess 4:13–18; 1 Cor 15:20–28), the account in Revelation 11 does not. In fact, Rev 11:1–13 could have been written by any apocalyptically minded Jew in the late Second Temple era (cf. Daniel 11–12; Zechariah 14; *Gabriel Revelation*).

If Knohl is correct in restoring the first part of line 80 as "By three days, live (חאיה), I Gabriel . . . ,"[41] it is still not clear to whom the angel speaks. Knohl argues that he commands the fallen Messiah ("prince of the princes"), the earthly leader of God's people, to rise from the dead on the third day.[42] Thus, the resurrection of a single individual initiates the miraculous deliverance of Jerusalem and God's people. But this interpretation is difficult to sustain in light of the fragmentary nature of the text and the more direct parallels we find in Daniel 11–12 and Revelation 11. In both cases, resurrection is not individual but corporate; it is God's vindication of all his martyred faithful. Properly understood, the two witnesses in Revelation 11 are not individuals whom God resurrects after three and a half days; they represent all believers who remain true to the end. If "live" (חאיה) is correct in *HazGab* 80, it is more likely a command for all the martyred faithful to be resurrected on the third day (following Hos 6:2), even if it is expressed in a collective singular. The phrase "prince of the princes" in line 81, then, is not the one addressed and therefore raised from the dead but the one who raises the dead, namely, God (cf. Dan 8:11, 24–25). This may well be confirmed by line 85, which reads: "then you [plural] will stand (אז תעמדו) . . . ." The verb עמד ("stand") is used to refer to future resurrection in Dan 12:13 and Ezek 37:10. If this interpretation is correct, line 85 then refers to the resurrection of God's martyrs in a not-too-distant future.

Finally, the *Gabriel Revelation* and the Revelation of John depict what may be variant versions of an accepted apocalyptic scenario regarding the future of Jerusalem. In the past, the holy city had fallen to the might and cruelty of various empires. But in the future, when all the nations of the world line up against her for one, final battle, the God of hosts will intervene decisively and reverse the shame of the past. Whether by resurrection, some miraculous incursion, or new creation, heaven will guarantee that Jerusalem will once again be the center of the world and her loyal citizens will rest safe in God's glorious presence.

---

41. Not all agree, of course. Qimron and Yuditsky read the word as "the sign" (האות). Likewise, Ronald Hendel, "The Messiah Son of Joseph: Simply 'Sign,'" *BAR* 35 (2009): 8. Matthias Henze also expressed doubt in his SBL seminar presentation (November 22, 2009) "*The Gabriel Revelation* Reconsidered: A Response to Israel Knohl."

42. Knohl (*Messiahs and Resurrection*, 26–28) bases his decision in large part on his reading of Daniel 8.

Bibliography

The bibliography consists of books and articles on the *Hazon Gabriel* that appeared prior to August 2010.

2007

Knohl, Israel. "In Three Days, You Shall Live." *Haaretz*. April 19, 2007.
———. "Studies in the *Gabriel Revelation*" (in Hebrew). *Tarbiz* 76 (2007): 303–28.
Yardeni, Ada, and Binyamin Elizur. "A Prophetic Text on Stone from the First Century BCE: First Publication" (in Hebrew). *Cathedra* 123 (2007): 155–66.

2008

Bar-Asher, Moshe. "On the Language of 'The Vision of Gabriel.'" *RevQ* 23 (2008): 491–524.
Blau, Gisela. "Révélation d'une stèle: La vision de Gabriel." *Revue Juive* 9 (2008): 9–12.
Bronner, Ethan. "Ancient Tablet Ignites Debate on Messiah and Resurrection." *New York Times*. July 6, 2008.
Collins, John J. "The Vision of Gabriel." *Yale Alumni Magazine* (September/October 2008): 26–27.
Goren, Yuval. "Micromorphologic Examination of the *Gabriel Revelation* Stone." *IEJ* 58 (2008): 220–29.
Knohl, Israel. "'By Three Days, Live': Messiahs, Resurrection, and Ascent to Heaven in *Hazon Gabriel*." *JR* 88 (2008): 147–58.
———. "The Messiah Son of Joseph: 'Gabriel's Revelation' and the Birth of a New Messianic Model." *BAR* 34, no. 5 (2008): 58–62, 78.
Yardeni, Ada. "A New Dead Sea Scroll in Stone? Bible-like Prophecy Was Mounted in a Wall 2,000 Years Ago." *BAR* 34, no. 1 (2008): 60–61.

2009

Bar-Asher, Moshe. "On the Language of 'The Vision of Gabriel'" (in Hebrew). Pages 193–226 in *Meghillot: Studies in the Dead Sea Scrolls VII*. Edited by Moshe Bar-Asher and Devorah Dimant. Jerusalem: Haifa University and Bialik Institute, 2009.
Hamidović, David. "La *Vision de Gabriel*." *RHPR* 89 (2009): 147–68.

Hendel, Ronald. "The Messiah Son of Joseph: Simply 'Sign.'" *BAR* 35, no. 1 (2009): 8.

Knohl, Israel. *Messiahs and Resurrection in 'The Gabriel Revelation.'* Kogod Library of Judaic Studies. London/New York: Continuum, 2009.

Rendsburg, Gary A. "Linguistic and Stylistic Notes to the Hazon Gabriel Inscription." *DSD* 16 (2009): 107–16.

Yuditsky, Alexey (Eliyahu), and Elisha Qimron. "Notes on the Inscription 'The Vision of Gabriel'" (in Hebrew). *Cathedra* 133 (2009): 133–44.

Hazon Gabriel.
Photograph by Bruce and Kenneth Zuckerman, and
Marilyn Lundberg, West Semitic Research.
Courtesy Dr. David Jeselsohn

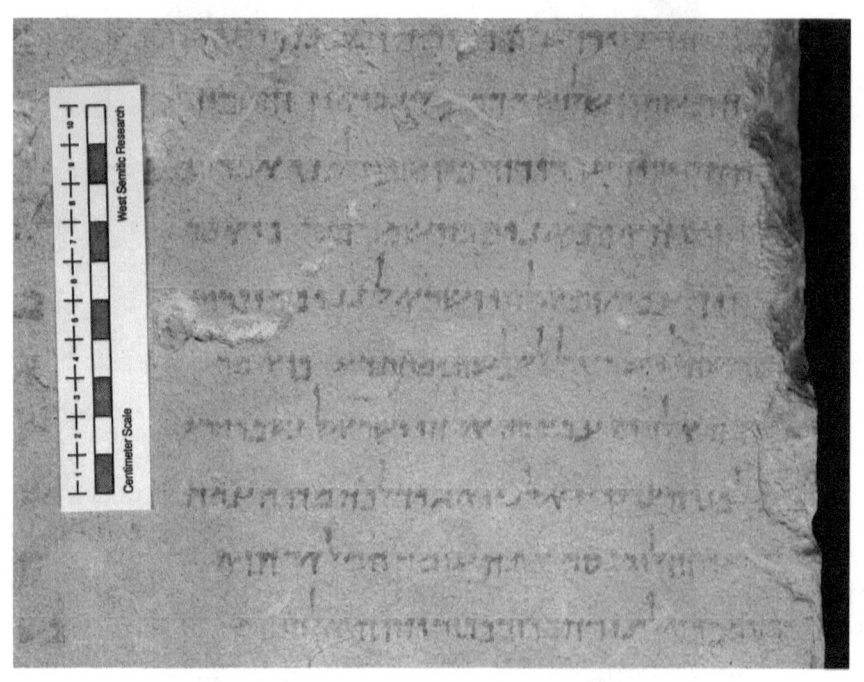

Hazon Gabriel, lines 15–23.
Photograph by Bruce and Kenneth Zuckerman, and Marilyn Lundberg, West Semitic Research. Courtesy Dr. David Jeselsohn

Hazon Gabriel, lines 15–18.
Photograph by Bruce and Kenneth Zuckerman, and Marilyn Lundberg, West Semitic Research. Courtesy Dr. David Jeselsohn

Hazon Gabriel, lines 23–32.
Photograph by Bruce and Kenneth Zuckerman, and Marilyn Lundberg, West Semitic Research. Courtesy Dr. David Jeselsohn

Hazon Gabriel, lines 76–83.
Photograph by Bruce and Kenneth Zuckerman, and Marilyn Lundberg, West Semitic Research. Courtesy Dr. David Jeselsohn

Hazon Gabriel, lines 76–82B.
Photograph by Bruce and Kenneth Zuckerman, and Marilyn Lundberg, West Semitic Research. Courtesy Dr. David Jeselsohn

Contributors

Kelley Coblentz Bautch
Associate Professor of Religious
 Studies
St. Edward's University

David Capes
Professor in Christianity
College of Arts and Humanities
Houston Baptist University

John J. Collins
Holmes Professor of Old Testament
 Criticism and Interpretation
Yale Divinity School

Binyamin Elizur
Dr. of Rabbinic Literature
The Historical Dictionary of the
 Hebrew Language
The Academy of the Hebrew
 Language, Jerusalem

Matthias Henze
Watt J. and Lilly G. Jackson Chair in
 Biblical Studies
Associate Professor of Religious
 Studies
Rice University

David Jeselsohn
Founder of the Epigraphic Center at
 Bar Ilan University
Independent scholar and collector
Zurich, Switzerland

Daewoong Kim
Graduate Student, Department of
 Religious Studies
Rice University

Israel Knohl
Yehezkel Kaufmann Chair of Biblical
 Studies
The Hebrew University of Jerusalem

Elisha Qimron
Professor of Hebrew Language
Ben-Gurion University of the Negev

Gary A. Rendsburg
Blanche and Irving Laurie Chair in
 Jewish History
Rutgers University

Adela Yarbro Collins
Buckingham Professor of New
 Testament Criticism and
 Interpretation
Yale Divinity School

Ada Yardeni
Researcher in Semitic Palaeography
 and Epigraphy
The Hebrew University of Jerusalem

Alexey (Eliyahu) Yuditsky
Researcher
The Academy of the Hebrew
 Language and Ben-Gurion
 University of the Negev

Index of Passages

1. The Hebrew Bible

Genesis
1:1–13	177
1:24	20
2:8–9	183
3:11	23
3:13	21
3:24	148
5:24	107
7:4	38
36	22
41:20	34
41:27	34
44:26	20, 23

Exodus
3:11	133, 146
3:12	119
4:2	21, 69
8:19	37, 170
13:21–22	177
14:19–20	177
16:15	69
19	165
19:11	165
19:15	19, 164–66
19:16–25	177
20:6	20, 41, 83, 180
32:15	50
34:5–7	127
34:7	41

Leviticus
11:27	78
11:28	78
16	57

Numbers
13:13	133
16:11	69
22:9	21

Deuteronomy
5:10	20, 41, 83, 133
6:5	22
9:5	34
10:21	117
28:31	80
32:7	74
32:15	123
32:17	75, 123
33:17	48

Joshua
5:14	145
7:8	69
9:16	69
23:1	69
24:20	69

Judges
5:29	157
6:12, 14, 16	167
6:17	167
6:23	135
19:23	69

1 Samuel
12:2	74
14:10	119
16:11	21
17:14	21
17:37	158
17:46	158
18:18	133, 146
23:27	133

2 Samuel
3:18	19

INDEX OF PASSAGES

2 Samuel (*continued*)		7:10–12	168
5:6–10	173	7:11	118
5:10	116	7:14	168
7	102	7:16	168
7:5	118	11:1–3	179
7:8	118	13:6	122
7:9	158	13:13	169
7:14	118	14:1	38
7:18	23, 133, 146	21:20	20
7:27	20	26:19	185
19:31	69	26:21	122
22:11	148	28:16	35
24:14	58	29:7	34, 83, 117
		29:7–8	74
1 Kings		29:8	117
6:19–20	182	34:2	80
7:27–37	143	37:16	20
7:33	143	37:35	126
11:12, 13, 34	126	38:7	167
11:13	20	38:22	167
11:32	19	40:1	122
14:4	74	40:1–10	170
14:8	19	41:10	21
15:4	126	51:19	122
19:10	116	52:9	35
19:14	116	53	94
		54:11–12	182
2 Kings		59:7	122
2	125	60:1–2	110
2:11	105, 125	60:5	177
8:19	126	60:18	122
9:37	44	60:21	120
19:29	119	61:3	120
19:34	126	61:6	177
20:6	126	63:9	74
20:8–9	167	63:11	74
20:9	119	65:12	80
22:3	19	65:22	35, 178
22:4	19	66:10, 11, 13	171
23:11	143	66:10–15	171
		66:15	170–71
Isaiah		66:15–16	144
3:16	66	66:20	177
6:2–6	148	66:24	40
7	108, 118–19, 129		
7:1	168	Jeremiah	
7:1–17	168	1:2	19
7:4	168	2:5	179

2:8	37	9:2–11	138
3:15	46	10	141, 148
5:14	116	10:1–22	148
6:7	35, 122	10:13	148
8:2	44	10:15	136
9:18	35	16:6	107
9:21	44	16:47	24
15:16	116	34:2–23	46
16:4	44	34:23	158
17:5–7	36	34:23–24	44
17:5–8	179	34:24	19, 158
20:8	35, 122	34:25	158
22:20	119	34:28	158
23:1	46	34:29	158
23:5	19, 21, 102, 120	34:30	158
24:1–10	38	37	185
25:33	44	37:10	128, 186
26:18	66	37:24	19, 158
31	42, 111	37:24–25	44
31–32	42, 129	37:26	158
31–33	40, 44, 49	37:27	158
31:8 [Engl. 9]	43, 48	38–39	149
31:17–19 [Engl. 18–20]	43, 48	38:12	173
31:20	110	40:1	69
31:31	42, 118, 176	45:9	122
32:17	55	47:1–12	183
32:17–18	37, 41, 42, 126, 133	Hosea	
32:18	20, 37	6:1–2	166
32:20	21, 42	6:2	186
32:36–42	37	6:2–3	165
32:37	37	11	111
33:3	19, 21, 40, 117	11:1	110
33:6–9	176	11:1–9	48
33:10	35	11:8	110
33:15	19, 21, 102, 120	13:1	48
35:17	116	13:14	48
38:17	116		
		Joel	
Ezekiel		2	104
1	136, 141, 148	3	117, 143
1:5–15	148	4:16	122
1:16	148		
1:29–2:2	135	Amos	
3:12	19, 35, 71, 87, 88, 122	4:4	19, 164
		7–8	100, 104
5:5	173	9:11	35, 64, 178

INDEX OF PASSAGES

Jonah		4:10–11	137
1:17	138	6:1	19
3:3	138	6:1–5	137
		6:1–6	142
Micah		6:1–7	136
1:3	122	6:1–8	144
3:12	66	6:7	142
		6:9–15	19
Habakkuk		6:12	21, 120
1:11	75	10:7	48
3:8, 12	171	11:8	19, 20, 46, 106, 126, 138
Zephaniah		12:10	109, 123
1:1	19	13:5	57
		14	39, 44, 101, 117, 129, 143, 149, 184–85
Haggai	3, 13		
1:13	133, 169		
2	129, 170	14:2	39, 176
2:4	169	14:3–5	40, 122
2:5	169, 177	14:5	176
2:6	17, 40, 71, 85, 122, 132, 144, 169, 176	14:8	183
		14:9	176
		14:10–11	177
2:6–7	177	14:12	32, 40, 117
2:7	24, 170	14:12–15	176
2:9	178	14:16–19	177
2:20–23	177		
2:21–22	144	Malachi	
2:22	170	2:7	133
Zechariah	3, 13	Psalms	
1–6	144	2	101, 102, 117
1:7–11	144	2:7	118
1:8–11 [LXX]	136, 142	2:7–8	109
1:9	138	8:16	17
1:12	35	9:21	17
1:17	35, 38	12:6	35
2:1–6	144	18:11	148
2:2	138	21:4	109
2:3–4	142	22:16	110
2:10	137	29:1	141
3	150	36:10	110
3:8	19, 21, 120	48	101
3:9	137	54:6 [Engl. 4]	56
4:1–7	144	59:6	76, 116
4:2–3	137	68:18	143
4:10	138	71:16	117

79:2–3	183	7	100
80:5	76, 116	7:9	142, 166
80:8	76, 116	7:13	145
80:15	76, 116	7:15–27	144
80:20	76, 116	7:16	166
81:4	57	7:22	166
83:11	44	7:25	52, 169
84:9	76, 116	8	100, 107, 129, 168, 179, 186
89:9	116		
90:15	74	8–9	24
94:2	74	8:8	119
106:21	117	8:9	161
140:6	74	8:10	161
149:5–6	18	8:11	145, 158, 161, 186
		8:12	122, 161
Job		8:13	124–25, 140
3–27	116	8:13–26	144
5:9	117	8:15–19	121
8:14	122	8:15–26	146
9:10	117	8:16	121, 145, 166
15:10	74	8:16–27	44
22:14	34	8:17	135, 163
26:9	57	8:17–18	44
32:14	157	8:18	34, 121
37:5	117	8:19	121, 154, 163
		8:23	44, 161
Proverbs		8:23–25	161
7:20	57	8:23–26	50
15:25	74	8:24	44, 161
16:19	74	8:25	19, 20, 44–45, 107, 128, 155, 158, 159, 160–62, 165
16:28	22		
22:21	34, 42, 83, 102, 120, 157		
		8:26	44, 104, 124, 163
Qoheleth		9:2	163
1:1	18	9:17	169
		9:21	145, 166
Esther		9:21–27	146
8:1	69	9:22–27	50
		9:23	163
Daniel		9:26	51
1:8	3, 13	9:27	51
2:28	87	10	105, 147
3:28	76, 97	10–12	101, 116, 129
4:10	136	10:8	135
4:14	125, 148	10:12	135
4:20	148	10:13	19, 34, 122–23, 145, 155
6:23	125, 148		
	136		

Daniel (continued)		25:1	65
10:13–14	122	29:17	38
10:18–19	34–35	32:9	66
10:19	122, 135	34:8	19
10:21	19, 123, 145, 154, 155	34:22	19
11–12	184–86		
11:2	154	## 2. The Apocryphal Writings of the Septuagint	
11:21–45	161		
11:22	51		
11:28	42, 51, 184	Ben Sira	
11:30	42	8:9	75
11:31	184	32:3	75
11:32	51	35:3	75
11:33	51	36:18	65
11:33–35	184	42:8	75
11:36	107	47:2	64
11:36–37	162	47:11	65
11:38	75–76	49:4	64
12:1	19, 123, 145, 155, 184	4 Ezra	101, 116
12:2–3	184	5–6	109
12:3	51	7:26	174
12:5–13	144	10:25–54	174
12:13	108, 128, 186	10:29–30	135
		12:23	138
Ezra		13	101, 117
1:1–4	177	13:36	174
8:8	133		
10:8	19, 163	1 Maccabees	
10:9	19	7:16–18	183
1 Chronicles		2 Maccabees	
3:5	66	7	185
5:13–14	133		
6:40	133	Tobit	
7:3	133	6:6–8	144
8:16	133	12:15	138
12:20	133	13:9–18	173
17:8	158		
17:16	23	## 3. The New Testament	
27:18	133		
28:18	143	Matthew	
		2:23	179
2 Chronicles		4:5	150
21:2	133	9:27	175
21:19	38	21–25	178

23:27	121	1 Thessalonians	
24:1–36	184	4:13–18	185
25:41	150		
		2 Thessalonians	
Mark		2:3–12	179
3:23	150		
8:31	97	Hebrews	
13:1–37	184	12:22	173, 182, 183
13:21–22	102–3	12:25–27	177
Luke		2 Peter	
1:13	135	2:4	149
1:19	146		
1:26	146	Jude	
1:30	135	6	149
4:3	150	9	145
13:16	150		
21:5–36	184	Revelation	
		1:3	183
John		1:4	137
6:70	150	1:12	137
13:27	150	1:12–17	135
		1:16	137
Acts		1:20	137
23:3	121	2:1	137
		2:7	123
Romans		3:1	137
8:38	148	3:12	180, 182
		4–5	142
1 Corinthians		4:4–10	137
3:16–17	180, 182	5:5–8	137
6:19–20	180	5:8–10	182
14:33	140	7:1–8	137
15:20–28	185	7:13	138
15:24	148	8:6	137
		8:13	138
2 Corinthians		11	111, 174, 185–86
6:14–15	150	11:1–2	181, 183
		11:1–13	183, 185
Galatians		11:3–7	184
4:21–31	178	11:8	181, 183
		11:9–13	181
Philippians		11:11–13	184
1:1	140	11:18	105, 141
		12:7–9	145
Colossians		12:9	150
1:16	142, 148	13	184

Revelation (continued)		Apocalypse of Moses	
13:10	105	13:2	155
14:1–5	183	28:4	123
14:1–20	182		
14:6–9	141	2 Baruch	116
14:8	180	4:1–7	174
14:12	105	25:2–4	119
16:6	105	32:2–4	173
16:12–16	182		
17:1–4	180	3 Baruch	
17:5	180	14:2	155
17:6	105, 180		
18	180	4 Baruch	
18:9	180	5:35	174
18:10	180		
19:1–4	180	1 Enoch	
19:11–16	183	6–16	149
19:11–21	182	7	150
19:14	184	9–10	136
20	182	9–11	145, 146, 147
20:1–3	181	9:1	123, 140
20:1–10	183	10:3	120
20:7–10	181, 183, 184	10:7 (Greek)	148
20:8–9	149	10:16	120, 159
20:9	181	14:25	135, 140
21–22	181–82	18:6, 13	137
21:1–22:5	183, 184	20	138, 144, 149
21:10	182, 183	20:1	148
21:15–16	182	20:5	123, 144
22:1	183	21:3	137
22:2, 14, 19	123	22:6	148
22:20	183	22:8–13	144
		24:2–3	137
4. The Pseudepigrapha		24:2–25:6	144
		24:6	155
Apocalypse of Elijah		25:1	138
5:6	123	25:4–5	144
		25:5	123
Apocalypse of Ezra		26:1	173
1:3	155	27:1–4	144
2:1	145	39–40	142
4:2	155	40:2–10	146, 149
4:7	145	40:7	150
		40:10	136, 146
Ascension of Isaiah		48:4	140
1:4	148	48:7	140
		54:6	150

61:10	142, 148
69	150
69:6	150
69:14–15	145
71:3	145
71:7	142, 148
71:9	123
81:5	138
87:2–3	141
89:1	134
89:59–90:19	105
90:21	138
93:1	159
93:5	120, 159
93:10	120, 159

2 Enoch 141, 143, 149
18:1	148
20:1	142, 148
21:2–6	135

3 Enoch 20, 149
18	138
23:18	123
30	142

Jubilees
1:16	120, 159
8:11	173
8:19	173
10:8	150
16:26	120
21:24	120
36:6	120, 159

4 Maccabees
17:5	185
18:16–19	185

Psalms of Solomon
17	111
17:21	175

Sibylline Oracles
3:401–6	159–60
3:401–10	169
8:459–63	147

The Syriac Apocalypse of Daniel
28	162

Testament of Abraham A
7–8	145
7:11	155

Testament of Dan
5:12	173

Testament of Isaac
2:1	145

Testament of Jacob
1:6	145

Testament of Levi
3	148
3:1–8	148
3:8	142, 148
8:1–2	138
18:2	138
18:4	150
18:10–11	123

Testament of Moses
	51–53
6:8–9	45, 52
6:8–10	45
7:1	52
9:7	53
10:2	52
10:8–9	46–47

Testament of Naphtali
3:5	148

Testament of Reuben
5:6–7	148

5. THE DEAD SEA SCROLLS

1QIsaᵃ	64

1QpMicah (1Q14)
5:2	122

1QpHab
9:4	65

1QpHab (continued)
12:7	65
12:7–9	174

The Genesis Apocryphon (1QapGen)
2:1	148
2:16	148
13:16	34

Book of Mysteries (1Q27)
1 i 5	119, 168

The Rule of the Community (1QS)
1:16–2:8	150
2:7	86
3:24	148
4:23	148
9:3–6	174
11:15	86

The War Rule (1QM)
1:3	123
1:10	148
1:11	148
1:13	150
9:14–16	136, 146
11:2	64
12:1	139
12:14	73
13	145
13:2	148
13:4	148
13:10	148
13:12	150
16:1	73
17:6–8	145

The Hodayot 1QH^a
10:18	150
10:24	150
11:20–24	134
11:21–23	140
11:23	139, 148
11:29	150
11:30	150
11:33	150
11:36	139
12:11	150
12:14	150
13:28	150
13:41	150
14:14	134
14:24	150
15:6	150
15:31	148
16:18	64
18:8	162
18:10	148
23:23	148

The Copper Scroll (3Q15) 27, 70, 89
9:2	79
10:9	79
10:13	79

The Damascus Document (CD)
2:18	148, 149
7:16	64
16:5	150

4QPesher Isaiah
4Q161 (4QpIsa^a)	102
4Q161 (4QpIsa^b)	
2:1–9	174
4Q161 (4QpIsa^c)	
23 ii 10–12	174

4Q164	174

4QPesher Nahum (4Q169)
3–4 iii 6–7	174

4QFlorilegium (4Q174)
1:1–2	174

4Q181
frg. 1.4	148

4QEn^a
1 iv	146

4QEn^b
1 iii	146

ID OF PASSAGES

4QEn^e		*4QMMT*	
1 xxii	148	4Q394 3:12, 4:5	86
		4Q396 1:3, 3:4–5, 4:2	86
4Q227 (4QpsJub^c?)		4Q397 1:7, 4:9	86
2:1	69	4Q398 frgs. 14–17 ii 4	87
4Q246	103	*Songs of the Sabbath Sacrifice*	
		(4QShirShab)	138, 151
4Q*Commentary on Genesis*		4Q403 1 i 30	148
4Q252	102, 120	4Q403 1 ii	142
		4Q403 1 ii 15	148, 149
4Q269	25–29	4Q403 1 ii 22	141
		4Q405 frg. 7 7, 8	141
4Q270	25–29	4Q405 frgs. 8–9 6	141
		4Q405 frg. 46.2	148
4Q280			
frg. 1.2	150	4Q448	28
4Q285	102, 120	4Q470	145
frg. 10.3	145		
		4Q491	145
4Q286			
frg. 1	142	4Q510	
frg. 7	150	frg. 1.5–6	150
4Q300		4Q511	
1 ii 2	124	frg. 10.1–2	150
		frg. 35.2–4	140
4Q365			
5:1	70	*Michael's Words*	
		4Q529	138, 144, 145,
4Q372			146, 147
2:12	34, 88		
		Book of Giants	
4Q373		4Q530	138
1:6	34, 88		
		4Q543	
4Q385 (4QpsEzek^a)		8	148
6:9	70		
		4Q560	150
4Q387 2 iii 5–6	119		
		5QNew Jerusalem ar (5Q15)	182
4Q389 8 ii 5–6	119		
		11QMelchizedek (11Q13)	
4Q390 1:11	150	2:5	141, 145
		2:12	148
4Q393 2:7	88	2:23–34	174

INDEX OF PASSAGES

11QShirShab (11Q17)
   frgs. 3:1–4:4   148

11QTemple
   29:6–10   174
   56:13   73
   57:7   73
   60:21   73
   62:12   73
   64:10   73

6. Philo

Det. 1.85   160

7. Josephus

Antiquities
   6.181   158
   17.6.2–4   46
   17.6.4   46
   17.10   45
   17.10.6   49
   17.10.8–10   175
   18.1.1   51

The Jewish War
   1.33.2–4   46
   2.1.1–2.2.1   126
   2.1.1–2.5.3   175
   2.1–5   45
   2.4.2   4, 47

8. Rabbinic and Jewish Medieval Literature

ʾ*Avinu Malkenu*   80

ʾ*Abot R. Nat.*
   ver. B, 47   18

Babylonian Talmud
   Ber. 57b   18
   Sukkah 52a   49, 95, 109
   Ḥag. 12b   19
   Ketub. 3b   80
   Ketub. 4a   80
   Sanh. 13b   21
   Zebaḥ. 62a   18

Genesis Rabba
   1   19
   20:2   22
   47:6   20

Hekhalot Literature
(Peter Schäfer, *Synopse zur Hekhalot — Literatur*, 1981)
   §30   22
   §31   22
   §39   22
   §§41–42   22
   §78   20
   §389   20
   §493   22
   §564   23
   §847   20

Hekhalot Rabbati   149

Maʿase Daniʾel alaw ha-Shalom   24

Maʿase Merkava
   57   23

Mekhilta de-Rabbi Ishmael
   Pisḥa 16–18   69
   Be-Shalaḥ 1–3   69
   Kaspa 20   69

Mishnah
Ber.
   1:5   74
   9:7   78

Ter.
   5:4   69

Šabb.
   1:9   78
   9:4   164

Šeqal.
   7:2   74
   8:1   74

INDEX OF PASSAGES

Sukkah		*Piyyutim*	21, 23
3:13	74		
4:8	74	*Prayer before the Thirteen Attributes, Selihot*	22
Moʿed Qaṭ.			
3:5	78	*Qoheleth Rabba*	
3:9	69	1,1,2	18
Giṭ.		*Re'uyot Yeḥezke'el*	143
3:5	69	11	20
Qidd.		*Sefer Zerubbabel*	95
3:5	69	*Sifra*	57
		ʾAḥare Mot 6:1	72
B. Meṣiʿa		Zavim 5:2	78
8:6	74		
		Sifre Deuteronomy	165
Sanh.			
3:5	78	*Talmud Yerushalmi*	
11:1	169	y. Ber. II 5a	21
		y. Taʿan. 2:1	58
ʿEd.			
4:7	69	*Tosefta*	
		t. Taʿan. 2:2	78
Bek.		t. Soṭah 5:13	72
9:7–8	84		
		Zohar	
Yad.		Vayakhel	36
4:8	69		

9. Targumic Literature

Midrash Tanḥuma		*Targum Chronicles*	
Huqqat 8	19	32:21	156
Qorah 3	19		
		Targum Esther I.	
Pesiqta de Rab Kahana		7:8	157
Va-tomer ziyyon	58		
		Targum Job	
Pesiqta Rabbati	95, 108, 119	25:2	19
26	19	37:11	57
36	49, 110		
36–37	19	*Targum Onqelos*	165
37	21, 110	Deut 20:3	34, 88
Pirqe Rabbi Eliezer		*Targum Psalms*	19
4	136, 146	137:8	156

10. Epigraphic Collections and Inscriptions

Bet ʿEmer [Eshel, Esther, Hanan Eshel, and Ada Yardeni, "A Document from 'Year Four of the Destruction of the House of Israel' in Which a Widow Declared that She Received All Her Rights," *Cathedra* 132 (2009): 5–24 (Hebrew)]

4–5	86

Murabbaʿat

24.2:7	71
30:24	64–65
43:3	86
44:6	68
46:9	69
174:5	86

Naḥal Ḥever

6:1	86
49:7	68, 86

Yadin [Yigael Yadin, "Expedition D — The Cave of the Letters," *Israel Exploration Journal* 12 (1962): 227–57]

45:6	86

Ada Yardeni, *Textbook of Aramaic, Hebrew and Nabatean Documentary Texts*, 2000

XḤev/SE 7:6	21

Bezalel Porten and Ada Yardeni, *Textbook of Aramaic Documents from ancient Egypt*, 1986–99

A6.2:22	21

Hazon Gabriel

1–10	61, 132
8	175
9	17
9–12	101
10	116
11	17, 20, 21, 34, 35, 38, 63, 64, 67, 72, 73, 75, 76, 79, 80, 84, 85, 91, 116, 134, 139, 155, 162
11–12	120
11–15	43
11–32	53, 61
12	17, 19, 21, 34, 40, 63, 64, 65, 70, 72, 75, 76, 79, 81, 117, 139, 143, 175, 178, 183
13	17, 20, 24, 28, 62, 66, 72, 73, 75, 77, 79, 82, 83, 101, 123, 155, 170, 176
13–14	40, 45, 70, 101, 117, 118, 143, 157, 159, 160, 183
13–16	39, 177
13–42	101
14	17, 34, 62, 63, 65, 80, 82, 83, 139, 143, 168, 175
15	34, 51, 62, 73, 74, 77, 82, 86, 91, 123, 129, 137, 138
15–16	18, 21
15–18	42
15–19	117–18
16	19, 21, 28, 29, 35, 37, 38, 44, 63, 63, 64, 67, 70, 72, 73, 75, 77, 79, 82, 83, 85, 95, 102, 108, 111, 114, 118, 119, 127, 143, 157, 167, 175
16–17	34, 42, 101–2, 119, 157, 176
16–18	48
17	21, 29, 34, 35, 37, 38, 41, 42,

INDEX OF PASSAGES

	63, 64, 65, 67, 70, 72, 77, 79, 80, 84, 91, 108, 119, 127, 157, 166–67, 170	23–24 24	84, 88, 122, 135, 168 71, 87, 126, 143 19, 24, 35, 63, 64, 67, 71, 73, 74, 80, 85, 86, 91, 158, 178, 183
17–18	17, 20, 118, 155		
17–19	176		
17–21	43	24–25	17, 40, 77, 103, 122, 132, 143, 169, 171, 176, 178, 184, 186
18	62, 64, 67, 70, 72, 73, 75, 101, 111, 128, 134, 139, 158, 167	24–26	144
18–19	34, 48, 49, 50, 51, 76, 101, 118, 165	24–29 24–31	39 39, 177
18–27	43	25	72, 73, 75, 76, 77, 82, 122, 143, 171, 176
19	19, 34, 37, 41, 70, 72, 73, 74, 75, 77, 78, 79, 82, 91, 123, 129, 137, 163, 165, 166	25–26 25–27 25–29 26	70, 76, 116, 139 170, 171 122 19, 64, 73, 75, 76, 77, 79, 86, 103, 123, 125, 134, 137, 138, 141, 142, 171
19–20	17, 20, 155		
19–21	119, 176		
20	64, 73, 75, 76, 77, 80, 101, 116, 134, 139, 163		
20–21	21, 34, 44, 85, 88, 168	26–27 26–29	123, 143 184
20–22	184	27	17, 35, 63, 65, 73, 75, 76, 79, 91, 122, 139, 142, 143, 164, 171, 175
21	21, 24, 34, 35, 42, 64, 65, 67, 68, 69, 70, 73, 77, 79, 80, 81, 84, 116, 154, 159	27–28 28	71 18, 19, 35, 56, 63, 63, 64, 70, 72, 73, 75, 76, 77, 79, 80, 82, 83, 91, 103, 104, 122, 125, 129, 133, 134, 135, 136, 141, 144, 150, 154, 155, 178
21–22	19, 21, 34, 44, 76, 77, 120, 159, 160		
22	34, 62, 63, 67, 68, 70, 72, 73, 77, 80, 85, 121, 129, 133, 135		
22–23	36–37, 44, 121, 134–35	28–29	35, 43
22–24	121	29	21, 28, 35, 56, 64, 72, 73, 75, 76, 79, 91, 101, 116, 123, 134
23	19, 21, 35, 62, 66, 67, 72, 73, 75, 76, 79, 80,		

INDEX OF PASSAGES

Hazon Gabriel (continued)

29–30	17, 20, 139, 155	57–58	155
29–32	144, 150	57–59	17, 20, 62, 139
30	62, 63, 75, 77, 82, 123, 129	58	64, 72, 73, 75, 79, 91, 134
30–31	138	58–59	155
30–32	21	59	38, 75
31	21, 35, 67, 69, 73, 80, 81, 91, 100–101, 104, 123, 129, 133, 134, 135, 137, 138, 150, 178	59–64	132
		60	38, 104, 175
		64	36, 77, 141
		64–65	36
		64–80	53, 61
		65	18, 22, 37, 63, 73, 76, 77, 78, 104, 124, 129, 129, 134, 136, 137, 140, 141
32	22, 29, 35, 36, 37, 70, 73, 74, 75, 76, 80, 81, 175, 178		
		66	22, 35, 36, 63, 67, 70, 75, 80, 82, 85, 125, 175, 179
32–33	184		
32–44	104		
32–56	132		
33	37, 129, 139, 143, 175, 178	66–67	36, 105, 179
		66–68	125
33–63	61, 104	67	22, 28, 46, 67, 68, 69, 70, 72, 73, 77, 91, 125, 134, 141, 142, 179
35	37		
36	17, 104, 123, 139, 143, 175		
37	18, 104		
37–38	38		
37–39	176, 178	67–68	125
38	18	68	18, 22, 35, 63, 64, 66, 70, 72, 73, 75, 76, 77, 80, 82, 83, 122, 134, 139, 180
39	17, 18, 25, 65, 123, 139, 143, 175		
39–40	139, 155		
40	46, 104, 134		
41	28, 38, 104		
41–42	39, 40	69	17, 20, 63, 64, 72, 73, 75, 79, 83, 101, 126, 129, 134, 139, 155
45–50	104		
50	155		
52	123, 135–36		
53	38		
54	104, 123, 129, 137	69–70	83
56–76	101	69–71	37, 126
57	17, 18, 22, 38, 44, 45, 72, 73, 75, 79, 80, 91, 101, 104, 124, 125, 134, 139, 143, 175, 178	70	18, 21, 22, 46, 63, 67, 70, 73, 77, 78, 79, 80, 82, 83, 105, 126, 129, 136, 137, 141

INDEX OF PASSAGES

71	22, 69, 70, 79	80	4, 7, 9, 17, 19, 37, 38, 43, 61–62, 63, 70, 72, 73, 74, 75, 77, 78, 82, 96, 106, 107, 115, 116, 127–29, 133, 137, 144, 146, 154, 166–67, 170, 179, 186
71–72	37, 126, 164		
72	19, 20, 63, 64, 71, 73, 75, 76, 77, 106, 108, 111, 126, 141, 143, 175, 179–80		
72–74	37, 126–27		
72–75	41	80–81	184
73	63, 67, 70, 72, 73, 77, 82	81	19, 20, 44, 47, 49, 96, 107, 128, 129, 145, 158, 160–61, 186
74	20, 37, 63, 66, 70, 72, 77, 80, 82, 83, 180		
75	18–19, 20, 22–23, 46, 63, 68, 70, 73, 75, 77, 78, 79, 80, 82, 85, 106, 126, 129, 136, 137, 141	81–87	61
		82	37, 38, 127, 167
		83	17, 21, 23, 38, 107, 116, 128–29, 133, 137, 144, 146, 154
		84	41, 134, 139
75–76	37	85	107, 128, 186
76	20, 23, 63, 67, 68, 70, 71, 73, 82, 91, 106, 124, 129, 134, 140	86–87	59

11. Early Christian Literature

Justin Martyr	149

12. Greek and Roman Literature

77	17, 23, 37, 67, 69, 75, 100–01, 106, 116, 127, 133, 144, 146, 154	Pliny the Elder *Natural History*	
		5.14	173
77–83	129	Tacitus *History*	
77–87	43, 50		
78	38, 63, 64, 67, 73, 79, 81, 84, 85, 86, 106	5.9.2	47
78–79	37, 127		
79	21, 23, 37, 62, 63, 65, 67, 70, 71, 73, 77, 78, 80, 82, 83, 106, 126, 128, 129		

Index of Names and Subjects

Ahaz, 119, 168–69
Alcimus, 183
Antichrist, 103, 121, 160, 179
Archelaus, 126
Armilus, 108
Augustus, 103

Bacchides, 183
Bar-Asher, Moshe, 6
Bar Kokhba, 24, 48, 65, 70, 109
Belial, 150
Ben-Zvi, Yad, 2
Boyarin, Daniel, 6
Bronner, Ethan, 5–6
Bultmann, Rudolf, 93

Cherubim, 148
Codex Panopolitanus, 146

Daniel, 44–45, 47, 50, 51, 53, 104, 153–71
DeConick, April, 131

Elijah, 97, 105, 125, 185
Elizur, Binyamin, 3, 8
Ephraim, 19, 40–45, 48–49, 50, 95–96, 102, 108–11, 119–20, 133, 157, 167, 175
Epiphanes, 50
Esther, 156

Fassberg, Steven, 61

Gabriel, 3, 4, 17, 24–25, 43, 44, 47, 50, 51, 53, 96, 101, 104, 114–15, 116, 121, 127, 129, 131, 133, 134, 138, 144, 145, 146, 147, 154, 156–57, 161–63, 166–71, 184
Geiger, Gregor, 61
Gideon, 167–68
Gospel of Judas, 5

Gospel of Mark, 96–97
Gratus, 47
Grigori, 148

Han, Eugen Y., 11
Harkins, Angela Kim, 131
Hasmonean Period, 27–28
Hekhalot, 2, 11, 13, 20, 22, 23, 131, 141, 142, 147, 148, 149, 151
Henze, Matthias, 7, 31, 131
Herod/Herodian Period, 25, 27–28, 45–46, 49, 58, 124, 126, 175
Hezekiah, 167
Himmelfarb, Martha, 110
Hoggard, Steven, 7
Houston Museum of Natural Science, 7

Ibn Ezra, 50
Idel, Moshe, 6
Israel Exploration Society, 5
Israel Museum, 5–6
Istrael, 146

Jeremiah, 43
Jerusalem, 3, 39, 45, 65–66, 96, 101–102, 104, 108, 111–12, 116–18, 122–27, 139, 143, 149, 156–58, 160–71, 173–86
Jeselsohn, David, 12
Jesus, 52, 93–97, 106–07, 114, 127, 180
John the Baptist, 95

Klütsch, Friedrich, 6

Lemaire, André, 2

Mastema, 150
Matthias ben Theophilus, 46
Melchiresha, 150
Menahem the Essene, 94

Merkabah, 23, 131, 141, 142, 147–49, 151
Messiah son of David, 25, 43–44, 48, 95–96, 102, 103, 108–11, 118–20, 175
Messiah son of Ephraim, 49, 108
Messiah son of Joseph, 4, 19, 25, 49, 95–96, 108–11, 114–15, 119–20, 184
Michael, 24, 52, 71, 104, 107, 122–23, 129, 131, 133, 134, 136, 144, 145, 146, 150, 154–55, 178–79
Milwaukee Public Museum, 7
Mor, Uri, 61
Morgenstern, Matthew, 61

National Geographic, 7
Numerals, 77–79

Ophannin, 148

Phanuel, 146
Pharisees, 51, 119
Philadelphia, 180
Phrygia, 159–60
Pompey, 111, 124
Porten, Bezalel, 3
Prince of Princes, 44–45, 47, 49, 53, 107, 128, 145, 155, 158–62, 168, 184, 186

Qumran Community, 51

Radovan, Zeev, 3
Rand, Michael, 11
Raphael, 146
Rihani, Ghassan, 2
Rihani, Tayeb, 2
Rösel, Martin, 113

Sadducees, 51
Samaritan Pentateuch, 35
Sariel, 146
Satan, 150
Sefer Zerubbabel, 95, 108, 119
Segal, Michael, 58
Sennacherib, 156
Seraphim, 148
Seth, 155
Son of God, 44, 50, 103
Steiner, Richard C., 24
Suffering Servant, 94
Syncellus, Georg, 146

Taxo, 52–53
Tchacos, Frieda, 5
Ten Commandments, 50

unio liturgica, 151
Uriel, 146
Uzziah (King), 28

van Bekkum, W., 11
Varus, governor of Syria, 45, 52, 111, 126

Wrede, William, 96

Xerxes, 156

Yardeni, Ada, 2–3, 8

Zangenberg, Jürgen, 6
Zealots, 51
Zedekiah, 145
Zuckerman, Bruce, 7
Zurich, 3, 4

Index of Authors

Adams, E., 164
Adler, W., 149
Alexander, P. A., 149, 150
Allison, D., 93–94
Andersen, F. I., 87
Atkinson, K., 52, 111
Aune, D. E., 137, 148
Azar, M., 78, 86

Bar-Asher, M., 8, 32, 45, 61, 62, 64, 65, 74, 80, 82, 99, 100, 107, 115, 116, 128, 131–52, 158
Barr, J., 63, 64, 68, 139
Bauckham, R., 164
Beentjes, P. C., 75
Ben-Ḥayyim, Z., 34, 66, 81
Ben-Porat, Z., 153
Bergey, R. L., 87
Berlin, A., 153
Berner, Ch., 137, 138
Betz, H. D., 148
Birnbaum, G., 65
Boustan, R. S., 142
Brekelmans, Ch. H. W., 140
Broshi, M., 79
Bultmann, R., 97

Charles, R. H., 52
Chazon, E. G., 153, 164
Clines, D. J. A., 57, 87
Coblentz Bautch, K., 123, 136–37, 138
Cohen, Ch. E., 84
Collins, J. J., 8, 47, 50, 52, 53, 95, 100, 101, 102, 103, 105, 107, 111, 120, 121, 140, 145, 147, 151, 159, 161, 166, 169

Dan, J., 108
Davidson, M., 139, 140, 145
Delsman, W. C., 85
Dibelius, M., 96–97

Díez Merino, L., 156
Dimant, D., 140, 151–52
Drazin, I., 165
Driver, S. R., 85

Ehrensvärd, M., 89
Elizur, B., 3, 32, 41, 42, 45, 53–59, 61–62, 65, 67, 69, 91, 99, 100, 102–12, 113–29, 113–52, 153–71, 174–75, 178–86
Eshel, H., 1, 119, 142
Even-Shoshan, A., 71, 87

Farmer, W. R., 45
Fassberg, S. E., 74, 85
Fishbane, M., 110–11
Fleischer, E., 21
Fletcher-Louis, H. T., 134
Flusser, D., 51, 103
Forbes, A. D., 87
Freedman, D. N., 64, 65
Frennesson, B., 134

García Martínez, F., 168, 174
Geiger, G., 86
Ginsberg, H. L., 161
Good, E. M., 165
Goodman, M., 46
Goren, Y., 4–5, 7, 47, 99, 100, 115
Greenstein, E. L., 75
Grossfeld, B., 157

Hamidović, D., 99–100, 101–12, 115, 121, 123, 124, 143, 145, 147, 151
Hanson, J. S., 102
Harkins, A. K., 134, 135
Hays, R. B., 168
Heinemann, J., 48, 109
Hempel, Ch., 152
Hendel, R., 32, 37, 43, 96, 107, 128, 146, 157, 170, 186

Hengel, M., 46, 118
Henze, M., 153, 161–62, 170, 186
Hollander, J. J., 168–69
Horsley, R. A., 45–46, 102
Hurvitz, A., 68, 87

Irwin, W., 153
Israeli, E., 52

Jastrow, M., 57
Jenks, G. C., 103
Jeselsohn, D., 1, 113
Joüon, P., 78, 81, 85

Kasser, R., 5
Katsumata, N., 21
King, P., 174
Kister, M., 119
Klijn, A. F. J., 173
Knohl, I., 4, 7–8, 32, 43, 56, 57–58, 61–62, 80–81, 93–97, 100–112, 114, 118–29, 132–52, 153, 157–62, 164, 166–71, 175–76, 178–86
Koester, H., 93
Kohut, A., 57
Kokkinos, N., 46
Kraus, T., 145
Krosney, H., 5
Kutscher, E. Y., 64, 66, 74

Larson, E., 145
Le Déaut, R., 156
Levin, S., 78
Licht, J., 53
Lietaert Peerbolte, L. J., 103

Mach, M., 132, 145
McGinn, B., 103
Meier, J. P., 97
Mettinger, T. N. D., 139
Meyer, M., 5
Montgomery, J. A., 128
Moore, G. F., 109
Mor, U., 65, 68, 69, 70, 71, 79, 83, 84, 86
Morgenstern, M., 67
Morrow, W. S., 162
Muraoka, T., 78, 81, 85

Murphy-O'Connor, J., 174
Murray, R., 148

Naeh, Sh., 83
Naveh, J., 150
Neusner, J., 169
Newman, C., 173, 180
Newsom, C. A., 132, 138, 141, 142, 151
Nickelsburg, G. W. E., 135, 137, 144, 148, 185
Niehr, H., 162
Nitzan, B., 120

O'Connor, M., 78
Odeberg, H., 20
Olyan, S. M., 142

Pérez Fernández, M., 69, 70, 71, 74
Perri, C., 153, 154
Piovanelli, P., 150
Polzin, R., 71, 78, 84
Porten, B., 21
Priest, J., 52, 53
Puech, E., 18

Qimron, E., 9, 40–41, 42, 43, 53–59, 61, 62, 64, 65, 66, 67, 68, 69, 69, 72, 73, 74, 76, 77, 79, 81, 82, 83, 84, 87, 88, 91, 95, 96, 99, 101, 102–12, 115–29, 134–52, 153–71, 175–76, 178–86

Rahlfs, A., 64
Rebiger, B., 148
Rendsburg, G., 9, 32, 61, 64, 67, 68, 72, 74, 76, 78, 86, 91, 99, 115, 116, 122, 132, 133, 139, 146, 155
Rezetko, R., 89
Rhoads, D. M., 52
Robert, J., 156
Roberts, J. J. M., 182

Sasson, V., 99
Schäfer, P., 11, 20, 22, 149, 150, 151
Schofield, A., 151
Scholem, G., 44
Schoors, A., 85
Schwartz, D. R., 46

Segal, M. H., 86
Segal, M. Z., 69
Seux, M.-J., 162
Shaked, Sh., 150
Sharvit, S., 65
Shmuel, E., 24–25
Slotki, I. W., 109
Smallwood, E. M., 47
Smith, M., 145
Sokoloff, M., 75
Sommer, B. D., 153
Stec, D. M., 57
Stern, M., 45, 46
Stuckenbruck, L. T., 120, 159
Sullivan, K., 132, 140

Tigchelaar, E. J. C., 168, 174
Tromp, J., 52
Tuschling, R. M. M., 132, 134, 140

van der Woude, A., 145
van Henten, J. W., 137
VanderKam, J. C., 149

Wagner, S. M., 165
Waltke, B. K., 78
Wassen, C., 139, 141
Weiser, A., 50
Wright, A. T., 149
Wurst, G., 5

Yarbro Collins, A., 46–47, 97, 102, 103, 174, 181, 182, 183
Yardeni, A., 3, 5, 21, 27, 28, 32, 41, 42, 45, 53–59, 61–62, 65, 67, 69, 91, 99, 100, 102–12, 113, 114–29, 132–52, 153–71, 174–75, 178–86
Yelinek, A., 24
Young, I., 89
Yuditsky, A. E., 9, 40–41, 42, 43, 53–59, 61, 62, 64, 65, 66, 67, 69, 72, 74, 76, 77, 81, 82, 83, 88, 91, 95, 96, 99, 101, 102–12, 115–29, 132, 134–52, 163–71, 175–76, 178–86

Zimmerli, W., 162

www.ingramcontent.com/pod-product-compliance
Lightning Source LLC
Chambersburg PA
CBHW021808220426
43662CB00006B/231